Florida A&M University, Tallahassee
Florida Atlantic University, Boca Raton
Florida Gulf Coast University, Ft. Myers
Florida International University, Miami
Florida State University, Tallahassee
University of Central Florida, Orlando
University of Florida, Gainesville
University of North Florida, Jacksonville
University of South Florida, Tampa
University of West Florida, Pensacola

Dr. Henry Nehrling in Naples, Florida, 1927.

Nehrling's Plants, People, and Places in Early Florida

 〜　〜

Abridged and Edited by Robert W. Read

University Press of Florida

Gainesville · Tallahassee · Tampa · Boca Raton

Pensacola · Orlando · Miami · Jacksonville · Ft. Myers

06 05 04 03 02 01 6 5 4 3 2 1

Library of Congress cataloging-in-publication data are available.
ISBN 0-8130-2428-5

The University Press of Florida is the scholarly publishing agency
for the State University System of Florida, comprising Florida A&M
University, Florida Atlantic University, Florida Gulf Coast University,
Florida International University, Florida State University, University of
Central Florida, University of Florida, University of North Florida,
University of South Florida, and University of West Florida.

University Press of Florida
15 Northwest 15th Street
Gainesville, FL 32611–2079
http://www.upf.com

This book represents selected portions of Dr. Henry Nehrling's *My Garden
in Florida and Miscellaneous Horticultural Notes,* originally published as a
two-volume work in 1944 and 1946 by Guiding Star Publishing House,
as taken from the writings of Dr. Nehrling published in the *American
Eagle,* Estero, Florida.

A companion volume, *Nehrling's Early Florida Gardens,* is also
published by the University Press of Florida.

"Every true happiness we enjoy three times—first in hope, second in truth and third in memory."

From Nehrling's "Horticultural notebook"

Contents

Illustrations

Foreword from the First Edition of
My Garden in Florida

I first met Dr. Nehrling on March 21st, 1917. He was working among his plants at Gotha. It was just after the great freeze of February 3rd and I had gone up from Miami to see how his garden there had come through the catastrophe of that day. This is what I wrote in my diary: "I went over the wonderful place of Dr. Nehrling and I was astonished at the number of things he has tested. He is a perfect mine of information regarding plants. . . . He has now a new place at Naples, south of Fort Myers, consisting of forty [*sic*] acres. The temperature there this winter did not go below 34°F. He expects to develop this more tropical place with the most tender species he can get and wants us to help him. Although he is now sixty-three years old, he feels able to undertake this big work. He is a real pioneer and student of nature of the old fashioned kind, and I want to have him recognized and propose to make him a collaborator of the office."

This, my first impression of Dr. Nehrling, has remained as a clear picture of him through a quarter of a century. I have not felt like changing it either, for it represents to me a personality the like of which I never met again in my travels. I have known many with a passion for plants. I have met many who were keen to collect and dry their fragments. I have known others who lived to make gardens, but none who quite so fully combined their passion for observation with their skill in the propagation and cultivation of a variety of species, keeping them under their constant attention so that they were able to accumulate through many years' observation clear pictures of their characteristics.

As the years have passed and I have seen more of the tropical plants which have, through one source or another, found their way into South

Florida, I have a growing respect for such series of observations as Dr. Nehrling accumulated. They can only be made by a man who is happy to live surrounded by his plants which he treats as pets. They are not such as one makes with his eye on the clock or his watch in his hand. They are such as a man makes who is out alone at dawn in his garden with not even a dog to distract his attention.

I am very glad that Mr. Andrews has taken the pains to preserve in Dr. Nehrling's own simple, but fascinating language, these stories of a great plantsman, one of the real pioneers in the fascinating field of plant introduction, a field in which my own life has been largely spent.

It is gratifying to think that the so-called "development of Florida" has not been quite synonymous with the destruction of its beautiful flora to make room for highways and cities; that some of the pioneers were busy with the study of the plants from foreign countries which are destined to make beautiful the gardens, parks, roadways and dooryards of those who have come to live in this paradise.

Dr. Nehrling's writings should be available to the young people who are making gardens around their houses, for they not only give the facts regarding a host of interesting plants from which they may choose, but they tell in narrative form how one who learns to recognize plants can explore for a lifetime the unlimited variety of beautiful forms which compose the plant kingdom. Dr. Nehrling got away from human troubles by putting his hand on the graceful spathe of a Butia Palm, or by walking through his beds of hybrid Caladiums or counting the Bromeliads on some Oak in the hammock near his home.

David Fairchild
The Kampong, Coconut Grove, Florida (1944)

Preface and Acknowledgments

Dr. David Fairchild clearly understood the true Henry Nehrling when he wrote that Nehrling combined "passion for observation" with skill in propagation and cultivation. Henry Nehrling was truly a great plantsman, mostly overlooked as a pioneer in the introduction and cultivation of plants in Florida.

This sage of turn-of-the-century horticulture published his original writings in the *American Eagle.* Now in this abridged edition of *My Garden in Florida,* he provides insight into the historical reports of the weather from 1894 to 1929, the people active or interested in Florida horticulture, and his sources of plant materials from around the world, and he supplies a record of the use of ornamental and native plants of central and south Florida. This is a personal narrative of his experiences with plants and worldwide correspondents.

Herein lies the colorful tale of one horticultural pioneer, a diary of historical horticulture in Florida's subtropical and tropical climes. Dr. Nehrling's horticultural practices and recommendations are as applicable today as they were a hundred years ago.

Henry Nehrling was a dreamer, visionary, teacher, researcher, writer, philosopher, and poet. But most of all he was an historian, writing of the environment, plants and people active in horticulture, many of whom assisted him in his quest for gathering exciting plants for his garden, so that his passionate love for growing, seeing, studying plants could be shared with others. Dr. Nehrling named his Gotha garden Palm Cottage Gardens and the one at Naples his Tropical Garden and Arboretum at Naples-by-the-Gulf or simply his Garden of Solitude. Although he waxed poetic at times in his enthusiasm for the beauty of Florida and plants, he was a keen observer, had a prodigious memory, and was a passionate note taker, accurate to minute details. Dr. Witmer Stone of the Academy of Natural Sciences in Philadelphia described him as "A typical German professor of the old school, of courtly manner and enthusiastically absorbed in his work, he made a host of warm friends and was pleased as a child when visitors admired his garden."

In 1933, under the title of *The Plant World in Florida*, the Macmillan Company issued a volume compiled by Colonel and Mrs. Alfred Kay from Nehrling's original articles in the *American Eagle*. As A. H. Andrews, editor of the *American Eagle* and compiler of *My Garden in Florida*, said of the Kays' work, "the personal narrative of Dr. Nehrling's experience with plants was necessarily omitted. Dr. Nehrling wrote with enthusiasm and a charm that held the attention of the reader from start to finish." Though many of the "Notes" that Andrews reproduced in the 1940s from Nehrling's "Horticultural notebook" have here been omitted, and a new biography of Nehrling has been added (chapter 1), the essence of the body of Nehrling's original work remains intact in the present edition; his personal narrative is preserved, including his inconsistencies of punctuation and style. I hope this effort may help to bring about a renaissance in the culture of some of the little-used or long-forgotten but beautiful and useful ornamental plants Nehrling so lovingly described.

This abridged edition has the nomenclature of the plants brought into line with modern botanical rules and concepts. It is what Dr. Nehrling would have done were he conducting the work himself. His identifications and knowledge of nomenclature were excellent, but as time and research progressed, in some cases older names were found to take precedence according to the rules of modern nomenclature. Nehrling's research and spelling of scientific names is very impressive considering the conditions at that time.

Technical manuals consulted during the preparation of the present work are cited in the Selected References. Corrections and editorial comments upon scientific names are presented in square brackets. The names used by Nehrling can be found in the index.

There has always been some misunderstanding regarding the treatment of cultivars: they may be indicated by the abbreviation cv. or enclosed in single quotation marks. Hybrids are indicated by an X next to the first letter of the name, which is capitalized and not underlined or italicized.

The two volumes of *My Garden in Florida* edited by A. H. Andrews (1944, 1946) contained over 750 pages of text, much of which had to be deleted due to size constraints in the present edition. I have tried to edit by deletion to avoid changing Nehrling's intent. By leaving out quotations, material about cultivars and varieties that probably are no longer applicable, repetition, and references to gardens outside Florida, I aim to present in Nehrling's own words his passion and love for plants in Florida. I have used my best judgment in determining if cultural practices or advice are applicable or possibly inadvisable. Had I read *My Garden in Florida* when I first moved to Naples, perhaps my own frustrations with freezes, soil, and seasonal drought and flood would have been less traumatic.

We have lost much beauty through not having preserved the gardens Nehrling describes. Botanical gardens are important for preserving species brought into cultivation because it is more and more difficult to import them, and many are being lost to cultivation, as with the plants Nehrling had in his collections. Many of the plants at Palm Cottage Gardens and the Naples garden are gone due to ignorance, carelessness, and theft. As of April 2001, Nehrling's Palm Cottage Gardens house and remaining grounds are being considered for preservation at Gotha near Orlando. Nehrling's Tropical Garden of Solitude is the site of Caribbean Gardens in Naples on the Gulf and is being restored as much as possible as a botanical garden and zoo.

Reading Nehrling expands our knowledge of tropical gardening and renews a feeling for the beauty of tropical plants. This is a historically and horticulturally important treatise by a passionate lover of the state of Florida, of its natural beauty and history, and especially of subtropical and tropical plants.

Acknowledgments

Great appreciation is extended to my colleagues Drs. Dan H. Nicolson and Dieter C. Wasshausen of the Department of Botany in the Natural History Museum of the Smithsonian Institution in Washington, D.C., for assistance with names of plants within their areas of specialty; and to Juan Chahinian, authority on the genus *Sansevieria,* whose collection in Naples, Florida, is one of the finest.

The chapter 1 biography of Henry Nehrling is from a previously unpublished manuscript by David J. Driapsa, a landscape architect in Naples, Florida. He graciously offered the manuscript as an opportunity to increase our knowledge of Nehrling.

Appreciation is also extended to Richard Nehrling, great-grandson to Henry Nehrling, who has worked so hard to bring about a new edition of his great-grandfather's writings and the restoration of Palm Cottage Gardens at Gotha. Richard has kindly contributed the black and white photographs in the present edition.

Very special appreciation is extended to my wife, Betsy (Elizabeth M. Read), for financial support for the pages of color photographs, adding so much to the book, for proofreading the final draft, and for her encouragement and patience during preparation of the manuscript.

Thanks go also to Dr. Richard P. Wunderlin and Roger Hammer, Jan Roby, and Jean McCullough for reading and making constructive and significant suggestions for improvement of the text.

Robert W. Read
Naples, Florida (2001)

Original Editor's Note from
Andrews' 1946 Edition of Volume 2

Volume 2 of "My Garden in Florida" completes the horticultural writings of the late Dr. Henry Nehrling, the original manuscripts of which were published serially in the *American Eagle* during the 1920's. The demand for Volume 1 so exceeded our expectations that a second edition became necessary to keep up with orders from public libraries, museums, universities, botanical gardens, nurserymen and plant collectors all over the country. A larger edition of Volume 2 has been printed in consequence.

Preparation of the Index has been particularly laborious due to the fact that many varieties of Orchids, Bromeliads and Ferns, and some species of Cacti were listed under the title of "Epiphytes" and had to be reclassified under their several headings. As many plants are mentioned, but with no description given, they were not included in the index.

It is a tremendous job to cull a mass of horticultural articles from hundreds of old papers and string them together in a semblance of orderly arrangement. Now that the task is done, I can readily see where some improvement could have been made, but altogether, I believe that we have done a fairly creditable job in producing an authoritative work by a great botanist that will be treasured by every collector and lover of tropical plants.

A. H. Andrews
Estero, Lee County, Florida (1946)

Henry Nehrling Biography (1853–1929)

David J. Driapsa

Florida historian Charlton Tebeau ranked Henry Nehrling among the most eminent pioneers of Naples, Florida, though he lived there for only ten years and then only part-time. Naples was a fledgling hamlet perched on a sand dune between the Gulf of Mexico and the vast Everglades frontier. Nehrling had arrived during what Tebeau termed the "third and final period of frontier Naples." Conditions were primitive at best. At first, he lodged at Bamboo Cottage, a sort of guesthouse and the only alternative to the Naples Hotel. The year was 1919. It was the dawn of the Roaring Twenties, but Naples was snoring. Nehrling was in his sixty-sixth year and beginning the last decade of his life. He went to Naples hoping to grow tropical plants outdoors year round. It was his life's dream and he accomplished it and more.

Up until the Civil War most Americans lived on farms and the landscape was mostly rural. Nehrling was of the generation who saw rapid industrialization of the American landscape. Interest was growing in wild gardens and naturalistic effects, in part to offset the changes that industrialization was causing. Famous landscape gardeners, such as William Robinson, Andrew Jackson Downing, Samuel Parsons, and Frederick Law Olmsted, used principles of design to harmonize man-made improvements with the setting and topography and to disturb the natural landscape as little as possible as they created new parks and suburbs. Natural gardening was presented as an American style of landscaping in books published in the early 1900s. Nehrling read widely on gardening, in both German and English, and would have been familiar with evolving trends. His own extensive library contained full sets of the *Gardener's Chronicle*, the *Garden*, *Garden and Forest*, and *Die Gartenwelt*, to all of which he was a contributing writer. He was an impassioned writer on tropical flora and Florida landscapes, and with keen perception of its natural beauty and delight in its loveliness, he inspired many to appreciate native landscapes and tropical gardening.

The period between the Civil War and the beginning of World War I has been characterized as a time of garden ferment. Plant collectors, botanists, and horticulturists introduced many thousands of showy and brilliantly colored plants from the far reaches of the tropics and subtropics. Horticultural professionals started special collections of newly introduced plants in glasshouses called conservatories. It became fashionable to create conservatory gardens resembling the native landscapes from which the plants came, giving their viewers a hint of places where summer never ended. Joseph Paxton created the world's largest conservatory at Chatsworth in 1840, Kew Gardens soon followed suit, and so the fashion spread.

The Victorian age saw many new manuals and specialized magazines devoted to gardening. Publications such as *Sunset Magazine, Southern Living,* and its south Florida counterpart the *American Eagle* of Estero were instrumental in spreading regional tastes. Nehrling wrote a weekly column for the *American Eagle* from late 1922 until his death seven years later. His articles covered topics about new introductions of tropical plants and gardening problems in the pinelands and swamps of south Florida, where Nehrling saw an opportunity to take the conservatory garden outdoors. With light botanical editing of his natural pine woodland and cypress swamp, he set out to create the prototypical tropical garden. Having worked out the prototype, he turned to spreading the gospel of the wilderness garden through the *American Eagle* to all who would listen.

Nehrling's gardens and articles were complementary in influencing public taste. He received numerous letters and constantly was approached by plant lovers asking for information. Before public botanical gardens and retail nurseries abounded, private plant collections strongly impacted gardens in the surrounding areas. Collection owners provided both the plants and the information to the public as well as their inspiration for design.

Between 1886 and his death in 1929, Nehrling created two outstanding gardens in Florida, one in the orange district at Gotha and the second in the southwest at Naples. For forty-three years, he experimented with growing plants from all reaches of the world's subtropics and tropics. He kept detailed records of the soil, water, and sun preferences of his plants, their color and time of blooming, and their growth characteristics under disparate conditions from one end of the state to the other.

Nehrling experimented with a regional expression of tropical garden design that few before him had ever attempted. Southwest Florida was a newly settled region, and gardening was a type of pioneering still beyond the reach of outside ideas. There were only a few trained gardeners working in south Florida at the time, and they were mostly in Miami. It was rare to meet anyone who knew the existing planting conditions at Naples.

He called his southern garden H. Nehrling's Tropical Gardens and Arboretum. The garden exists today in the heart of the Caribbean Gardens. Some of the trees Nehrling planted, such as the very large Araucarias, have grown into the largest specimens of their kind in Florida. According to David Fairchild, the garden is significant in the annals of American garden history: "With its keen historical interest, as well as its undisputed botanical significance, Dr. Nehrling's old Naples homestead can be imagined as a second Fairchild Gardens."

Nehrling's decision to avoid the English park rules of sweeping lawns with scattered clumps of trees and instead to adopt a garden style responsive to the subtropical environment was in part due to his personal situation. First, his monetary resources were always limited. Working his improvements with the setting and topography required less outlay of resources to mold the land. Disturbing the natural landscape as little as possible allowed him to use the existing native plant material as the foundation for his new garden. He utilized the process of elaboration, of intensifying original features and melding his cultivated areas into the natural landscape. Additionally, Nehrling was keenly attracted to the low rich hammock forests and palm glades of the Florida Everglades and to the vernacular landscapes of the pioneers. He enjoyed rambling about his wilderness garden admiring the many tropical plants, the orchids and bromeliads and the ferns growing on the forest trees, and the feeling in his garden—the impression of aloofness, of wide separation from humankind and a deep remoteness from the modern and conventional of his world. There were no lawns and broad open spaces resembling an English garden. Single specimens, groups and dense masses of trees, shrubs, palms, and bamboo were the main features. There were wild portions with narrow paths leading from one place to another. Native shrubs and trees formed the structural foundation, while Japanese and Chinese evergreens, hardy bamboo, and leafy palms ornamented the garden.

Henry Nehrling's father was Carl S. Nehrling and his mother was Elizabeth Ruge Nehrling. They were German immigrants to the United States and had settled in a German community in the town of Herman near Howard's Grove in Sheboygan County, Wisconsin. Henry was educated at home by his mother and grandfather and spoke only German until age eleven, when he entered Lutheran parochial school in 1864. He went on to Teacher's Seminary at the State Normal School in Addison, Illinois, at age sixteen and upon graduation in 1873 entered a career of teaching at Harlem, Illinois. For the next sixteen years he taught at various schools in Illinois, Missouri, and Texas.

Nehrling married Sophia Schoff on July 20, 1874. He moved with his bride to Chicago in 1875 to teach at a branch school of the Emmanuel Church until another teaching assignment with the Lutheran Church took them to Houston, Texas, in 1879.

Living in Texas enabled Nehrling to flower as a scholar of horticulture, ornithology, and the broader field of natural science. It was in a Houston garden that he first saw the Amaryllis (*Hippeastrum*) in full bloom. Apparently the experience was a transcendent moment for the young Nehrling. Years later he recalled the moment to his son, implying that he would never forget the impression that first Amaryllis had made on him. It did enflame his enthusiasm for horticulture. Over the next quarter century Nehrling helped to make the plant popular among plant enthusiasts. Starting with a few specimens of *Hippeastrum johnsonii*, he produced the modern form of *Amaryllis* through crossbreeding and created many thousands of hybrids. He became an authority on the plant and in 1909 he published a book in German titled "Amaryllis, or Knight Stars (*Hippeastrum*)." In 1934 the editor of the American Amaryllis Society, Hamilton P. Traub, dedicated the first issue of the society's journal to Nehrling for his pioneering work with the Amaryllis. Nehrling's friend Henry Pfister, who was in charge of the White House Conservatory, named his most popular Amaryllis hybrid 'Henry Nehrling.' When a new teaching assignment in 1881 took the Nehrlings to the town of Fedor in Lee County, Texas, Nehrling resumed his studies of bird life. He had enjoyed nature since his youth and observing birds was a favorite pastime. Texas provided excellent bird-watching, and moving from town to town allowed him to notice that bird life varied from place to place;

he wrote articles describing it. Nehrling's articles were recognized by the ornithological societies, and he soon gained acceptance by scientific societies as an authority on birds. He became a charter member of the American Ornithological Union in 1883. By 1893 his own work in ornithology was gaining him the reputation of a "Wisconsin Audubon." In 1891 he published *Die Nordamerikanische Vogelwelt* (North American Birds) in German. A two-volume edition in English followed in 1893 and 1896 under the title *Our Native Birds of Song and Beauty.*

His success as a writer and the backing of literary and scientific societies had helped him gain appointment as deputy collector of customs at the port of Milwaukee, Wisconsin, in 1887. When a vacancy opened three years later he became the temporary acting secretary and custodian of the Public Museum of Milwaukee. The following year he was appointed to full custodianship. It was under his able leadership that a new public library and museum were built. Nehrling traveled to Chicago in 1893 to the Columbian Exposition to purchase displays at the closing of the expo for commissioning the museum with natural history exhibits.

The Columbian Exposition was staged as a classical city set in landscaped gardens. Participating states and many foreign countries created theme gardens representing their regions. A five-acre conservatory contained many rare plants from the subtropics and tropics. Nehrling spent several days viewing the exhibits, where he met Adolf Leitze from Brazil. Leitze was a plant scientist from Rio de Janeiro and had made his specialty the hybridization of a fancy-leafed Brazilian plant called the Caladium, characterized by colorful foliage. He created many beautiful varieties of the native plant and brought them to the expo on behalf of his county. At the closing of the expo Nehrling acquired many hundreds of Lietze's Caladiums and unknowingly set himself up as the center of distribution in the United States. Nehrling shipped Leitze's Caladiums to his 21st Street residence in Milwaukee, where he had already built a greenhouse for breeding tropical Amaryllis and orchids. It was not long before visitors were traveling from near and far to obtain Nehrling's rare colorful plants.

Nehrling left the museum in 1904 and by 1906 again entered public service, this time in Florida as a collaborator with the United States Department of Agriculture's Bureau of Plant Industries, with the assignment of scientific specialist. In 1884, wishing to grow tropical plants outdoors year round, Nehrling purchased a forty-acre farm sight unseen in central Florida. The property was selected for him by Francis von Siller one year earlier. The land lay half a mile north of the village of Gotha, known for its population of German intellectuals. From that year onward Nehrling set his mind to making Florida his permanent home. He first went to Florida in 1886 to inspect his land and thereafter visited for a month or two each year until moving there permanently in 1904. He set out the first orange tree in 1889 and the following year set out to create a tropical garden. The property adjoined small Lake Audubon and offered a favorable setting for a tropical garden. The land had once been covered with a pine forest, but only about a dozen tall trees, small oaks, willows, and brush remained. He carted a wooden structure in piece by piece and reassembled it on his property to make a home for his family, and he surrounded it with plants collected from around the world. Franz Barthels, a nearby neighbor and kindred spirit, cared for the garden while Nehrling was away. David Fairchild described Palm Cottage Gardens as one of the most interesting places in all of Florida. The remaining homestead and some of the plantings set out by Nehrling still hint of the beauty that once existed there.

Nehrling constructed a one-roomed cabin for his library and office, where he spent many hours each day poring over his scientific studies. The small pine-walled room was all he needed for checking over the results of his experiments with plants. In the solitude of his well-stocked library he documented his findings and concentrated on building his worldwide network of correspondence with eminent botanists, plant collectors, and breeders to obtain seeds of new plants to test in his garden.

His wife Sophia died in 1911, and he must have struggled caring for their children alone. On June 7, 1916, Nehrling married Betty B. Mitchell. He took her son Robert as his own and sent him to Missouri Botanical Garden for an education in horticulture.

Nehrling hybridized many beautiful varieties of Leitze's fancy-leafed Caladiums at Palm Cottage Gardens and built a considerable market for them. By 1913 he grew eight hundred varieties and had more than fifty thousand seedlings for sale. Unfortunately, a severe freeze in 1917 caught him unprepared, with over two thousand named varieties planted out in raised beds. Seventy-five thousand plants were ready for sale. More than half were killed outright. It was another devastating blow and caused him to question the direction his life should take.

South Florida is the only region in the continental United States where tender plants may be grown outdoors throughout the year. From 1906 onward, with the encouragement of his sons, Nehrling had considered moving his plant nursery operations to Miami, where frost occurs only infrequently. They reasoned that the real estate boom in Miami would support his plant business. When David Fairchild visited Palm Cottage Gardens after the freeze to assess the damage, Nehrling laid out his plan to establish a southern garden at Naples. He had in mind rebuilding his Fancy-leafed Caladium business and expanding into growing orchids. In connection with his commercial crops, he proposed to work again in collaboration with the U.S. government to create a truly tropical botanical garden in the south of Florida, where he could introduce frost-tender ornamental tropical plants into cultivation. With this plan in mind, Nehrling resumed his position as collaborator with the U.S. Department of Agriculture.

He had visited Fort Myers on earlier trips through Florida and had been attracted to the beautiful natural landscapes of the region. The landscape around Miami was being devastated through land development, and that was not yet happening in southwest Florida. Nehrling likely heard of Naples through real estate advertisements that the Naples Improvement Company was posting. He wrote letters to the company inquiring about a suitable piece of land where he could rebuild his caladium business. The company thought Nehrling, with his solid reputation, was "the type" who would benefit their community by taking up residence there. William Birch Haldemann, a son of Naples founder William Haldemann, and his wife, Lissie C., both plant lovers, befriended Nehrling and were instrumental in persuading him to reestablish his business at Naples. They loaned Nehrling and his new wife two thousand dollars for buying property and starting a nursery.

The Nehrlings purchased a small farm just outside the northeast corner of the city limits. The eastern side of the land fronted on a canal of the Gordon River. It was waterfront property with access to the Gulf of Mexico, and Nehrling believed the future growth of Naples would eventually allow him to sell it for a profit. At 13.35 acres it was the smallest parcel in the Naples Little Farms subdivision. The legal description was lot number 5 of the Naples Improvement Company Little Farms Plat, a subdivision of sections 15, 22, 27, and the north half of the northeast quarter of section 34 and Township 49 South of Range 25 East. The deed was recorded in Lee County on June 1, 1921, and witnessed by Walter O. Shepherd and Maimie E. Nicholson, according to Lee County records for 1921. The Nehrlings paid fifty dollars an acre for the land, one hundred dollars to clear it of brush, and another hundred and twenty five dollars to set out the first plants. Nehrling and his wife sold the property on May 1, 1923 to Tom I. Shadle of Orange County, Florida, and bought it back the same day, clearing Mrs. Nehrling's name from the mortgage.

At sixty-six years of age Nehrling became a pioneer. He entered an isolated and obscure colony of about two hundred full-time residents at Naples, mostly fishermen, farmers, and cattlemen, and a winter colony of wealthy seasonal visitors and their guests. Mrs. Nehrling viewed the frontier conditions at Naples with disdain and left her husband to suffer there without her. Florida pioneers risked slowly wasting away from malaria and rapid illness or death from yellow fever. Saltmarsh mosquitoes were so vicious that business districts closed down during the summer. Mrs. Nehrling lived at Gotha to manage Palm Cottage Gardens, while her husband divided his time between Gotha and his Naples camp, traveling between them in a Model T Ford automobile, making stops at plant nurseries along the way. Life was hard for him in Naples. He complained about the mosquitoes, his diet of rice and bacon, and the absence of good human company through summer months.

His closest friends in Naples, in addition to the Haldemanns, were John Hachmeister and Robert R. Fohl, Sr. Hachmeister was Nehrling's neighbor and of German descent. The two men had had similar backgrounds on the midwestern frontier. They likely met at the Bamboo Cottage in Naples, making temporary quarters while establishing their own places. Hachmeister became wealthy managing horse-racing associations and had retired to Naples. He knew something about landscaping from improving the racing grounds and used his talent to beautify his own property, which was described as a sixty-acre "showplace" of palm trees, shrubs, and roses. Like Nehrling, he was passionate about palms and cycads. Fohl was the grounds superintendent of the Naples Hotel and golf course. He, Nehrling, and Hachmeister all had in common an interest in growing things.

Nehrling had successfully grown his plants on the dry sand hills of Palm Cottage Gardens, but at Naples conditions differed in climate and geography and caused him difficulty. His initial efforts were frustrated by wet soil during the long and rainy summer and presented the opposite problem of drought all winter. The shallow water table made it impossible for deep-rooted plants to do well, and he learned to dig deep, broad ditches to lower the water. The soil appeared good, but in working it he found nothing but sea sand lacking organic matter. The abundant humus in the cypress swamp looked black and rich, but it lacked essential minerals and required expensive fertilizer. He learned to make garden soil by digging pits three feet deep and five feet wide, hundreds of them, and filling them with compost to age before planting anything in them. It was difficult work, but as long as he could get compost, he could grow plants successfully.

In unraveling the mysteries of gardening in the subtropics, he learned to love his southern garden and delighted in the cypress swamp with its edges lighted up by the red flowers of *Ixora coccinea* and the yellow flowers of *Ixora lutea*. With great effort he resumed production of his fancy-leafed Caladiums, and by 1923 he had many for sale. He constructed a shade house. Two hundred wheelbarrow loads of mulch from the cypress swamp were spread over the beds and mixed with a ton of castor pumice to improve the growing condition of the soil. Many tropical plants grew outdoors with little or no protection from the winter cold; he quickly expanded his plant collection. The excellence of his plants was immediately recognized and his garden became a mecca for all gardeners, horticulturists, and botanists who came to Florida. It was a perpetual source of wonder and delight for all who visited it.

Having started his Naples garden to grow Caladiums, orchids, bromeliads, and other strictly tropical plants, Nehrling quickly increased his collection until quarantine was imposed in 1924 on importation of exotic plants into the United States. The quarantine eliminated his unofficial sources, making it impossible to obtain new plants through independent collectors and forcing him to add to his plants in a long, roundabout official way through the federal government. He already had ten times the plants of all commercial growers put together, and he believed ten times as many more were necessary for his work. By 1925, in spite of the quarantine, he had amassed in his collection of tropical plants at Naples more than three thousand different species.

Nehrling's effort to widen his collection of plants created for him many financial and labor problems, and his advanced age frustrated many of his efforts. In 1925 he suffered from pneumonia and typhoid. He was feeling old and work had become a terrible burden. In 1928 his failing health forced him to turn over the care of his "government" plants to C. W. Codwise, a graduate of Union College. The arrangement met Nehrling's obligation as collaborator and freed him from everything but the most essential work.

The famous inventor Thomas A. Edison and his wife Mina visited Nehrling in April of 1927, spending the day with him in his garden. They were enthusiastic about his plant articles in the *American Eagle* and spent several hours looking over his books and photographs. During the day Edison systematically and thoroughly inspected Nehrling's Ficus collection, more than one hundred species, and tested each one for the quality and quantity of rubber that it might produce.

Edison hired Nehrling to improve the gardens of his winter estate in Fort Myers. Their agreement was for a period of one year and for the sum of eighteen hundred dollars. Edison agreed to allow Nehrling one gardener and all the fertilizer needed to take care of the place. Nehrling agreed to add all the plants of beauty and interest for which he could find room.

Nehrling loaned his expertise to solve the interests of Barron Collier in Naples when his company was investigating future parks and landscaping projects in what became Collier County. The officials at the City of Everglades retained him, though for only a limited time, to advise them on appropriate native and tropical trees for landscaping their new city. Everglades City lay on terrain reclaimed from mangrove swamps by dredging drainage channels, and the salt content in the soil was so high that growing anything was seemingly impossible. Nehrling undertook a research project to identify the tropical trees growing in the Royal Palm Hammock area that would flourish and beautify the new city. He studied plants growing along the littoral zone of the bay to determine which would grow well given the existing concentration of salt. Growing dissatisfied with the time it was taking to conduct the research and make his recommendations, the Collier company released him. Had they taken his suggestions, Nehrling claimed, Everglades would have been the "most beautiful and unique town in Florida."

Nehrling also consulted on the plants of Vizcaya, the palatial estate of industrialist John Deering on Biscayne Bay, when the gardens, designed by Chicago landscape architect Ossian Cole Simonds, were carved out of a mangrove forest.

When the Florida land boom of the 1920s necessitated construction of miles of new highways connecting the state's growing cities, Nehrling recommended Ficus trees for shading the roadway and Royal Palms for ornamenting them. The road building also spawned new roadside attractions featuring the state's unusual natural flora, fauna, and geography, and Nehrling's gardens became a stop on the roadside itinerary.

Nehrling's Naples home was described as a small "backwoods" shack standing on piers, containing one large living room with windows looking over the garden and another very small room where he kept his books and photographs.

The weather in Florida was severe during the decade of the twenties. There was a freeze in Naples January 1926, another in January 1927, and another in 1928. Each one killed some of his most delicate plants but did not destroy his garden.

A catastrophic hurricane struck Florida on May 6, 1926, and uprooted Nehrling's garden, tearing it to pieces. His water tank was demolished. When drought followed the storm, conditions became so dry that the humus on the ground burned and filled the air with smoke. Several men from the neighborhood helped him contain the fire, but hundreds of his plants were destroyed before the men had the fire in check. He noted that although his losses were large, they could have been worse, and almost all the plants killed could be replaced from his reserve stock. Wind took the roof off his house and forced it off its piers. His clothes, bedding, books, papers, and manuscripts were badly damaged in the downpour, though the best of them survived unharmed.

Nehrling drafted his last will and testament the day following the hurricane. He asked that the land not be sold as long as one of his five sons remained living. He wanted the property to be managed by his son Arno, to whom he left all his plants, the plant business, and all liabilities from it. He requested that his extensive library be protected in a fireproof building within the garden.

After the hurricane came help. Mr. McIntosh of Sebring Ornamental Nurseries sent five of his men to clean up the mess and help with the Caladiums. By May 28 three men were working full-time in the garden and four to six men at a time lived in the little house. The main worker was named A. Dare. He had been employed in Philadelphia and in the Edison garden in Fort Myers. Other workers included a Canadian, a colonel from the U.S. Army, an agent from the Hollywood Company, and a graduate of Ann Arbor Normal College. Nehrling's association with Mr. McIntosh is surrounded with intrigue and controversy that has never been fully explained.

Many hundreds of rooted cuttings from Nehrling's plants were either loaned or sold outright and were delivered by truckloads to McIntosh's nursery. Nehrling apparently never felt that he recovered whatever was due him.

Nehrling knew his time on earth was growing short. As he said in his column in the *American Eagle*, "My vision depicts wonderful landscape effects and glorious specimen plants, but alas! I am an old man. The time of building air-castles has passed. I have done my share in the building up of Florida. My financial resources have always been limited. All I achieved along the lines of ornamental horticulture was connected with much hard labor, with constant study and painfully insufficient means."

On his last birthday Nehrling received a greeting from his friend Robert Fohl, Sr., in Naples, and replied from Gotha that he had been sick for quite a while. On July 2 he wrote asking his son Arno to administer his estate.

On November 12 of that year Nehrling leased his Naples garden to his stepson, Robert D. Mitchell, and Mitchell's partner R. W. Wheeler for a period of two years, one month, and eighteen days. Mitchell, who was the manager of Everglades Nursery Company in Fort Myers, leased the property with the purpose of propagating Nehrling's plants.

The Florida Federation of Garden Clubs honored the failing Nehrling in 1929 with their Frank Meyer Medal Award at their annual meeting in Palm Beach. The award was bestowed in recognition of his distinguished service in the field of foreign plant introduction.

Henry Nehrling died at his home in Gotha on November 21, 1929. According to Arno Nehrling, his father "was honored by a public memorial service, on Nov. 28, 1931, at Rollins College, under the auspices of the Quest Society. The principal speakers included Dr. Harold Hume, later Dean of the College of Agriculture of the University of Florida, and Theodore L. Mead, hybridizer of orchids, now commemorated by the Mead Botanical Garden in Winter Park" (quoted in Morton, *Some Useful and Ornamental Plants*).

Nehrling owed eight thousand dollars in mortgage obligations on his Naples property when he died. The property was sold at a sheriff's auction on the steps of the Collier Courthouse in Everglades City a few years later for six thousand dollars and his possessions were dispersed. The Florida Audubon Society purchased a large part of Nehrling's personal library from his estate and donated it to Rollins College in Winter Park, where Nehrling had once lectured on horticulture. Housed in the Special Collection Library, the Nehrling Papers consist of more than seventeen hundred books, manuscripts, periodicals, pamphlets, photographs, letters, and other documents in both English and German. Hedwig Michel, of the Koreshan Unity Foundation in Estero, amassed numerous documents, articles, and manuscripts about and by Nehrling in the foundation's archives. That collection is comparable in size and significance to the Rollins College collection. Michel honored Nehrling posthumously with title "Patron Saint of Florida Gardens."

The Garden Club of Palm Beach sponsored a book titled *The Plant World of Florida,* edited by Alfred and Elizabeth Kay and published by the Macmillan Company of New York in 1933, as an abstract of the horticultural information from Nehrling's articles originally published the *American Eagle.* The book became one of the most valuable references for Florida gardeners. In 1944 and 1946, Allen H. Andrews edited two volumes of Nehrling's articles originally published in the *American Eagle.* The books are titled *My Garden in Florida,* volumes 1 and 2.

Nehrling was listed in *American Men of Science* and *Who's Who in America.* He penned numerous articles for *Gardener's Chronicle, Garden and Forest, Die Gartenwelt, Florida Fruits and Flowers,* the *Florist's Exchange,* and the *American Eagle.* He published books on bird life and horticulture. He was an active and honorary member of many learned societies and a fellow of the American Ornithological Union from its inception. He is ranked among the eminent natural scientists of his time, such as Dr. Harold Hume, Dr. David Fairchild of the U.S. Department of Agriculture, Dr. Wilson Popenoe of the United Fruit Company, and so on. That those great men sought his counsel despite his lack of formal horticultural qualifications is testimony to his natural talent, inclination, knowledge, and authority in subtropical horticulture.

The Naples property lay untended until 1952, when Julius Fleischmann brought the sleeping beauty back to life as the Caribbean Gardens. Dedicated to reviving the gardens, he invested a good deal of money (a luxury Nehrling never had) in restoring and enlarging the gardens. The property was described as a "veritable Garden of Eden" when Fleischmann purchased the land and planned to preserve Nehrling's plants as a memorial to the pioneer horticulturist. He saved the Nehrling garden and combined it with property to the south, creating a unique botanical and zoological attraction. In 1955 Julia F. Morton, of the Morton Collectanea at the University of Miami, published a booklet titled *Some Useful and Ornamental Plants of the Caribbean Gardens*, drawing heavily upon and celebrating Nehrling's work.

Ironically, despite his many achievements in plant propagation and research, it was not for horticulture but for his impressive work in a second field that Nehrling received the academic recognition of an honorary degree. His son Arno, by then executive secretary of the Massachusetts Horticultural Society, is quoted in Morton's pamphlet: "His principal ornithological writing was his *Die Nordamerikanische Vogelwelt*, illustrated with color plates by Prof. Robert Ridgeway of the Smithsonian Institution and two German artists, Goring and Muetzel. . . . It was in recognition of his work as an ornithologist that an honorary doctorate was conferred upon him."

2

Oriental Trees and Shrubs

There is no country in the world where flowers, trees and shrubs are so universally beloved as in Japan. They are inseparable from the life, art and literature of the people, and to deprive the Japanese of their flowers would be to take the sunshine out of their lives. Beautiful plants are enjoyed equally by the high and the low. The charming natural landscapes of the mountain sides, of glades and glens and along the lakes and rivers are a continuous pleasure to one and all. The richer classes, in the seclusion of their well-kept gardens and pleasure grounds, can feast their eyes almost constantly on the beauties of plant life, while the poor have the benefit of the public parks, temple gardens and flower shows, and even the poorest of the poor devote a few coins of their earnings to the gratification of their taste.*

Flowers and shrubs, and even dwarfed trees in beautiful and tasteful pots or vases, are everywhere present, and the private grounds,—particularly the temple gardens,—are replete with floral treasures, having been grown by them since times immemorial. They were the delight of the first explorers. The pioneer botanists and horticultural collectors raved over the many new and extremely beautiful plants which they discovered in the gardens and forests of this island empire. In fact Japan, and more recently also China, have been almost inexhaustible treasure grounds for the plant collector. Our gardens are replete with plants from the far-eastern countries. I have room here only for a rough outline. It would take volumes to treat the subject in the way that it deserves. I mention only a few.

The Japanese and Chinese Lilies are the most exquisite and the most enchantingly fragrant in the world. The Chrysanthemum reigns supreme in our flower shows in November. The Japanese or Kaempfer's Iris with its huge flowers in many fantastic colors is a glory in many of our water gar-

---

*A discussion of the forest flora of Japan is included in the companion volume, *Nehrling's Early Florida Gardens.*

dens, while the Peony is the undisputed queen of June in the North. Unfortunately only a few of these plants succeed well in Florida. But we have the gorgeously glorious Camellia or the Japonica. We have the deliciously scented Banana-Shrub, the Pittosporum, the Gardenia or Cape Jasmine and the Loquat, the Hortensia or Hydrangea, the wonderfully beautiful evergreen Azaleas, the lovely Fortune's Double Yellow Rose, the two Banksia Roses and many others, all hailing from Japan and China. For our subtropical gardens most of these, including many beautiful Bamboos, are ideal plants in every respect. They are extremely beautiful when used in combination with our native species.

For the benefit of my readers I shall quote a really classical discourse from A. B. Freeman-Mitford (Lord Redesdale) from his *Bamboo Garden* (p. 199). He writes:

He who would lay out for himself a paradise,—I use the word in old Parkinson's sense,—cannot do better, having the needful leisure, than set out to drink in wisdom in Japan. Not in the Japanese gardens, for, as we shall see presently, nowhere is the gardener's work more out of tune with nature than in that country of paradoxes; but on the mountain side, in the dim recesses of the forest, by the banks of many a torrent there the great silent Teacher has mapped out for our instruction plans and devices which are the living refutation of the heresies of stone masonry. There are spots among the Hakone Mountains, not to mention many other places, of which the study of a lifetime could hardly exhaust the lessons.

One reason which makes Japan such a rich field for observation is that perhaps in no other country will you find so many types of vegetation within so small an area. The somber gloom of the Cryptomerias, the stiff and stately Firs; Pine Trees twisted and gnarled into every conceivable shape; flowering trees and shrubs in countless varieties, combined with the feathery grace of the Bamboo, and all arranged as if the function of each plant were not only itself to look its very best, but also to enhance and set off the beauty of its neighbors, present a series of pictures difficult to realize. Fancy a great glen all besnowed with the tender bloom of Cherries and Peaches and Magnolias in spring, or blazing with the flames of the Maples to warm the chill October, and in the depths a great waterfall leaping from rock to rock for some hundreds of feet! Here and there the soft brown thatch of some peasant's cottage, or the quaint eaves of a Buddhist temple jut out from the hillside, while far down below you see the emerald green patches of paddy fields, while great white cranes stalk about in solemn state. In such a glen you may sit hour after hour, feasting your eyes in wonder, and learning how to get the fullest value out of your treasures at home. Few if any of the plants which you are admiring are too tender to be grown in England, and the fair landscape before you furnishes the key of their successful adaptation.

The Japanese are true lovers of scenery; no people have a keener feeling for a beautiful landscape; to them a moon rising over Mount Fuji is a poem, and their pilgrimages to see the Almonds in blossom or the glories of the autumn tints are almost proverbial,—and yet, strange to say, in their gardens they seem to take a delight in setting at defiance every one of those canons which nature has laid down so unmistakable for those who will be at the pains to read them.

The Japanese garden is a mere toy that might be the appanage of a doll's house. Everything is in miniature. There is a dwarf forest of stunted Pines with a Lilliputian waterfall running into a tiny pond full of giant goldfish,—the only big things to be seen. There is a semblance in earth and stones of the great Mount Fuji, and in one corner is a temple to Inari Sama, the god who presides over farming, and is waited upon by the foxes. Stone lanterns of grotesque shape spring up here and there, and the paths are made of great flat stepping-stones set well apart so as not to touch one another; shrubs, Cycads and dwarf Conifers are planted, not without quaint skill and prettiness, but there are no broad effects, no inspiration of nature. It is all spick and span, intensely artificial, a miracle of misplaced zeal and wasted labor!

Attached to some of what were the Daimios' palaces in the old days, there were some fine pleasure grounds, well laid out, rich in trees, and daintily kept. The gardens of the Mikado, by the shore of the Bay of Yedo, are beautiful. But the average Japanese garden is such as I have described it,—a mere whimsical toy, a relic of an art imported from China, and stereotyped on the willow pattern plate.

None in this country, save a Japanese himself, can hope to have a veritable Japanese garden; and none should for a moment aspire to have one. For the true Japanese garden is a national outgrowth of rare sentiment, tradition, and not infrequently religion, and requires years of unbelievably careful planning and minute attention to details before it reaches completion. Moreover, when it is at last complete, the most admirable example of the Japanese garden might seem very bare and flowerless and unlike a real garden to our untrained, hence perhaps unseeing western eyes. (*Garden* magazine, August 1920, p. 376.)

It is not the imitation of the Japanese garden that I am trying to recommend: It is the Japanese poetic love for gardening, for plants and plant beauty,—for nature,—that I want to bring before my readers as an example to follow. And it is preeminently my desire to call the attention of American plant lovers to the incomparable wealth of the wonderful Japanese and Chinese broad-leaved evergreen trees and shrubs that are available for our southern gardens. Long before the present and the preceding generations,—in ante-bellum times,—the gardens along the south Atlantic and Gulf were celebrated for their Chinese and Japanese Roses, for their masses of Camellias and Azaleas, for their Banana-Shrubs, Loquats, Pittosporum, Viburnums and many other species hailing from the Far East.

As I have already pointed out, the native plants should form the foundation of every American garden. But variety is the spice of life, and in horticulture we look constantly for variety. The larger the number of species we grow, the more different and impressive their forms and flowers, the greater and the more lasting will be our interest and pleasure. There cannot be the least doubt that the beautiful Japanese and Chinese plants happily supplement our own native species.

Among the many celebrated botanical collectors we find the names of Robert Fortune Maries, Dr. Hall, Ernest H. Wilson, Dr. Augustine Henry, Forrest, our own Frank W. Meyer, R. F. Rock and many others.

Chinese and Japanese Hollies

Many of our native evergreen trees and shrubs are very beautiful, yet they exhibit comparatively little variety. China and Japan possess a wealth of beautiful plants that are positively bewildering. Since more than a century and a half we have been acquainted with the flora of the coast regions, and many Roses, among them the exquisite tea-scented species, Camellias and Azaleas, Gardenias, Photinias, and most lovely Magnolias, etc., have been inmates of our gardens for more than a hundred years. It is only lately that the regions of Yunnan and Szechwan have been explored, especially the sub-tropical mountainous regions. The flora seems inexhaustible, and so many of the trees, shrubs and perennials are highly ornamental.

There is probably no other place in the world that would yield so many plants adapted and worth cultivating in our southern and gulf states and Florida. Keen collectors like Dr. Augustine Henry, E. H. Wilson, Rock, Forrest and others, have sent,—mostly to England,—grand collections of new plants and seeds. New species of new genera have been discovered, and new and most beautiful species of old genera, such as *Camellia, Symplocos, Azalea, Rhodazalea, Ligustrum, Magnolia,* etc., have been added.

There are also new Hollies (*Ilex*), not yet perhaps, introduced, though in the course of time they will adorn our southern gardens with new and distinct charms. I am only hinting in a most cursory way what a wealth of new and beautiful evergreen trees and shrubs is in store for a future plant loving generation. No other botanical collector has written so charmingly and so vividly about his discoveries as Mr. E. H. Wilson (Chinese Wilson), the present assistant director of the Arnold Arboretum, in his book, *A Naturalist in China,* and in his contributions to the *Gardener's Chronicle* (London). Among the older and better known Chinese and Japanese evergreen shrubs the various beautiful Hollies occupy a foremost rank.

Ilex cornuta: The subject of this sketch is a native of northern China, particularly in the neighborhood of Shanghai. It was introduced to this country by the late indefatigable botanical collector F. N. Meyer from Soochow, Kiangsu, China, and distributed by our Bureau of Plant Industry. Mr. Meyer described it as "a very ornamental bush or small tree, loaded in winter with scarlet berries. A slow grower and probably not hardy north. Chinese name, Ta-hu-tse." At Chico, Calif., it has succeeded admirably and promises to be one of the best Hollies for regions where the winter is not too severe. (See "Plant Immigrants," No 117, under number 22979.)

I received two small plants of this fine evergreen, April 9, 1919, from Washington. They were planted out in my garden at Naples in well drained soil and have made a fine dense growth, being at present (November, 1925) about 3 feet high. Both are beautiful, compact and very conspicuous specimens. The leaves, strongly spined, remind one of those of our native *I. opaca,* but they are larger, of a somewhat lighter green, hard and leathery, almost always furnished with three strong spines at the end, which assume the appearance of horns. When young, one or two more spines are added at each side, but they disappear in older plants. Undoubtedly this beautiful Holly is hardy. As it grows so well in our southern states, even in south Florida, it should find a place in all good gardens. It is easily grown, even in poor sandy soils, but responds quickly to good cultivation and fertilizing.

Ilex crenata, (*I. fortunei*), Dwarf Japanese Holly: A beautiful evergreen Holly from Japan and fully as hardy as the foregoing. Several specimens, directly imported from Japan, among them a few with beautifully variegated leaves, did very well at Palm Cottage Gardens for many years. Growing thriftily in the rather dry sandy soil, but doing much better in moister and richer ground. It is a very slow grower, my largest plant not having attained more than 3 feet in height within twenty years. In Japan, where it grows on sandy barrens, and is found in nearly every part of the empire, it is usually also a low, much branched, rigid shrub, though under cultivation in the Japanese gardens it attains not infrequently a height of 20 feet. The leaves are rather light green, very lustrous, about one inch long, ovate-acute with crenate margins. The fruit, which is produced in great abundance, is black, ripening late in autumn. It is an excellent plant for rockeries or for grouping with some of the larger growing species. Its slow growth is probably the reason we do not see it more often in gardens or nurseries, for though readily propagated, it takes some time to attain to saleable size. While a great many of the Hollies do not strike root readily from cuttings, this dwarf species can be easily propagated in this manner. It really matters little at what season of the year the cuttings are taken, but a very good time is towards the end of summer or early in autumn.

Ilex integra: In the spring of 1896 I imported a large number of Japanese evergreen trees and shrubs directly from Yokohama. This consignment included a few small specimens of the above named Holly. In the fall of the same year the late Mr. P. J. Berckmans of Augusta, Ga., sent me several small bushy plants of *Othera japonica* [?] for experimental purposes in my garden at Gotha. In the course of time both of these plants turned out to be identical. I have called them the Othera Holly. This is a most beautiful species, very dense and upright in growth, with slightly reclining exterior branches, and a moderately fast grower. My specimens are from 12 to 15 feet high and very hardy and distinct. It is said that this holly eventually attains the size of a small tree. Specimens in Japan, 30 to 40 feet tall, are not rare. It grows equally well (at Palm Cottage Gardens) on high and low land. One of our distinguished pioneers of ornamental horticulture, the late Mr. E. H. Hart of Federal Point, informed me years ago that he had an Othera Holly in his grounds fully 22 feet high and of a dense and compact habit.

My plants are pictures of beauty, elegance and symmetry. They form, in company of *Ilex latifolia,* Chinese and Japanese Magnolias and *Michelia* [*figo*] (Banana-Shrubs) ideal groups. They do not at all remind one in their garb of the typical Hollies. The leaves are rather laurel-like, narrow obovate, 3 to 4 inches long and quite entire. In Mr. Hart's garden it has flowered and borne its vivid red berries in great abundance. I have only been lately successful in seeing one of my specimens adorned with its red berries.

As the Hollies are dioecious, care must be taken to plant the male and female specimens not too far apart, or crops of the beautiful red berries will not be produced. This fine species should be planted in groups of from five to ten and they should be about 12 to 15 feet apart. If seedlings are set out there will always be a sufficient number of both sexes represented. Though a most elegant evergreen, even without fruit, it is an extremely charming object when covered with an abundance of its brilliant red berries during the winter. It is a perfect success in our Florida gardens, and it is equally at home as far north as Augusta, Ga., and is also found in many gardens of South Carolina. All these specimens came originally from Mr. Berckman's Fruitland Nurseries at Augusta, Ga.

Ilex latifolia, the large-leaved Japanese Holly: This is a gem among broadleaved evergreens, and is perfectly at home in our Florida gardens, though a slow grower on high, dry pineland. In rich hammock land or in soils containing a sufficient amount of humus it grows much faster. It is the finest and most beautiful and distinct of all the Hollies, and Prof. C. S. Sargent, an authority on Japanese trees and shrubs, says that it is probably the handsomest broad-leaved evergreen tree that grows in the forests of Japan. It is much cultivated there in private gardens and in temple grounds. The leaves are about 6 inches long and 3 to 4 inches broad, and coarsely serrated along their edges, very thick and leathery, dark green and very lustrous. The large scarlet berries of this tree, which eventually assumes a height of 30 to 40 feet, do not ripen until late in autumn or early in winter and are produced in the greatest abundance in axillary clusters, remaining on the branches until the beginning of the following summer.

In order to enjoy the abundance and the beauty of these brilliant red berries it is advisable to plant quite a number of specimens in groups to make sure that male and female plants are represented. In 1896 I imported from Japan a dozen fine bushy plants and all were set out in my garden at Gotha. I made the mistake of scattering them around on high and low land, instead of planting all in a group. The largest ones, in good soil, have attained a height of about 12 feet and as much in diameter. One female specimen has borne a crop of berries,—a most beautiful sight on Christmas and New Year's Day.

This Holly forms beautiful dense, well-shaped specimens in our gardens and it should be largely planted, not only on account of its brilliant berries, but also in consideration of the size and the character of its abundant foliage. It requires rich and rather moist soil and responds well to well balanced applications of organic and commercial fertilizers. My largest specimen at present,—a female plant,—is about 12 to 14 feet high, being of dense, upright growth and of globular form.

Ilex rotunda (*I. microcarpa*): Also from Japan, this is a fine dense shrub or small tree, 20 to 30 feet high in its native home. The lustrous leaves are oblong or elliptic-acute, pointed and quite entire. The berries are small and red, and appear in pedunced clusters. As I imported only one plant in 1896 I never had an opportunity to see the fruit. It grows well in good sandy soil in central Florida, being very dense and quite distinct.

There are about two hundred species of Hollies known to science, mostly natives of North and South America, tropical and temperate Asia and Europe. Only a few have been discovered in Australia and Africa. With the exception of *Ilex paraguariensis* (the Mate) none is of any special economic value, but almost all are very interesting and beautiful shrubs or trees, many of them evergreen, others deciduous.

Crape-Myrtles

Lagerstroemia indica: This is one of our floral gems. I cannot conceive of anything more beautiful than a well-grown and well-shaped Crape-Myrtle in full bloom. During three months of the year,—June, July and August,— my garden at Gotha, southeast of the house, shows a picture of such dreamy and vivid beauty, of such glorious charm, and at the same time so uniquely magnificent that no pen and no pencil are able to give a correct idea of it. It has to be seen to fully understand and appreciate it. In all my rambles I never found even a remote rival of it. At this time quite a large and dense specimen of the rose-colored form of the Crape-Myrtle, about 20 feet high and 15 feet in diameter, is a sheet of brilliant rosy-red. It is in all its beauty. I do not remember a similar floral picture of such impressive brilliance and loveliness. This specimen forms the background of a shady group of [*Michelia figo*], and the Florida-Myrtle, which have again a foreground of some large and healthy *Cycas revoluta* and clumps of *Zamia floridana*. Up to a recent date a very large and most effective specimen of *Dioon edule* stood also in the immediate foreground. In the not far distance, forming a background for the Crape-Myrtle, grows a tall, broad and dense evergreen Cypress (*Cupressus* [*lusitanica*]). In this frame of Cycads, broad-leaved evergreen and the Cypress, the picture of this tree in full bloom reminds one of fairyland.

I often wonder, when I see the sheets of rosy color, why this glorious plant is not used in groups as well as in single specimens in our parks and gardens for the formation of exquisite landscape pictures. It is true the Crape-Myrtle loses its leaves in winter, and it is also true that it flowers in the summer months, but we need the latter class of plants just as much as the winter bloomers, and as for its deciduous habit, it can be planted in the background of fine bushy evergreens, such as Banana-Shrubs, Myrtles, Hollies, Illiciums, *Viburnum odoratissimum,* and some of the finer Privets. Its deciduous habit is scarcely evident when thus grouped.

My favorite specimen, the rose-colored form, has panicles of flowers almost a yard long if the many axillary clusters are also taken into consideration. They form an almost unbroken sheet of color, as there are many upright flaming branches. This form is undoubtedly the most showy one. There are, however, quite a few distinct varieties, among them scarlet, purple blush and even pure white sorts. None of them is quite as floriferous and as showy as the rose-colored variety. My specimen of the latter is surrounded by many vigorous seedlings which are constantly coming up from self-sown seeds.

The rage for winter-flowering evergreens in Florida,—to please the tourists,—has unfortunately pushed this gem into the background. In the gardens of Georgia, South Carolina and as far north as Baltimore, in Alabama and even in southern Tennessee the Crape-Myrtle is highly valued for its flowers. In Houston, Texas, I found it one of the most common ornaments of the gardens, and it also was much used as a street and avenue tree. In these gardens I often saw most effective combinations in which it was used to great advantage, fine dense evergreen shrubs, such as Gardenias and Hollies, forming the foreground. In Mobile I admired a group of the dwarf, dense and very elegant *Bambusa gracilis* [?] and in the background a large group of various Crape-Myrtles. In another garden in Pensacola I saw it as a background of Camellias and Azaleas. Such pictures—and they can be varied manifoldly to suit the individual taste—should be found everywhere in the gardens of Florida. Scattered around in the grounds they do not show their full beauty. This is only possible when massed, or planted as a background to rather medium sized evergreen shrubs.

In the South the Crape-Myrtle is often also called the Indian-Lilac. The genus *Lagerstroemia* (named by Linnaeus after his friend, Magnus N. Lagerstrom) consists of about twenty species, all inhabitants of tropical Asia. We grow in tropical Florida the most exquisite Queen's Crape-Myrtle ([*L. speciosa*]) a very tender evergreen species. The present species, though much grown in India, is a native of China, particularly the southern part of the Celestial Empire, where it evidently has been grown in the gardens since times immemorial. As far as I know, it never and nowhere has actually been found wild of late years. Its leaves are rather small, about 2 inches long, elliptic or oblong, acute, sessile and deciduous. The flowers are either brilliant rosy-red, blush, white, crimson or purple, the rose-colored variety being by far the most popular, as it is the most floriferous.

The flowers are arranged in upright lilac-like racemes and also in axillary clusters. The structure of the flowers is very different from that of the Lilac, the petals being nearly one inch broad with crimped edges, while the base is narrowed to a slender stalk-like claw. They are very beautiful, but they are scentless. The bark of the tree is smooth as if polished. It is much grown in our northern parks. I have seen large beds of dwarf plants in full bloom. As soon as the cold weather approaches the plants are taken up and wintered in cellars. As soon as warm weather again approaches they are planted out in beds in sunny spots. They are much admired when in bloom.

Under cultivation in Florida and all over the South, the Crape-Myrtle needs little care. A rich sandy loam and now and then a good application of old manure is all it requires. Of course it responds, as most plants do, to good cultivation and fertilizing.

Azaleas and Camellias

Azalea indica, Indian Azalea, Chinese Evergreen Azalea: One of the most precious jewels of all flowering shrubs, of incomparable beauty and of an ornamental value without a rival. Perfectly hardy and most successfully grown out of doors in the Gulf Coast and South Atlantic regions and in northern and central Florida, where the conditions of soil are beneficial for its growth.

A famous botanist and scholar, a man of culture and high ideals, the late Dr. Carl Mohr, of Mobile, Ala., has the following to say about this Azalea in his model book, *Alabama Plant Life*: "Of the large number of hardy shrubs only the most frequent and prominent can be mentioned, the hybrid Indian Azaleas taking the first place. These shrubs, loaded with a profusion of flowers running from pure white through all shades of dazzling flame color, vermilion, pink and purple, are produced from the beginning to near the close of spring in a perfection scarcely ever surpassed."

Only those who have seen the color-masses of these Azaleas in April and May in the wonderfully rich southern gardens, pervaded with the delicious perfume of [*Michelia figo*] and *Magnolia grandiflora,* and made still more charming by the song of the mocking-bird and the cardinal redbird, can have a real idea of this gorgeous and wonderfully lovely beauty. I must confess the reality far outrivaled my expectations. While passing through southern Georgia, early in April, 1904, I enjoyed sights of flowering Azaleas in the gardens that neither pen nor brush can bring before the eyes of my readers. This beauty must be seen to be fully understood and appreciated. There is nothing like it anywhere in the more northern parts of the country. In China, in regions not severely cold, *Azalea indica* is indigenous, attaining a height of from 4 to 6 feet and bearing numerous small evergreen leaves, which are cuneate-lanceolate, finely crenulated, covered with sharp, close-pressed rigid hairs. The branches are also covered with these rigid hairs. The campanulate flowers are terminal, solitary or twins and in the wild form seem to be of a purplish-lavender color.

Since times immemorial the Chinese have nursed and cultivated this Azalea in their gardens, attending to it with loving care and deep interest. New varieties in many colors, either by hybridization or selection, made their appearance and were carefully preserved. When the first European botanical and horticultural collectors entered China they were not only greatly surprised at what they found, but they were overwhelmed by the brilliancy of the color masses that was placed before their astonished eyes. [Botanically the Azalea is considered a true Rhododendron, however, traditional usage requires the distinction of *Azalea* for horticultural purposes.]

This Azalea was one of the first treasures that went to Europe (1808), very likely by way of India. Hence its botanical name, *A. indica*. When it first flowered in England its wonderful beauty and its sheets of color created a veritable sensation and deep interest which is still evident in our present day. Gardeners in many lands, especially in England, Germany, Holland and Belgium, took the plants in their hands, and raised many hundreds, each one different from the other and each one more beautiful than its forebears.

There is now a long list of glorious varieties, double and single, and from the purest white to the deepest and most glowing scarlet and crimson, and there are hybrids galore which are beautifully spotted and strangely marked. They are all so very floriferous that scarcely a leaf can be seen when in full bloom. Even in England the best plants for forcing purposes are obtained from the continent where they are grown in enormous quantities. Many thousands,—in fact hundreds of thousands,—were annually imported, as they cannot be grown so cheaply, so easily and with such perfection in this country.

The old and reliable firm of Henry A. Dreer, Inc., in Philadelphia, imported annually about thirty carloads of *Azalea indica*. They were sold for a low price, mostly as little round-headed trees in full bloom, to flower lovers all over the country, everywhere finding enthusiastic reception and bringing into many a poor family home, love, hope and happiness. The Azalea shows in spring were features of national interest. In fact this Azalea was everywhere extremely popular and a great favorite. When I saw the great show,—thousands of them in full bloom,—at the World's Columbian Exposition of 1893, the sight was so bewildering, so grand, so brilliant and so overpowering that it really staggered imagination.

Azalea indica is indeed one of the most precious jewels of our southern gardens, growing extremely well in the rather low coast regions from Charleston, S.C., to Savannah and Jacksonville, Fla.; and even as far south as Orlando and Kissimmee and probably even to Tampa. All along the Gulf Coast from Pensacola to Mobile and New Orleans and all through southern Louisiana it is a much appreciated garden ornament. In Texas I have not seen it in the open. The Magnolia Gardens on the Ashley, in South Carolina, have a world-wide fame for their grand old specimens of Indian Azaleas. When in full bloom thousands of visitors come and enjoy the sight.

I do not hesitate to declare that the beauty of these Azaleas in a number of gardens at Orlando and vicinity outrivals every other floral show that may present itself. And here they are winter bloomers. My Horticultural notebook shows the following entry: "March 10. *Azalea indica* gloriously in bloom in quite a number of gardens in Orlando. There is a specimen on a lawn in one of the side streets near Lake Lucerne, being about five feet high and almost as broad, which is a sheet of dazzling rosy-scarlet, and in another garden nearby is one that is covered with a snowy-white garb. The very interesting Carpenter place near Lake Cherokee is replete with the most exquisite specimens of various colors from the purest white to the most brilliant red. And there are also a few double varieties."

Azaleas, like Rhododendrons and other members of the family Ericaceae, do not grow in soil that contains lime. They need a compost of a mixture of peat, leaf-mold, good fibrous loam and sand. When well established a little,—very little,—old well decomposed cow manure is quite beneficial. The soil must be well drained, and it never must dry out. As a rule the Indian Azalea, and also [*Rhododendron molle*] (with rather large yellow, orange or pink flowers) is of easy culture. Thrips and red spider must be kept down by frequent syringings mornings and evenings. In all cases, the roots near the stems must be above the soil, so that the water may not sink in next to the stem. They must not be cultivated, as the roots are near the surface. A good mulch of old leaves is essential. Propagation is effected by cuttings and grafting, both operations being very easy. In fact, the scions of these plants are among the easiest and quickest to form a union with the stock of anything that we know. [Nehrling's original text includes an extensive list of varieties and cultivars.]

Camellia japonica, Camellia: Called "Japonica" in the South, the Indian Azalea and Camellia are the glories of our southern gardens,—the gardens of the Gulf Coast and South Atlantic regions. No pen and no pencil can do justice to these color displays. The Camellia is even more uniquely beautiful on account of its deep evergreen, leathery, glossy foliage and its mostly very double, richly colored and beautifully marked flowers. The two cannot be compared, so distinct are they. Each group has an individuality of its own.

The Camellia, in its wild form much like a single red rose, has been cultivated by the Japanese and Chinese since times immemorial. The Chinese Camellia gardens were a bewildering sensation to the first European plant hunters. Numerous and wonderfully rich and varied in colors were these double and half-double varieties. The often very large specimens were covered with thickly scattered flowers of many colors which formed a most delightful contrast with the large leathery foliage. Many of the flowers were so double and formal that they looked more artificial than natural, but they fitted in well with the life and culture of the people. They were favorites with all,—rich and poor, old and young. The temple gardens also were replete with them. When it made its first appearance in Europe in 1739 it met with a royal reception and was universally admired for the rich and pleasing contrast afforded by the dark green, rather large leaves and their superb double flowers, which latter were largely used to enliven the greenhouses throughout the winter and spring months. For more than a hundred years it was called the "Queen of Flowers."

The literature on the Camellia is very extensive. Dr. B. Seeman wrote the first monograph of the genus, and Curtis, in 1819, another one on the cultivated varieties. Then followed in 1828 Baumann's *Bollweiler Camelien-sammlung* and in 1831 Chandler's *Camelliaceae*. Berlese's *Monograph du Genre Camellia,* with 300 colored plates, appeared in 1839, and Verschaffelt's *Nouvelle Monographie du Camellia* with 576 beautifully colored plates, between 1846–1860. Robert Halliday's *Practical Camellia Culture* (Baltimore, 1880) is the only American book on the subject.

The above titles, only a few of the many, show plainly how immensely popular the Camellia has been as a glasshouse plant. It had first been made known to the western world by George Joseph Kamel, or Camellus, a Moravian Jesuit, who traveled in Asia in the seventeenth century.

In this article I can only touch the subject from the open air point of view, the Camellia being one of the most important, one of the grandest and most charming garden ornaments of the South. Old Camellia Trees in Charleston, S.C.; in Augusta and Savannah, Ga.; in the famous Magnolia Gardens on the Ashley in Quincy and Tallahassee, Fla.; in Montgomery and Mobile, Ala.; in New Orleans and other places in southern Louisiana and Mississippi, show plainly that the "Japonica," as it is universally called in these southern localities, must have been introduced into the South even before the Revolutionary War, or early in the nineteenth century. I have seen trees, particularly in Tallahassee, Quincy and Monticello, that were 35 feet tall, and in some cases there were specimens 20 to 25 feet high and 65 feet in circumference. This was in 1886, and old inhabitants told me then that they had been planted a hundred years before.

They always made a very delightful impression, especially when they were growing in groups. Even without flowers these dense evergreen specimens were highly ornamental in their garb of broad, glossy green foliage, but when in full bloom in this latitude in February, March and April, the sight was enchantingly brilliant. Near Mobile I was directed to a place that was called "Japonica Glen" or "Japonica Gardens." This was surrounded by tall old Magnolias, very beautiful large Banana Shrubs, large cone-shaped specimens of *Viburnum odoratissimum,* masses of Gardenias and fine Loquats, and in the broad center, surrounded by a green smooth lawn, there were several hundred Camellias in full bloom, from the purest white to the deepest carmine. These big blossoms reminded me somewhat of large double roses, but they were of better, waxy substance, though more formal. The largest bushes,—in some cases small trees,—were from 12 to 15 feet high and often 10 feet in diameter. Azaleas in separate beds were also in bloom, and the delicious perfume of the Banana Magnolia pervaded this entire garden. Mocking-birds sang joyously; painted buntings uttered their sprightly notes, and cardinal redbirds made the deep green foliage of the Magnolias alive by their glowing color and loud strains. It all seemed to me like fairy-land. I wish I had the ability to describe it with all its glories, but this is beyond me. The master mind of a Charles Kingsley or Lafcadio Hearn only could succeed to give a real idea of what I saw.

Such paradises along the South Atlantic and in the region of the Gulf coast should not be the exception; they should be the rule. Where such glorious plants as the Camellia (and many others almost equally beautiful) are available this earth can be made a most beautiful place to enjoy life and make it a happy spot. I know that these grand evergreen shrubs have endured a temperature of 15°F and even 10°F for a short time without bad results. I think that where [*Michelia figo*] can be grown successfully, the Camellia will also be hardy. It delights in a rather heavy, rich soil. The finest specimens I ever saw were growing in Tallahassee in a tenacious clay-like loam. In Jacksonville, where I also have seen many fine large Camellias, the soil was very sandy, but rich in humus and this holds true in respect to soil conditions at Orlando, where many dense bushes adorn the lawns. They require a soil rather moist and rich in humus, and they should be mulched during the rainy season with old cow manure. Deep hoeing around the plants should be avoided. I have always flat-hoed the surrounding soil,—not deeper than an inch,—so that the roots near the surface were not injured.

People with ideals, enthusiasm, love for plants, leisure, and last but by no means least, with ambition and the necessary means, should plant Camellias in masses, by the hundreds and in many varieties, in separate beds. They should be planted 10 to 12 feet apart each way and should be carefully nursed. They need careful watering during dry spells, else the buds will drop unopened.

The Camellia is a very slow grower, and specimens 30 to 35 feet high may be 75 or even 100 years old. I have about fifty different varieties in Palm Cottage Gardens, many of them almost forty years old, but none of them is taller than 7 or 8 feet. A rose grows in six months as much as a Camellia in six years. This is one of the minor reasons why it went out of fashion and why these plants were always much more expensive than common commercial plants.

During the past twenty-five years my Camellias have been a constant source of intense joy when in bloom and they were likewise a revelation to the many visitors who come and go. The greatest trouble with the visiting public is to keep your bushes or trees intact,—not to cut the flowers or to tear off entire branches. The Camellia cannot stand such treatment. Flowers should never be cut with their stems as this greatly injures not only the plant, but is particularly detrimental to next season's flowering. A Rose you can,—you really must cut with a long stem; a Camellia should remain where it blooms. I have seen fine dense bushes utterly ruined by cutting the flowers.

How far south the Camellia can be cultivated successfully in Florida I do not know. At Gotha (Orange County) they thrive exceedingly well, even with very little attention and on high, poor pineland. I am quite sure that they will do equally well at Kissimmee, Lakeland and Winter Haven and that they will grow splendidly in the rich phosphate region of Bartow. Many years ago very fine and large specimens were dug up in the above mentioned Camellia garden in southern Alabama, and were transported with big balls of soil around their roots to Tampa where they were set out in the grounds of the Tampa Bay Hotel. For one reason or another they did not thrive. All disappeared in the course of time, and I am not aware of one single specimen in that city, large or small. But this conclusion is by no means final. In well prepared soil and under half shade it may be grown perhaps in localities where we do not see it now. Some of the causes why we see these noble and proud plants so rarely in our present day gardens can be summed up in the following:

There are no Camellia specialists in this country; they are never advertised, and in consequence few of our present generation know anything about them; they are slow growers and therefore more expensive than common garden plants.

The Camellia is a comparatively expensive plant, even in Europe where it is grown by specialists in immense quantities. The beauty and variety of many of the gardens of middle and south Georgia is due to the late Mr. P. J. Berckmans. He was the leading spirit of ornamental horticulture in the South Atlantic states for almost half a century. The most beautiful Chinese and Japanese evergreens were distributed by him, and the Camellia was one of his special favorites. He propagated them largely and his importations from Japan, China, and Europe ran into many thousands. In 1894 he sent me a collection of such beautiful hybrids as *Camellia* 'Donckelardii,' 'Chandleri Elegans,' 'Contessa Lavinia,' 'Maggi Rosea,' 'Lady Hume's Blush,' 'C. M. Hovey,' old double white ('Alba Plena'), 'Countess of Derby,' 'Fimbriata,' 'Jenny Lind,' 'La Maestosa,' 'Mad. Ambrose Verschaffelt,' 'Marchioness of Exeter,' 'Rubens,' 'Thomas Moore' and others. A friend of mine at Orlando was anxious to add a few large specimens to his collection, and I wrote Mr. Berckmans about it. He informed me that specimens 6 to 8 feet high could not be dug up anywhere in Georgia for less than $250 to $500 each, and that people, even at that price, hesitated to part with them, and they are worth it.

The Camellia is one of the noblest of the plant aristocracy, occupying a foremost rank among the most magnificent of all garden ornaments. I imported large consignments directly from Japan in the early '90's of the last century, among them *Camellia sasanqua* and *C. reticulata,* and I scarcely ever lost a single plant. How much they were in favor is shown by the fact that the late Mr. C. M. Hovey of Boston had made the Camellia his specialty and that he obtained wonderful results by cross-breeding and selection. Some of the finest hybrids still in existence were raised by him. Hovey was a great lover of fine rare plants and his *Rhodoleia championii* was the only large specimen in the country. Another specialist was the late Mr. Samuel B.

Parsons of Flushing, N.Y. He had, at one time, a most beautiful subtropical nursery on an island in the St. John's a little north of Palatka. Here he grew mostly Azaleas and Camellias in large quantities.

For more than a century the Camellia was the special favorite of the horticultural world, just as the Orchid and the Rose are the fashionable flowers of the present day. On account of its lack of perfume, its stiff formality and its slow growth and tedious propagation it lost the favor of the general public as a glasshouse plant, but in our southern gardens where it can be grown and associated with a multitude of many elegant and highly fragrant flowers, these objections do not hold. Of late years many of the more graceful semi-double kinds, showing their profusion of yellow anthers conspicuously, have again come to the front. Many of these new forms come directly from China and Japan and they are much grown in England and elsewhere.

We need Camellia and Azalea specialists in the South,—specialists of Japanese and Chinese plants,—to take hold not only of the old favorites but also of the many new discoveries by such collectors as Mr. E. H. Wilson, Dr. Augustine Henry and others. Cultured and ambitious young men, enthusiasts and plant lovers like S. B. Parsons, C. M. Hovey and P. J. Berckmans should take up the cultivation, hybridization and distribution of these garden jewels.

The propagation of the Camellia, though slow, is quite easy. Single red Camellias can be raised by the thousands from imported seeds, and these seedlings form an ideal stock to graft the finest varieties on. They also can be propagated from cuttings of the ripe growth late in summer.

My Camellias were never troubled with diseases, but there are a few insect pests that must be kept down. Mealy bug and scale insects are often found on the underside of the leaves and aphids sometimes attack the young foliage. Thrips and red spider are best kept in check by syringing. With the usual care and insecticides the plants can easily be kept clean.

There are hundreds of most exquisite hybrids and it would require quite a number of pages to describe them. [Nehrling gives a listing of hybrids and cultivars of the era.]

Camellia sasanqua, Sasanqua: Known as the Susan Kuwa in Japan, where it is a native, it has been a favorite in gardens for centuries. Many beautiful varieties, single and double, originated with the Japanese, but only a few of them have reached England or America. I imported my plants,—five named sorts,—directly from Japan in 1897. Two of them, a double and a semi-double red one, were rather weak and did not thrive, while the specimens of the single red typical species started into growth most vigorously, and the same holds true of the snowy-white double Sasanqua. A third variety, with deep pink flowers and a white center, is only a medium grower. All of them are still growing well and form wonderful ornaments in Palm Cottage Gardens. The following is quoted from my Horticultural notebook:

This morning (Nov. 7) a cool breeze from the north makes the air delightfully pure. The whole garden is alive with hundreds of yellow-rump or myrtle warblers, which arrived in swarms last night. It is undoubtedly the mission of plants and flowers to spread beauty, fragrance, sunshine, happiness, love and sympathy over our lives. I feel this most strongly this beautiful cool morning. The air is heavy with the delicious carnation-like perfume of the many dense evergreen Oleasters (*Elaeagnus* [*pungens* 'Reflexa'] and *E. macrophylla*), clambering vigorously in intricate masses over many an Oak and which are in full bloom now. The Night-blooming Jasmine (*Cestrum nocturnum*) saturated the air of the entire garden during the night with its powerful fragrance, and it still lingers near where it grows.

Hundreds of other plants are still in full bloom, notably the Allamanda and Love's-Chain (*Antigonon leptopus*) along the verandah. The single red *Camellia sasanqua*, however, is the glory of the day. It is in full bloom and is the brightest, most brilliant and most conspicuous of all the flowering plants near the house. The bushes are from 8 to 10 feet high and from 5 to 6 feet in diameter, and are provided with dense upright branches from the ground. They are covered with thousands of flowers of a very delightful brilliancy. They are single, of a lovely deep pink or rose color, their form and color, as well as their orange-yellow stamens, suggesting a Wild Rose. They exhale a pleasant delicate fragrance when we pass the shrubs, but on taking one of the blossoms in your hand and inhaling its odor, you will find that it is a little musty. The leaves are much smaller than those of the common Camellia, being of leathery texture, laurel-like, deep glossy green and growing in dense masses upon the shrubs. I have had the single Sasanqua in bloom as early as October 20 and as late as December 15. They are excellent as cut flowers.

The beautiful double white Sasanqua is a much more open and straggling grower. It commences to open its flowers early in December and is in full bloom at Christmas time, for which reason it has been called the Christmas Camellia by many flower-loving visitors. When at its best the entire plant seems to be covered with a pure white sheet. These flowers have so much substance, are so double, of such fine form, so pure and fragrant that they stand at the head of all winter-flowering plants. This flower of purity is verily the Queen of Christmas.

My Sasanquas all grow in poor, dry sandy soil, being supplied with very little fertilizer, but often receive liquid manure in various forms. Of all my Camellias the single red Sasanqua is the tallest, most upright and most vigorous grower. They are not troubled with insect pests, nor with diseases. Comparatively slender shoots strike roots much more readily as cuttings, than those of *C. japonica*. It appears to be extremely rare in cultivation, and my specimens seem to be the only ones in Florida. It is not in the trade, though it is a precious jewel as a subtropical winter flowering shrub.

[*Camellia sinensis*] Tea Shrub, Tea Plant: The Tea Plant is a native of China, Japan and India. Though mostly a shrub, it attains a height of 30 feet. Its growth is naturally dense and bushy, and its appearance very attractive. The leaves are elliptic-lanceolate, acuminate, serrate and somewhat wavy. There are two different varieties, [*C. sinensis*] var. *bohea* and var. *viridis*. The flowers are described as fragrant, white and nodding. The yellow stamens, seen in masses in the center of the blossom, add to their beauty. In my specimen, which flowers most profusely from November to early spring, I never have detected any odor. It grows on high dry pineland and is a fine sturdy, dense shrub about 5 feet high and almost as much through. When in good health and bushy and full of its nodding white flowers it is quite attractive. It is now and then found in the gardens of all the South Atlantic and Gulf Coast regions, and at Orlando I met it several years ago as a dense hedge plant. In Mobile I was delighted to enjoy the sight of a very dense specimen 12 to 15 feet high and grown in cone-shaped form.

Fine tea, as good as the best imported, has been grown in South Carolina and it can be grown in many other localities along our southern coast regions, but on account of the too expensive, unreliable, inefficient labor, it cannot be grown profitably here. In India, Ceylon (in the mountains), in China and Japan, where good and efficient labor can cheaply be had, the conditions are very different. All our tea comes from there. The Tea Shrub is well adapted for ornamental planting where soil and climate are conducive to its growth.

Camellia oleifera: Another very attractive species from China with fine evergreen leaves and numerous white, fragrant, solitary flowers. It attains a height of from 6 to 8 feet and was introduced to cultivation in 1820. I have never seen it.

Chinese and Japanese Magnolias

The Magnolias belong to one of the noblest plant families. All our native species,—eight in number,—are the aristocrats among the trees of our forests, and the evergreen *Magnolia grandiflora* is the undisputed queen,—the most glorious of all subtropical broad-leaved evergreens. The Chinese and Japanese species are mostly deciduous, but as all of them flower in our winter months, and as all of them do well in northern and central Florida, I shall briefly describe them here. Most of them form a very conspicuous picture when in full bloom at Palm Cottage Gardens, which is from Christmas to March. They even grow and flower beautifully in south Florida. Dr. G. W. Tyrrell in his interesting garden on the banks of the Caloosahatchee, near LaBelle, had very fine specimens. Unfortunately they were destroyed a few years ago by a long-lasting flood.

The genus *Magnolia* was named by Linnaeus after Pierre Magnol, director of the Botanical Gardens at Montpellier (1638–1715). There are about twenty-five species known to science. All are found in temperate eastern North America, and in temperate eastern Asia, being almost entirely confined to Japan and China, though a few occur in the Himalayas. All grow best in rich, moist well-drained soils. At Palm Cottage Gardens I have, or have had, most of the following species in my collection.

Magnolia campbellii, Campbell's Magnolia: Introduced in recent years by the Bureau of Plant Industry, but raised by me from seeds which I received from the late Mr. Kennedy of Darjeeling, Sikkim, Himalayas, in 1895. My seedlings grew well in pots, but were lost after having been planted out in the poor sandy soil of my hill-side. It is the most brilliantly colored of all Magnolias, and flowers before the leaves appear. Its large blossoms are rose-colored. Sir Joseph D. Hooker describes them as rosy-purple. The leaves are eight inches long, glaucous-green and ovate. Maries, the well-known English horticultural collector, wrote many years ago: "Forests of Evergreen Oaks and *Magnolia campbellii*. I should mention that I was here in March (near Darjeeling) and that the hill-sides were complete masses of the magnificent rosy flowers of this Magnolia. Here it really constitutes the beauty of the upper mountain forests (8,000 feet altitude)." It is a large and abundant tree in the Himalayas, where it attains a height of 80 feet. It will undoubtedly be hardy as far north as Charleston, S.C., and should thrive admirably all along the northern Gulf Coast. Fine flowering trees are today found in southern Ireland and in southwest England.

Magnolia delavayi: A most beautiful species as described in the *Botanical Magazine* and figured on plate 8282. Though I have tried to add it to my collection, I always failed. Attempts should be made by our Bureau of Plant Industry to introduce it in the near future. It will very likely prove hardy where our *Magnolia grandiflora* is found. It is an evergreen shrub or small tree with creamy-white, fragrant flowers. A native of southwestern China.

[*Magnolia heptapeta*] (syns. *M. conspicua, M. denudata,* M. *yulan*): A beautiful deciduous tree, attaining a height of 50 feet, with spreading branches and an abundance of large obovate-oblong leaves. I received my first specimen from my late friend, Thomas Meehan, of Germantown, Pa., in 1892, and a few additional ones from P. J. Berckmans of Augusta, Ga., in 1896. It is a strong grower at Palm Cottage Gardens. Though growing well in my dry, sandy soil, it should be well cultivated and fertilized. Only with good care will all these Magnolias show their full and distinct beauty. If neglected the scale insects get the upper hand and finally destroy them. My specimens began to flower profusely when only a few feet high, and always at Christmas and New Year's time. The flowers are large, pure white, campanulate, upright and sweet-scented. A large specimen in full bloom is a magnificent sight. Its variety, M. [*heptapeta*] var. *purpurea,* has flowers of a rose-red color which are pale pink within. Both are natives of central China.

Magnolia hypoleuca: One of the grandest of all Magnolias. A large Japanese tree, attaining a height of 100 feet, of broad pyramidal form, the handsomest of all deciduous species. The large leaves, eight to fourteen inches long, are of a fine green color above and silvery-white beneath. The showy white flowers display stamens with purple filaments. It is hardy even in the northern states, and will probably do well also in the lower South. My specimens, imported directly from Japan, did not thrive. It may grow more successfully, probably, in some of our rich, shady hammocks.

Magnolia kobus: A fine Japanese species which grows exceedingly well at Palm Cottage Gardens, flowering from January to late in March. It is not as abundant a bloomer as most other species, but there are always a number of open flowers evident. The flowers are pure white and appear before the leaves, as is the case with all deciduous Magnolias. The growth is upright, quite dense and pyramidal.

[*Magnolia quinquepeta*]: I received it in 1897 from P. J. Berckmans under the name of *M. obovata*. It is a rather large upright shrub. The large scentless flowers appear in great abundance during January and February and are upright, bell-shaped, white within and purple on the outside.

[*Magnolia sieboldii*]: A small tree from Japan. A very handsome species. Flowers white with crimson stamens, sweet-scented and produced in great abundance late in February and during March at Palm Cottage Gardens.

Magnolia pumila (*M. coco*) [These names do not appear in *Hortus Third*.]: The late Mr. P. J. Berckmans sent me in November, 1897, a fine small specimen of this little evergreen Magnolia. On account of the wonderfully strong and indescribably delicious fragrance exhaled by its rather small waxy-white flowers, this is a first-class gem. Unfortunately it is of straggling growth, never forming dense, well-shaped specimens. It is an extremely slow grower. My specimen attained only a height of four feet within fifteen years. In its native home, southern China, especially in and around Canton, its ultimate height is about 12 feet. The flowers are not at all conspicuous, being small, one to 1½ inches in diameter, somewhat nodding, white, slightly suffused with green and produced not very plentifully. They are intensely and powerfully fragrant. There is nothing among flowers that I can compare to it. This perfume is entirely its own, very characteristic and penetrating. Especially during the night, this perfume can be inhaled many rods distant. One flower perfumes the entire house if put in a vase. A lady friend of mine described it as a mixture of the odors of the Tuberose, the Gardenia, the Sweet Olive, the Golden-banded lily and the Tea Rose. My opinion is that this fragrance is entirely its own, and different from any other.

This gem only can be grown in rich, moist, well-drained, partly shaded soil. It grows particularly well in lath-houses among such plants as *Chamaedorea* palms, *Phoenix roebelenii*, Ixoras and similar plants. My plant was killed by the rising of Lake Audubon, and I never have been able to replace it. Mr. Berckmans has distributed it quite largely, but I know of not one plant at present under cultivation. It should be grown in all good gardens in Florida, though it is no winter bloomer, flowering late in spring and during the summer months. Earnest attempts should be made to re-introduce it on a large scale.

Magnolia salicifolia: A rather dense small tree from Japan, hardier than most of its congeners, but less showy when in bloom. It flowers with me at Christmas time and throughout January and February. Flowers white, cup-shaped, upright, solitary. Grows well in Central Florida and attains a height of about 20 feet.

Magnolia XSoulangiana and its various fine varieties are the most showy, as well as the most vigorous, the most floriferous and the most easily grown of all the deciduous Magnolias. The subject under consideration is a hybrid between *M.* [*heptapeta*] and *M.* [*quinquepeta*] and begins to flower at Christmas time at Palm Cottage Gardens, and continues throughout January and February. The entire tree is a sheet of bloom when at its best. The flowers are large, upright, bell-shaped, white, more or less suffused with rosy-red or purplish, and pleasantly, but not very strongly fragrant. Wherever this Magnolia has been largely planted, it is, with its varieties extremely popular. My particular favorite is *M.* XSoulangiana 'Lennei,' which flowers a little later. The fine large blossoms are deep crimson outside, lighter colored within and quite fragrant. Other fine forms are 'Alexandrina,' 'Alba Superba,' 'Grandis,' 'Norbertiana,' 'Rustica,' 'Speciosa' and 'Triumphans.' All are extremely beautiful. All flower during the winter and all are very showy and easily grown with a minimum of care.

Magnolia stellata: In 1893 I received a specimen of this Magnolia under the name of *M. halleana* from the, at that time, very famous nursery of S. B. Parsons, Flushing, L.I. It is quite distinct from all my other species. It requires rich, moist soil, and a somewhat shady position. All other deciduous Magnolias flower before the leaves appear, but in Hall's Magnolia the new foliage is fully developed when the first flowers open. They appear in great numbers, but are quite small (3 inches in diameter), and are sweet-scented, spreading and finally reflexed. Though forming a small tree about 20 feet in its native home (Japan), it grows slowly in Florida. My specimen, planted in 1893, is scarcely more than 20 feet in height, quite dense, with spreading branches, and an abundance of leaves, each about 4 to 5 inches long, oblong-ovate and pubescent beneath when young. This is a beautiful and distinct Magnolia, discovered and introduced by Dr. George R. Hall.

Magnolia 'Watsonii': Named in honor of W. Watson, late famous curator of the Kew Gardens. A most beautiful small tree-like Magnolia from Japan. It is a most lovely plant when well grown. The flowers are large, white, sweet-scented. The appearance is much heightened by the crimson center of bright-colored stamens. I had it for years in my collection, but lost it during a protracted drouth.

Other Notable Imports

Illicium anisatum (*I. religiosum*), Star Anise: All the Illiciums are aromatic plants, including our two native species. They belong to the Magnolia family. I have dense, beautiful specimens of the above in Palm Cottage Gardens. Whether or not it is the true Star Anise I am not prepared to decide, though they flower and fruit abundantly every year. Its star-shaped clusters of fruits are very aromatic. In oriental countries the seeds are much used in cookery, and the Germans use them most profusely in some of their fine Christmas cakes. All these seeds come from China, while my plants were imported from Japan, where they are native, grown much in temple grounds and regarded as sacred.

In my garden the Star Anise is a very dense bushy grower, an altogether beautiful and very interesting evergreen large shrub or small tree. The leaves, elliptic, short-petioled and some acuminated, are of a peculiar beautiful green color. When crushed they exhale a very strong and pleasant odor, reminding one of that of Sassafras. The small, nodding, yellowish green flowers are scentless. Some of my specimens have attained a height of 15 feet. The lower growth is very broad and spreading, and at the top it tapers to a narrow point. From the powdered bark, mixed with resin, are prepared the "smoke candles," with which incense is made in the Japanese temples.

All my specimens grow on high dry pineland, among palms, Magnolias and Bamboos. Some are associated with [*Michelia figo*] (the Banana-Shrub) and fine specimens of the Laurel Cherry (*Prunus caroliniana*). A large group, consisting of about half a dozen specimens, and planted in 1895, is particularly effective, covering at present a space of about 75 feet square. It is very dense and almost impenetrable. The lower, wide-spreading branches, resting on the ground, have struck root at various points and in consequence many new vigorous plants have pushed up on all sides around the parent specimen. This is a most lovely spot among the large Magnolias on one side and an avenue of various Date Palms on the other.

The Star Anise is not only a very handsome, highly interesting and aromatic Japanese evergreen, but is also one of the easiest grown on our high and dry sandy soil, requiring scarcely any care after it has been well established. It thrives as well in shady spots as in full sun. I took a small plant with me to Naples, where it is perfectly at home, growing very vigorously in the new soil of my garden. This plant deserves the attention of all plant lovers. It is at present rarely found in our gardens, though it always attracts attention of the winter sojourners on account of its fine, dense, fragrant foliage.

Bischofia javanica: The name suggests that this beautiful dense shade tree is a native of Java, but it is also found abundantly as far north as Canton, China, and other tropical parts of the Celestial Empire. It is much hardier than its name would make us believe, as we presently shall see.

The honor of its introduction into Florida belongs to Mr. E. N. Reasoner of the Royal Palm Nurseries, Oneco, Fla. In his letter to me he several times mentioned it and referred to its great beauty, telling me that it was perfectly hardy in his grounds and that it formed an ideal shade tree. A number of years ago I had the opportunity to see and study this unique tree in Mrs. Reasoner's grounds. I was at once struck by its distinct beauty, its outstanding individuality and its fine form. In fact, it was one of the most beautiful, one of the densest and noblest exotic trees it ever had been my good fortune to see. Its superb, wide-spreading crown of dark green foliage was so dense that not a ray of sunshine could reach the ground. Its trunk, only about 10 to 12 feet tall underneath the head of leaves, was quite massive and covered with dark brown bark, soft to the touch and shedding in thin, large scales. The leaves are alternate, trifoliate, quite smooth, but not very glossy. The greenish-white flowers along the branches are insignificant. The beauty of this tree never faded from memory.

I planted it out at Palm Cottage Gardens, but while it grew well, it never assumed that fine form which I have described. Its growth was always quite open and leggy. In order to induce it to make a fine dense growth it must be planted out in rich, somewhat moist soil and in the full sun. It refuses to reveal its full beauty in the shade. For its expansion it needs room and a space where it is not crowned by other more aggressive trees. It is much hardier than I expected it to be. The heavy freeze in early February, 1917, only killed back some of its branches, and it soon fully recuperated. Had it been planted in an open, well-protected place it would not only have grown into a beautiful dense specimen, but it would, very likely, not have suffered much from the cold. The small plant I set out in my Naples garden soon died, on account of the stagnant water in the soil. It needs a rich well-drained spot in order to develop its full beauty.

The *Bischofia javanica* should be planted largely as a shade and avenue tree in extreme south Florida. Plants raised from seeds that came from Canton, Hong Kong and other parts of subtropical China will undoubtedly be much hardier than those from seed coming from Java and the Malaya Archipelago.

[*Hydrangea macrophylla*]: Common names Hydrangea and Hortensia. This Hydrangea was introduced from Japan to France in 1790, and named after Hortensia, the daughter of Empress Josephine and mother of Napoleon III. One of the most cherished flowering shrubs under glasshouse culture and very popular as a garden plant in our southern states. It grows and flowers abundantly in all the gardens of northern and central Florida where its requirements are met,—shade and a very rich, rather moist soil.

Before Orlando became commercialized,—in the good old days when it could be called the real "city beautiful" as far as gardens and rare plant growth is concerned,—Hydrangeas formed in many gardens wonderful ornaments during April, May and June. I have in mind a particular garden where a wealth of Hydrangea blossoms, on bushes 6 to 8 feet tall, formed a magic sight worthy of traveling far to see. The bushes, dense and very luxuriant, formed the foundation planting along the north side of a large dwelling. The soil in which they grew was dark, mellow, moist loam made very rich by an abundance of old, well-rotted cow manure. The specimens were extremely dense, and the huge flower trusses displayed a rich deep indigo blue, surmounting and even hiding in superabundance the fine large foliage.

It must be kept in mind that all the forms of *Hydrangea* [*macrophylla*] are shade and moisture loving plants. They will not grow in sunny spots, nor in poor dry soil. Only when planted in shady situations, in very rich moist, well drained soil they will show their full beauty.

The Japanese grow many distinct forms and value all of them highly. The majority have beautiful pure white or rosy-red flower clusters, but as far as I have experimented with them, all change to a pretty deep azure blue, or even to a decided indigo blue in our Florida soils. There is no doubt that certain soils have the property to change the normal color in consequence of the presence of some chemical constituents. While living in the Ozark Mountains of southwestern Missouri, I added alum, and in another experiment iron filings to the potting soil with the result that I obtained dingy-blue flowers,—never the deep, clear blue we see as a rule in Florida. Mr. E. N. Reasoner says: "The color of the pink and blue sorts is variable, according to the acidity of the soil; for the blue color use plenty of humus and organic manure and add a little powdered alum to the soil, for pink use lime and chemical fertilizer,—no humus."

3

Cacti and Succulents

The Cactus family is a large and varied one. It is strictly an American family of plants. Since the discovery of the New World most all of its members have been of general or particular interest to all who have come in contact with them. The various species of Cacti native of the state, or introduced from the American tropics, belong to the most wonderful and charming plants we grow in our gardens. [While cacti are succulents, not all succulents are cacti.]

Cacti

Only a comparatively few select amateurs revel in the beauty of their forms, the symmetry of their spiny armor and the charm of their gorgeous flowers. I can scarcely recollect a greater delight in my life than when coming suddenly upon groups of [*Echinocereus reichenbachii*] and *Echinocactus texensis* in full bloom in the Post Oak woods of Texas, or when seeing for the first time the large, pure white and deliciously fragrant flowers of the Queen of the Night (*Cereus grandiflorus*) on the trunk and among the leaves of a large Cabbage Palm in a garden of Palm Beach. Along the Indian River the intricate masses of [*Cereus pteranthus*] and *Cereus triangularis* in full bloom during the glorious Florida moonlight nights were a revelation to me.

For many years I have cultivated the choicest and most exquisite of these plants in my garden. Unfortunately only a very few are perfectly hardy here [Gotha], while the majority of them are killed outright by a heavy freeze. I have often saved the lower part of the stems by banking them with dry sand. This is easily done in the case of species of *Cereus* and *Pereskia,* but impossible with *Epiphyllum, Phyllocactus* and *Rhipsalis* which I always have grown as epiphytes on the trunks of Cabbage Palms, Coconut and Date Palms. In extreme south Florida all are perfectly hardy.

All the species of Cacti adapted to our climate require little care. The strong growing climbing and upright species of *Cereus* do exceedingly well in a fairly moist, well drained sandy humus. When in vigorous growth they are benefited by a little old cow manure. All the Epiphyllums, a few of the epiphytal species of *Cereus* and all the *Phyllocactus* species and hybrids grow vigorously and flower abundantly as epiphytes on the rough trunks of various palms. Small pieces can be easily wedged in between the old leaf remnants (boots) and the trunk where they soon strike roots. If planted in pots all form beautiful ornaments on verandahs or in rooms. The pots must be filled at least one-third with broken potsherds or broken shells. The best soil consists of equal parts of sand, good loam, leaf mould, and broken pieces of old dry cow manure. The drainage must always be perfect, or plants will soon decay. This is the most important point in cactus culture. Water should be supplied, but never excessively, when the plants are in vigorous growth during summer, but only very little should be applied when they are at rest during winter. I know of no other plants which can stand so much neglect. You may leave the place for weeks and even for months, and when you return they are in as good a condition as when you left. They resent coddling and pampering.

The Opuntias, or Prickly-Pears,—also known as Indian Figs,—are familiar to every tiller of the soil in Florida, being common in field and forest, and the best and most effective tall or arborescent species are common garden plants. They are looked at with contempt by the orange grower, their spines being abundant, long and exceedingly sharp and their small cushion-like prickles, provided with hooks, deeply penetrate the skin. Woe to the hand reaching out for one of the brilliantly beautiful yellow flowers. Many bear quite large pear-shaped fruits. Though interesting in their way, as Opuntias undoubtedly are, they are far outrivaled in beauty by the species of *Cereus, Epiphyllum* and *Phyllocactus.* The flowers of these cacti are so large, so beautifully formed, the fragrance of many so delicious, and the colors so brilliant and blended that no pen and no pencil can give an idea of their splendor.

I have several times been asked why we do not grow the Tuna (*Opuntia tuna*) in Florida. It is a cactus of a very dry country, and our climate in Florida is too humid and the soil too light and sandy. We have, however, several species of closely allied forms—the Prickly-Pear—the finest of which can also be used for preserves and other purposes.

While living in Texas, from 1879 to 1882, we made frequent use of the beautiful, but rather insipid fruits of [*Opuntia ficus-indica*], a species that grows in immense masses in the prairies. The sap shows a very vivid purple color. The plants are provided with innumerable sharp spines and clusters of fine sticky bristles. The preserves and jams made of these Prickly Pears are very palatable when lemon juice is added in their preparation.

In Mexico two species are of great economic value—*Opuntia tuna* and *O. ficus-indica*. The fruits, as large as small pears, ripen from June to Christmas and they are consumed by all classes of people. The bunches of fine bristles covering the fruit must be carefully removed, before handling them, or they will deeply penetrate the skin and cause much irritation. In Mexico the sweet Tunas are eaten raw or as excellent preserves, and a good light wine is also produced from the sap.

The genus *Cereus* has been split up into quite a number of new subgenera by recent botanists. (See Alvin Berger, "A Systematic Review of the Genus *Cereus*." Sixteenth Annual Report, Missouri Botanical Garden, 1905.) For convenience sake and to avoid confusion, I shall in almost all cases strictly adhere to the old names of the species [revisions follow Benson, *Cacti of the United States and Canada,* where possible]. In this connection I would like to call attention of the reader to the fact that six [four] different species are found in Florida as natives. Three are climbers, immense specimens often being found on Cabbage Palms, particularly along the Indian River. [*Cereus pteranthus*] reminds one in its growth of the Night-blooming *Cereus,* while the three-angular stems of [*C. undatus*] readily distinguish it from the former. A certain species was at no distant time common on Key West, but is now exterminated. Another night-blooming species, dense and upright in its growth and provided with an armor of very sharp spines, is known as the Dildoe (*C. pentagonus*). It is a common plant in the coastal regions of south Florida. In addition to the above we have two species of very striking Tree Cacti in the extreme part of south Florida,—[*Cereus robinii* var. *robinii*] and [*C. robinii* var. *deeringii*].

I shall give room here to the upright-growing and tree-like cacti first. Planted in groups in extreme south Florida, where they are perfectly hardy, they form imposing features. The soil should be very light and rich and rather dry. In their native haunts most of the species are apparently growing in a rocky soil, which insures perfect drainage. All are sun-loving plants and all can endure considerable drouth.

I received [*Cereus robinii* var. *robinii*], the Key West Tree Cactus, many years ago from Reasoner Brothers under the name *Cereus monoclonus*. It was at one time very common around Key West. With destruction of the hammock for building sites, this interesting cactus has become scarce until at present it is on the verge of extermination in its natural habitat. A dozen years ago many fine and robust trees, some of them over 20 feet high, stood in the hammock east of the city. These have long since disappeared (J. K. Small). Dr. Small counted a score of prostrate skeleton remains scattered over the hammock floor which were either cut down by the wood hunters or blown down by storms. Many small plants and a few small trees remained standing as late as 1915. "The trees have now been destroyed, and nearly all of the small plants have been exterminated during the past year by the construction of a baseball field and by the clearing of building lots." Fortunately, a number of fine small specimens have been secured by Mr. Charles Deering and planted in a certain tropical hammock in the Miami region. I have found it very tender here.

A new species, [*Cereus robinii* var. *deeringii*], was first seen and admired by two of the most ardent and enthusiastic plant lovers of Florida, Prof. Chas. T. Simpson and Mr. John Soar. They thought it identical with the former. In comparing the two, Dr. Small found this to be different. It is a feature in the rocky hammocks of lower Matecumbe Key. When Dr. Small visited this key no tall Cactus was observed at first, and it was assumed that a recent hurricane had blown down all the plants.

"However, a landing near the southern end of the island in March, 1916, gave opportunity for further search, and then an abundance of the cactus was encountered. As had been suspected, all the older and large plants were prostrate on the hammock floor as a result of the hurricanes, and the younger plants had not yet grown up as high as the tree tops. Considering the slight foothold, the habit of growth, and the weight of the stems and branches, it is difficult to understand how the plant can ordinarily maintain its erect position." (Small.)

While the former species is copiously and intricately branched, the stems of Deering's Tree Cactus are nearly simple-stemmed or with few straight, erect or ascending branches. It is a slender plant, often 30 feet tall, deep green, usually ten-ribbed, with rather short spines. It flowers in the afternoon, but very likely also during the night. The berry-like fruits, over an inch in diameter, are dark red. "The plant is named for Charles Deering, whose deep interest in the botanical exploration in Florida, and in the preservation of its hammocks from destruction and its rare native plants from extermination, enabled us to rediscover, study, and satisfactorily determine the relationship of this cactus." (Small.)

Cereus peruvianus (*Piptanthocerus peruvianus*), Hedge Cactus, is common in many parts of South America and the West Indies. A beautiful columnar Tree Cactus, reaching a height of 50 feet with stems 5 to 8 inches in diameter, branching freely toward the base. The young growth is of a beautiful blue color, which changes to a deep green when older. The eight inch wide white flowers open at night. This fine species should be largely planted in all the finer gardens of extreme south Florida. It grows well in spots where the lower stem is somewhat shaded.

The subgenus *Hylocereus* is characterized by its very large and showy funnel-shaped flowers, white or red. They are all climbers and produce roots all along their triangular stems. The flowers are in evidence only at night and are among the largest and most beautiful of the whole family. The fruit is large, red, and covered with foliaceous scales, which increase in size during the growth of the fruit.

Cereus lemairei (*Hylocereus lemairei*), from Antigua in the Lesser Antilles, is a tender species and one of the finest in my collection. It climbs trees to a considerable height, and is particularly adapted for bare palm trunks to which its stems adhere by a network of tough rootlets. The long-tubed, large flowers are bright yellow inside, the sepals on the outside being lemon yellow, margined with red. The blossoms exhale a strong and pleasant aromatic odor.

Cereus triangularis (*Hylocereus triangularis, H. tricostalus*) is very common all along the Indian River and in the hammocks farther south [probably *C. undatus,* which escaped cultivation and occurs along the Indian River]. One of the most vividly beautiful pictures in my mind is a certain tall, dense specimen of the Triangular Cactus, which I saw in full bloom during one of the beautiful July nights on the Indian River, in company of *Cereus boeckmannii* [probably *C. pteranthus*].

One beautiful Sunday morning in July, while speeding along the highway close to the ocean between Delray and Palm Beach, the smooth water showed the most intense colors of red, violet, purple and blue. I have never seen anything like it before or after. At Palm Beach it began to rain and showers were frequent all the afternoon. North of Fort Pierce the highway leads along the Indian River through forests of Cabbage Palms, many of which were covered from bottom to top with luxuriant dense masses of these climbing cacti, full of buds. About 9 o'clock in the evening the spotlight of the automobile fell upon a huge specimen showing hundreds of large, open, glistening white flowers. The picture was so wonderfully, impressively beautiful, so perfect, so fairy-like that my eyes could scarcely part from it. I admired this glorious scene,—such a one as I never had seen before,—in the stillness of the night for hours. I made quite a number of cuttings from this immense specimen, which are now growing finely here in my garden and at Naples-on-the-Gulf.

About ten years ago, while roaming around in the tropical Brickell Hammock near Miami with my friend, Prof. Chas. T. Simpson, he pointed out to me the first wild specimen of this cactus which I had ever seen. It was a very large plant, growing in an intricate, dense mass in the rather flat top of a large, low forest tree. Though growing as an epiphyte, it was in the most perfect health, finding sufficient nourishment in the old leaves and rotten wood that accumulated among the dense network of stems and branches. A little later I admired the many large specimens adorning the trunks and the leaf-crowns of Cabbage Palms all along the Indian River. In Punta Gorda, a row of Gumbo Limbo Trees is covered with it, and it is quite common in the gardens of Fort Myers. An immense, massive, densely intricate specimen grew on a Palmetto I often admired in the garden of Mrs. W. B. Haldeman at Naples-on-the-Gulf. The plants often reach a height of 30 to 35 feet.

In Hawaii it is the most common and most admired climbing cactus. The flowers are very large,—over a foot long and often 15 inches in diameter, when fully open. The outside (or the sepals) exhibits a brownish color. They open only during the night. The fruit is large, often as large as a goose-egg, brilliant red, covered with a rather soft grayish-white prickly substance. All the climbing species of night-blooming cacti do best in rich, rocky, well-drained soil, fairly moist and somewhat shady. They dislike dry sandy soils, and refuse to grow in moist, mucky composts.

Nothing to me is so fairy-like, so enchantingly beautiful in the way of flowers, as the great blossoms of these night-blooming Cerei by the brilliant southern moonlight, or by strong artificial light in the stillness of the night. They do not look like ordinary flowers, for every petal seems to be chiseled out of alabaster and sparkles as if beset with myriads of crystals. The beautiful way in which the long white petals hold themselves up in a symmetrical cup-like form is admired by all who love exquisite form in flowers. I had the flowers of *Cereus triangularis* [probably *C. undatus*], *C. boeckmannii* [probably *C. pteranthus*], *C. grandiflorus*, *C. nycticallus* [= *C. pteranthus*] and *C. macdonaldiae* all open in one night. The sight was so charming that it will never be forgotten. The air was pervaded with the strong and delicious odor of the Queen of the Night, the powerful perfume of the Night-blooming Jasmine and numerous blossoms of *Magnolia grandiflora* and the mockingbird sounded its sweet night song through the air. They grow easily in pots, but they do much better in south Florida when planted out on Palm trunks or trees, on verandahs and on pots in plant sheds.

[*Cereus pteranthus*], from Florida and Cuba [Mexico], is the rope cactus of the Floridians. When I first saw the large specimens and climbing masses of this species I was strongly reminded of the Night-blooming Cereus and the Moon Cactus, as the growth is very much the same. Only a close examination reveals its distinct character. I found it very common as a climber on Cabbage Palms all along the Indian River. It often grows on rocky soil in deep, moist, but well drained humus, and specimens 20 to 25 feet tall are not uncommon. Even the most indifferent is impressed by the immense specimens which adorn the palms. When in full bloom, in June and July, the large white blossoms make a magnificent show in bright moonlight nights.

This species makes a fine companion plant to the Triangular Cereus, as it flowers at the same time. Both are often seen together in the wild, but usually each species occupies a separate tree. The stems are very round, ribbed, often over one inch thick and are provided with many tough roots which tightly adhere to the trunk upon which it climbs. I have collected quite a number of cuttings and planted them out on my place at Naples-on-the-Gulf. It is perfectly hardy here.

Cereus grandiflorus (*Selenicereus grandiflorus*) of Jamaica and other West Indian Islands is the celebrated Night-blooming Cereus, the Queen of the Night, so common in cultivation as a greenhouse plant in northern regions. The snake-like stems are somewhat uncanny, but words are not adequate to describe the glories of the expanded flowers, with their outer segments of cinnamon-brown passing gradually through cream-color to snowy-white and with crowds of delicate white thread-like stamens moving gradually around the projecting style. And then the perfume! It is like the most fragrant of incense. If one saw but one flower in the year, and that one flower were one of the Night-blooming Cereus, it would remain as a vision of beauty and a wonder of wonders for many a day. It is undoubtedly the most celebrated of all cacti and one of the largest of its class in growth, reaching in south Florida, where frosts are slight and far between, a height on Palm stems and live oaks of 20 to 30 feet, and flowering profusely every summer. It climbs, as all its congeners do, by means of tough adventive roots which are abundantly produced along the 5 or 6 angled somewhat spiny stems.

The flowers are very large and extremely elegant and beautiful. I have measured many that were a foot in diameter and some even measured 15 inches. The flower tube is 8 to 12 inches long, covered with short scales and brown hairs. The calyx is composed of numerous narrow spreading sepals, bright yellow inside, brown outside. The petals form a broad cup and are of the purest crystalline whiteness. The vast number of recurved yellowish stamens in the center add considerably to the beauty of this immense and chaste flower. The delicious vanilla-like perfume exhaled by the gigantic blossoms pervades a very large garden. This most delightful perfume has a great charm, and for this reason particularly it is more grown in gardens than any other night-blooming cactus. The flowers open about 9 o'clock in the evening and fade just before sunrise, never to open again, but during this short existence there is hardly any other flower of such exquisite beauty or such unrivaled magnificence.

The Queen of the Night should be grown in every good garden in extreme south Florida. I have had it for years growing on posts in my lath house. Small plants set out in good, rich soil make a rapid growth and usually bloom in the second year. A temperature of 24°F kills it to the ground. I always protected my plants by banking them with dry sand. In this way about a foot or more of the lower stem can be saved, which soon sends out a number of vigorous new sprouts.

This species should be used largely by the hybridizers. In *Paxton's Magazine of Botany*, almost a century ago, a hybrid between the Night-blooming Cereus and *Cereus speciosus* was figured, and described as having the climbing habit of *C. grandiflorus*, whilst the flowers are 11 inches in diameter and of rich red color. They are as freely produced as in *C. speciosus,* and they have the excellent habit of remaining expanded for about three days. I am not aware that this hybrid is in cultivation in this country.

Cereus [*C. pteranthus*], Moon Cactus from Mexico, is perhaps the most common in Florida gardens, being often distributed under the name of Night-blooming Cereus. It is a strong and luxuriant climber, the lower stems being frequently as thick as a man's wrist. The stems are 4- to 6-angled. They are provided with numerous adventitious roots which tightly cling to the support on which it climbs. The flowers are as large as those of *Cereus grandiflorus.* The tube is covered with white hairs, and the spreading sepals are colored bright orange, while the petals or the inside flower are pure white. While the flowers of some of my plants are nearly scentless, others are strongly and deliciously fragrant. They usually last twelve hours in full beauty. The young shoots are bluish-green. Very strong plants of this species are not uncommon in south Florida. With me it is almost hardy, though a freeze of 20°F cuts it down to the ground. In good soil it attains a height of 25 to 30 feet, but, like all these plants of the subgenus *Selenicereus,* it revels in rather warm, moist well drained spots. On high pineland it is no success, unless given half shade and water.

Cereus pentagonus (*C. variabilis, Acanthocereus pentagonus*) is the Common Dildoe of our Old Settlers. Several years ago I had an opportunity to study this variable species on Pine Island, where it grows in dense thickets and among other shrubs and trees all along the coast, and particularly on shell mounds. When I saw it first I was reminded of what the late Pliny W. Reasoner wrote about it many years ago.

The most plentiful, and at the same time the most "murderous" species of *Cereus* found in Florida, is *Cereus variabilis.* This is only found below the Caloosahatche, but it occurs there on all the high land in sufficient quantities to strike terror in the heart of every adventurous "Conch" (Bahamian) who essays to start a tomato patch or a pineapple plantation. The stems are about the size of those of *Cereus triangularis,* and are three, four, five or six-sided, a peculiarity indicated by its name. They are of upright, scrambling, creeping or any other style of growth, and are armed with most formidable spines an inch or more long, and so strong as to penetrate thick leather. It is in Cactuses, as in other things that grow, that Florida demonstrates its wonderful adaptability and wide range.

With the treasures of the tropics ought we not be proud of our land of flowers? If only the occasional freezes were not the serpent in our Eden, how happy we would be!

The young shoots are very different from the old ones, being round and covered with flat, soft spiny clusters reminding one of a young *Cereus serpentinus*. The flowers are large, pure white and quite handsome. The color of the plant is always a glossy yellowish-green.

Cereus speciosus (*Cereus speciosissimus, Heliocereus speciosus*) is the most beautiful, the most important, and the most common species of this group,—in fact, one of the most brilliant and most valuable of all Cacti. A fine specimen plant in full bloom is a sight which is always remembered. It is a noble species with upright 3- or 4-angled shoots, attaining a height of from 6 to 9 feet and provided with some aerial roots which attach themselves to rocks or to the trunks of trees. It branches freely from the base. The stems are provided with clusters of short spines. Under pot culture the shoots need a support. A bamboo stick, about 4 or 5 feet long, is best adapted for this purpose, and the stems should be neatly tied to it. The flowers are large, widely open, very symmetrical and of a most brilliant and glowing scarlet, sometimes with a purple or violet sheen, and with numerous spreading white stamens. The single flower lasts in full beauty for 3 or 4 days.

This beautiful and easily grown Cactus, known here as the Cardinal Cactus or Cardinal Cereus, has been used to a large extent by the hybridizer. Some of our most vivid climbing day-blooming sorts, like *Cereus* XMallisonii, were raised from it. The fine modern race of Phyllocacti can almost be traced back to this superb species. Its blood appears to be in the veins of most of them. In the first quarter of the last century, the late C. M. Hovey of Boston, one of the most famous gardeners of his time, an enthusiast and real plant lover, used this species largely in cross-breeding and obtained quite a number of marvelously beautiful hybrids, the best of which he named. All seemed to be lost. The whims of fashion relegated them into oblivion. But the love for these plants again has found a foothold. Many more than a hundred new and beautiful hybrids have been offered by the trade in recent years. The species under consideration is not only a fine pot plant, but it grows well when planted out under a palm, or it even thrives as an epiphyte on rough palm trunks. It revels in a temperature warm and moist enough for orchids. High and dry pineland culture is always a failure, though it bears more neglect than any other plant outside the cactus family.

Cereus XMallisonii is a hybrid raised from the former, fertilized with the pollen of *Cereus flagelliformis*. A rather tall climber and one of the most brilliantly gorgeous cacti in cultivation. Rather tender, but easily protected as a pot plant or on posts in plant sheds. In south Florida it grows luxuriantly on palms in the same way as the Night-blooming Cereus. A large plant of this day-blooming hybrid in full bloom is a magnificent sight. According to the light in which these flowers are seen, they are brilliant scarlet, glowing purplish crimson, or of an indescribable mixture of all these hues. The large number of stamens show a light yellow color. The flowers open wide and are finely formed.

The sub-genus *Aporocactus* contains a few species only, but they are exceedingly handsome and very popular, being much grown as pot plants in northern regions and are often grafted on other strong growing stock such as the Triangular *Cereus*.

Cereus flagelliformis or *Aporocactus flagelliformis,* the Rat-tail-Cactus or Whip-Cactus, is often seen in cultivation as a grafted plant. In its native haunts, in Mexico, it seems to creep and clamber over rocks and is also found as an epiphyte. I have grown it on Live Oaks, large limbs of *Grevillea robusta* and in the old leaf pockets of Cabbage Palms, and wherever it was planted it made a luxuriant growth with down-hanging shoots, often 2 to 2½ feet long and as thick as one's little finger. The flowers are small, somewhat irregular and brilliant red. The shoots send out aerial roots.

I have seen similar long ("4 to 5 feet long") shoots on a grafted plant in Mr. John Soar's place at Little River, Fla. A gigantic *Cereus triangularis* is climbing up into a large Live Oak, and in some of its stems this cactus and Epiphyllums are grafted, and when in full bloom they form a magnificent sight. The operation of grafting is very simple: a slit in the point of the stock, the scion cut into a wedge and inserted, and a thorn to keep it in place, are all that are needed.

Phyllocactus [= *Epiphyllum*], the next group of cacti, contains a large number of most beautiful, brilliantly colored species and hybrids. They all have flat, two-edged branches, leaf-like in form, crenate or serrate on their margins, and spineless. The flowers appear always on the edges of these leaf-like branches; they are usually large, mostly nocturnal, white, yellow or red in color, and sometimes deliciously fragrant. The bright red, juicy, smooth fruit adds another interesting characteristic to the plants. Modern botanists have referred to them as *Epiphyllum*. I shall adhere to their old name which has become a popular one in the course of time.

This genus consists of species that are all epiphytes in their native haunts; that is, they all grow on the trunks, branches and large limbs of forest trees, especially where old leaves and rotten wood have accumulated, and where mosses, orchids, bromeliads, Aroids and ferns are growing. All the species and hybrids which I had an opportunity to experiment with made a fine growth and flowered profusely on the rough trunks and among the remnants of old leaf stalks of my hardy species of Coconut [*Butia*] and Date Palms and on the various Cabbage Palms. All like half shade. Several of the species are quite hardy here, though I lost all of them early in February, 1917, when the thermometer registered as low as 18° F. Only a few short stems of [*Epiphyllum strictum*] survived. The following species did well in ordinary seasons, several of them having been in my possession for at least ten to fifteen years:

[*Nopalxochia ackermanii*], the King-Cactus, from Mexico, is one of the most vividly colored in cultivation, the flowers being rich crimson, very satiny, and somewhat lighter outside. Quite a number of still finer hybrids have been raised from it. It is very tender. When the brilliant flowers open, usually when the rainy season begins, the show is indescribably beautiful, and the massive trunks of the palms appear as if bespangled with the richest red ornaments. It is a day bloomer.

[*Epiphyllum anguliger*], like all the species of this genus, is found as an epiphyte on palms and other trees in Mexico. Hartweg discovered it near Matanejo, a village in Western Mexico, not far from Tepic. It grew on Oaks together with some species of *Epidendrum,* an *Oncidium* and an *Odontoglossum.* The leaf-like stems are quite serrate on their margins, somewhat like the teeth of a large saw. I have had fine specimens on my palms. A large clump nestled underneath of the leaf-crown of a Cabbage Palm is a noble sight when the large flowers with white petals, and orange or yellowish narrow and spreading sepals have opened in numbers. They always expand during the daytime, emitting a powerful and most delicious fragrance. This fine and rather hardy Leaf-Cactus grows about 3 feet high, and is easily raised to a large size in pots with good soil and perfect drainage.

[*Epiphyllum crenatus*] is a native of Guatemala, southern Mexico and Honduras. I received my first plants from Mr. Erich Wittkugel, San Pedro Sula, Honduras. In his rambles through the forests he found masses of them on the lower limbs of large forest trees. It is a very tender plant here. Like all the Leaf Cacti it has flat, strongly crenate stems, growing 3 to 4 feet long. The flowers are creamy-white in the center, very satiny, and the exterior segments are of a light orange color and quite narrow. They open during daytime and exhale a very strong and delicious perfume. A number of fine hybrids have been obtained from this fine species, in having employed the pollen of [*Nopalxochia ackermannii*] and *Cereus speciosus*.

[*Epiphyllum oxypetalum*], as its old name [*Phyllocactus grandis*] implies, is certainly a grand species, a native of Mexico, Honduras and Guatemala. It is a very large plant when fully grown, with shoots sometimes 20 feet long and with many short side branches. It is night-bloomer with very large fragrant flowers, often a foot in diameter and almost as long. One evening, after a fine rainy summer day, the bright moonlight induced me to stroll around in the garden. When passing a large massive [*Syagrus romanzoffiana* var. *australis*], I inhaled a new and strange perfume, an odor very distinct, very aromatic and extremely delicious. At first I had no idea from whence this fragrance came. I searched for quite a while, but always in the wrong place. Finally I discovered its source. In looking up I perceived an immense pure white flower just underneath the leaf crown of the Palm,—the first blossom of [*Epiphyllum oxypetalum*] I ever had seen. It was so large, so pure and its fragrance, so charming that I was immediately reminded of the Night-blooming Cereus. Such are very often the surprises and delights of the lover of nature. Since that time I have often had the species in bloom, and enjoyed its fairy-like beauty and its delicious perfume in the stillness of a Florida summer night.

[*Epiphyllum latifrons*], the Queen-Cactus, is one of the most popular of all cacti, and a great favorite with many amateurs. It is supposed to be a Mexican species. In Milwaukee I have seen many fine and perfect specimens grown in pots in private homes, and their possessors always pointed it out to me with much pride as the Night-blooming Cereus (and the Queen of the Night), from which, however, it is vastly different, though the flowers of both are somewhat similar. Here in my garden it grows most luxuriantly all around the trunks of many palms, climbing high up in the leaf crown and hanging down in long drooping masses. Some of the leaf-stems are fully 6 to 8 feet, and even 10 feet long. One single flat leaf-branch often displays, at times 3 to 4 fully open, pure satiny-white and very large blossoms 6 to 10 inches long and as much in diameter when fully expanded.

A flower which I measured today (October 1, 1920) was over a foot long and twelve inches broad. The flower-stem is of a beautiful orange-brown and the sepals, or the outer parts of the flower, are also orange-brown with a slight tint of violet intermixed. The petals are of a crystalline whiteness and the style and stigma are pure snowy white. A rather strong and delicious odor is exhaled by the open flower. The plant flowered constantly throughout the summer and there are four or five unopened buds still developing. As in all the Phyllocacti they are produced along the serrated or notched margins of the leaves and are powerfully aromatic. They open usually at 8 or 9 o'clock in the evening and close just before sunrise. I have often had 50 and 60, and on large plants, even 100 flowers at one time on the same plant. Seen by artificial light in such large numbers suspended from the trunks of palms just underneath the leaf-crown the sight is enchantingly beautiful. This is the most rampant grower of all the Phyllocacti, and the easiest to cultivate. It is also the hardiest here. Late in summer the large, smooth, brilliant red fruits, somewhat oblong in form and of the size of a hen's egg, contribute an additional charm to the plants growing on the palm trunks.

[*Nopalxochia phyllanthoides*], the Rose-Cactus, is another species from southern Mexico having been in cultivation for more than a century. It is a very beautiful cactus with rather small flower, 3 to 4 inches in diameter, colored rose and white in irregular streaks. It grows from 2 to 3 feet high, and is the most floriferous of all the species, and a day bloomer. It is easily established on rough palm trunks. A few years ago a most exquisite hybrid from it—*Phyllocactus* XDeutsche Kaiserin—has appeared in the trade—a first rate gem, with flowers of the size and color of the LaFrance Rose. The flowers appear in such large numbers that the entire plant is covered with them.

Scarcely any other plant is so easily grown and flowers so profusely as *Phyllocactus* [*Epiphyllum*] and its hybrids. Here in Florida a place on the verandah or fixed to the trunks of large palms suits them perfectly. As tender plants they must be protected from frost. A light sandy soil, mixed with some loam, a little dry cow manure and crushed potsherds, comparatively small pots and a perfect drainage is all they require. In winter, water is rarely necessary, but as soon as they begin to show buds and throughout the summer an abundant supply is essential, also a little fertilizer in the form of weak manure water. In strong sunlight a thin shading should be given, as all the species of *Phyllocactus* in their wild haunts grow as epiphytes on the branches of trees or among the rotten litter accumulated on palm trunks, where they are well shaded from the fierce rays of the sun. They seem to prefer a good letting alone during the winter months. Set in an out of the way corner, giving them only enough water to prevent shriveling, and don't allow them to be brushed or washed in the least during their rest. When new growth commences in spring shower them thoroughly and give them more light and heat, and buds may be expected in due time.

In our time of unrest these easily grown plants, without which the cozy rooms of our grandmothers cannot be imagined, should be found in every window in the North, on every verandah in the South and in every good garden of Florida. Because they are so easily grown, require so little care and can be propagated so readily from cuttings these cacti had been pushed in the background. In the time of C. M. Hovey of Boston, about 1837, beautiful hybrids raised by him were the pride of the day. It is only recently that large plant establishments, such as James Bornemann of Blankenburg and Harz, Germany, have again taken these plants in their hands. A new and very beautiful race of hybrids has been the result. Henry A. Dreer of Philadelphia also offers fine collections of the best hybrids.

By crossing the various species of *Phyllocactus* [*Epiphyllum*] among themselves and even with the finest species of *Cereus* (such as *C. speciosus* and *C. grandiflorus*), and vice versa, a new and brilliant class of plants has made its appearance. Again the attention of a flower loving public has been called to easily grown and indescribably brilliant Leaf Cacti,—the favorites of our ancestors. The size of the flowers of some of the hybrids is enormous, and their scintillating splendor and brilliancy indescribable. Not a few are deliciously fragrant. We have now all the colors from the purest crystalline whiteness to the most dazzling orange-scarlet, and from the faintest softest pink and rose to the most vivid and brilliant light and deep crimson. Some hybrids even show brownish-red, lilac and even blue tints in their colors, while others are primrose and canary-yellow.

The genus *Phyllocactus* [*Epiphyllum*] is closely related to several groups of the genus *Cereus,* which is characterized by angled spiny stems, while in the former they are more or less flattened and free of sharp prickles. So many hybrids have been obtained from the two that no line of demarcation can be drawn, some showing a leaning towards one genus and some to the other. As there are new and beautiful hybrids constantly raised and as the list is long already, I shall only mention those that I have grown at one time or another. Almost all are very interesting and beautiful, and all are day bloomers.

Phyllocactus [*Epiphyllum*] hybrids P. J. T. Peacock are magnificent hybrids. The colors are so varied and iridescent that every description and even a water color painting must fail to give a correct idea of its hues. The flowers are very large, 10 to 12 inches in diameter and the color is an indescribable blending of vermilion, dazzling purple and violet, appearing to be of as many different hues as the standpoint from which it is viewed. To me the outer segments often appear crimson, the inner ones of a lovely pellucid satiny purple. This hybrid is a poem of color, form and beauty.

[*Epiphyllum*] XWrayi is large, yellow, and fragrant. In 1906 F. Weinberg, a cactus specialist of Woodside, Long Island, issued a beautiful catalogue of Cacti and other succulents, containing all the species and hybrids worthy of cultivation. In this catalogue I find all the species and many hybrids,—about fifty,—listed. Unfortunately lack of interest in these plants in this country forced him to discontinue his business and a successor has never filled his place. The catalogues of the late firms of James Veitch & Sons, London, and G. Bornemann, Blackenburg, Germany, list a very large number of the best new and old hybrids. Henry A. Dreer, Philadelphia, offers also a collection of fine hybrids.

[*Schlumbergia* and *Zygocactus,* both confined to southern Brazil, are allied with *Epiphyllum,* and have been hybridized with each other], are found as epiphytes on large old forest trees, growing in large clumps on the flat surface or in crotches of large limbs, together with orchids, bromeliads, ferns and aroids. When in full bloom large plants present a magnificent sight in their wild haunts. The often dazzling colors and the fine leaf-rosettes of the bromeliads and the many flowering orchids heighten the effect.

There is nothing in our plant collections more delightful or more worthy and easy of cultivation than these Crab Cacti. They are mostly seen as grafted plants, the stock used being almost invariably the Lemon Vine (*Pereskia aculeata*), though I prefer for this purpose the tall climbing, robust stems of *Cereus* [*undatus*] [*C. pteranthus*] and the erect shoots of *C. speci-*

osus. They are, however, most beautiful and dainty on their own roots in small pots or, in south Florida, as epiphytes on the limbs of large forest trees in rather moist localities. They refuse to grow on trees of high pinelands. The stems of all of them are flat, two-edged, thin, fleshy, somewhat crenated, smooth and green. All are tender and are easily lost in a heavy freeze.

Schlumbergera gaertneri (*Epiphyllum gaertneri*), the Easter Cactus, has rather upright stems with drooping branches. The flowers are borne singly or in groups from the ends of the joints. Their regular form reminds one of Cereus, while that of [*Zygocactus truncatus*] is irregular. This fine species was discovered by H. Gaertner of Blumenau, Brazil, in the Organ Mountains, and was sent by him to Haage & Schmidt, Erfurt, Germany. Dr. E. von Regel described and named it and published a fine colored plate of it in his *Gartenflora* (1884, tab. 1173). It flowers in cultivation in March and April. The color of the blossoms is a brilliant scarlet, shaded with violet. I have grown it on its own roots and as an epiphyte on large trees, and whe ever it was seen in full bloom it made always a very fine show. As a strong grafted plant, with heads one above the other, it presents a most charming picture when in full bloom. Here in Florida it can be easily grafted on the strong stems of various night-blooming cacti, one above the other, so that a chain of flowering specimens can be admired at the same time. *Epiphyllum makoyanum* is identical with this species.

Schlumbergera russelliana (*Epiphyllum russellianum*) has flowers that are rosy-red, opening early in May. Quite a number of varieties of this species have been described. A beautiful plant.

Rhipsalis pachyptera (*R. alata*) from Brazil is a much branched, erect Mistletoe-Cactus growing from 2 to 3 feet tall. The joints or branches are usually 5 inches long, flat, crenated and from 2 to 3 inches broad and often of a distinct purplish red color. The flowers are small and of a yellowish color. They always appear in the crenatures of the flat branches. A good grower, particularly on palms.

Rhipsalis paradoxa from Brazil is an interesting little cactus that grows about 2 feet high and is sparingly branched. The branchlets are from 1 to 2 inches long and from one-half to one inch in diameter and much twisted at their joints, three to four angled and the margins of a purplish color.

Rhipsalis pentaptera from Southern Brazil, Uruguay, and Argentina has greenish-white flowers. Fruit white, rosy-red above. Plant sub-erect, about 2 feet high and much branched. Branchlets 2 to 5 inches long, 5- to 6-angled or almost winged.

Rhipsalis rhombea [not *R. rhombea;* perhaps *R. virgata*] also from Brazil is a very dainty, dense and interesting Mistletoe-Cactus, perfectly hardy here and an excellent plant for growing on Palms and shade trees, where it soon forms dense masses of yellowish-green growths, about a foot high and as much in diameter. All the branches and small joints are cylindrical. It is difficult to describe the plant. One must see it to form an idea. The inconspicuous flowers are small, greenish-yellow. The small berries are white. It grows well in pots. In my garden at Naples I have masses of this species, and *R. cassutha* [= *R. baccifera*] growing on the trunks of Cabbage Palms, together with bromeliads, orchids and ferns and the effect is very striking.

Rhipsalis warningiana from Brazil is particularly common in the Province of Minas Geraes where it was first found (in 1854) by G. A. Lindberg. Ten years later Dr. Warning found it at Lagoa Santa in the same province. It is a beautiful plant, much like *R. houlettiana* in appearance, but quite distinct. The two to four-angled, much crenated stems and branches remind one strongly of a *Phyllocactus*. The flowers are pure white, almost an inch in diameter and exhale a faint Narcissus-like fragrance. One flower is scarcely noticeable, but when a large plant is in full bloom the perfume is quite strong and very lovely. The plant grows well in pots, but it is a gem as an epiphyte on large trees and palms in extreme south Florida, where the long slender branches hang gracefully down in dense masses.

[*Rhipsalis salicornioides*], from Brazil, is a very pretty and interesting little epiphyte. I received my specimen from Dr. G. T. Moore of the Missouri Botanical Garden, under the above name. It is a dense, erect plant. Branches short, arising in twos and threes from the tops of the older branches, cylindric, club or flask shaped with slender base. The small flowers are orange-yellow, and the berries are white. A full-grown plant is about 20 inches high. It grows well in pots but is especially adapted for growing on palms and other trees as an epiphyte. [This was known to Nehrling as *Hatiora salicornioides*.]

The genus Pereskia consists of a number of very interesting and formidably spined cacti, all tropical American. Their stems are scarcely succulent, and unlike all other cacti, they bear large green leaves. In the axils of the leaves we find groups of sharp thorns and hairs. These groups of thorns are known as areoles. New spines are produced in each areole every year. So formidable is the armor of these plants that they can be handled only with great care. The flowers are borne in panicles. In other cacti they are solitary. Several species are very ornamental not only as dense climbing foliage plants, but also on account of their large conspicuous flowers. The fruit of several species is excellent for culinary purposes, reminding one of the common Gooseberry both in appearance and flavor. In greenhouse culture they are best known as stocks for grafting Epiphyllums, particularly *Pereskia aculeata,* although *P. bleo* is better adapted for supporting large plants, being of much stronger habit than the former. Here in central Florida all can be grown successfully in the open. They make a most luxuriant growth in good rich soil, doing well even on high pineland. Though very tender and easily cut down by a heavy freeze, they soon send up new vigorous sprouts and are as beautiful as ever after a season's growth. After having been cut back by frost the injured stems should be removed immediately.

Pereskia aculeata (Lemon-Vine, Blade-Apple, Barbados-Gooseberry) is widely spread in tropical America and common in south Florida as a climbing and verandah plant. When the masses of pure white, strangely fragrant flowers open the sight is a very beautiful one. Each blossom is as large as a silver dollar. The foliage is very thick and glossy and has a peculiar luster which must be seen to be appreciated. The fruit, which appears in great abundance on large vines in extreme south Florida, is lemon-colored and of the size of an olive. It can be used in the same way as the Gooseberry is used, and is just as good in every respect. Here in Orange County it is not so much grown in gardens as it was years ago. This is due to its being very tender, but many people are much opposed to it on account of its formidable spines. They call it the "Cherokee Cactus Vine" in allusion to the Cherokee Rose, which has been banished from most gardens on account of its spiny armor. The variety *Pereskia aculeata* var. *godseffiana* with richly colored leaves is now and then found in gardens.

Pereskia bleo (*P. grandifolia*), the Rose-Cactus from Panama and Colombia, is now grown in many warm countries. The growth is much stouter than the former, and the leaves are larger, about 5 inches long. The flowers appear in large clusters and are of a beautiful rosy purple, being about 2 inches in diameter. They have little or no fragrance. The pear-shaped fruit is about 2 inches long. Usually this species grows as a tall shrub, but it can be used on posts or verandahs as a clambering plant. It is much more tender there than the Lemon-Vine, and as the flowers always appear on the old wood and this is often destroyed by a frost, flowers are not often seen here in my garden. It thrives to perfection in extreme south Florida.

Sansevierias and Agave

Three species of Bow-String-Hemp, or Sansevierias, are extremely popular pot plants and are grown quite extensively in south Florida. The oldest one, forming fine, tall, dense specimens in not too large pots, is *Sansevieria zeylanica* [= *S. trifasciata*], a native of tropical Africa where most of the other species seem to occur. Its tall narrow leaves are dark green, transversely marked with grayish-white. *Sansevieria guinensis* (*S. thyrsiflora*) has much broader, shorter and lighter green leaves. They are also transversely marked with grayish-green. It also forms a very fine pot plant. *Sansevieria* [*trifasciata* 'Laurentii'], a plant now grown in immense numbers for the northern market, has a band of creamy-yellow along its margin beside the transverse markings. It seems closely allied to the first named species. All these are highly valued as pot plants, standing the dry air of rooms and corridors very well, and grow freely even in shade. For verandah decoration they are invaluable.

A species with round leaves is *Sansevieria cylindrica* [var. *patula*]—an interesting plant, but the leaves never stand upright as in the other species named, and for this reason it is not much in demand. I have also had *Sansevieria spicata* and *S. subspicata*, both very interesting, rather small-growing species. The largest and most imposing species I have grown is *Sansevieria kirkii*, a native of Zanzibar [now part of Tanzania], which has leaves 9 feet long. All the species are excellent fiber plants, but this one is particularly valuable. As a garden plant it is of importance, its stout lanceolate leaves, mottled with various shades of green and its large heads of grayish, long-tubed flowers are very attractive. All require very rich [well drained] soil. They ought to be planted in pots or tubs, where they soon form dense masses of fine upright leaves. If given too much space the clumps increase rapidly, but they are never dense, and therefore lose their elegance and attractive compactness.

I have been repeatedly requested to say a "few kind words" in favor of the Agaves, or Century Plants, and if and how they can be grown in Florida. Many of the species (the genus *Agave* consists of over [300] species) thrive splendidly in Florida, though little has been done by amateurs and specialists to bring together large collections. A few years ago, Dr. Geo. Stone of Fort Myers had a fine collection of the most beautiful small and broad-leafed species in his front garden, which attracted much attention and caused a great deal of enthusiastic comment.

There are two fine species growing wild in Florida—*Agave neglecta* [probably *A. decipiens*] and *A. decipiens,* the latter usually occurring on shell mounds near the beach. The Sisal (*A. sisalana*), a rather coarse-growing plant, is found in many gardens. It was introduced almost a century ago from Mexico on account of its valuable fiber, known as "Sisal Hemp." For ornamental purposes the common American Century-Plant (*A. americana*) and its variegated form (*A. americana* 'Variegata') is an old and much admired strong growing, formal plant. It is often found in gardens all along the Gulf Coast, particularly in very dry and otherwise barren situations. I have seen it quite frequently from Houston, Texas, to Mobile, Pensacola and as far north as Charleston, S.C.

There are a few other equally attractive species now and then found in our southern gardens, but not by far as many as the ardent plant lover may expect.

The late Dr. J. N. Rose says that "Amateurs often cultivate a greater number of species than are described" in the current literature. "Agaves," he goes on to say,

> are essentially fancier's or amateur's plants. This noble group of plants has never received the attention it deserves, and yet no genus of plants in America furnishes so many suitable decorative plants. Sir Joseph Hooker places it next to the Palms and Aloes, but the former is a great family of 1200 [2,000] species. While in the United States we think of the Agaves only as decorative plants, yet in Mexico, their native home, they are most useful of plants. Many species furnish fiber, others soap, while still others produce the two great Mexican drinks, pulque and mescal. Pulque, which is a fermented drink, is obtained from several species, especially *Agave atrovirens.* Mescal, which is a distilled drink, is usually not ob-

tained from the same species as pulque, although there is a general belief to the contrary. The species from which is made most of the mescal used in Mexico is unknown.

As a rule many of the fine large growing Agaves thrive with astonishing vigor in our Florida gardens. All they demand is a rather dry, well-drained soil in the full sun. The rocky soil along the lower East Coast is particularly adapted for their culture. The different species vary so much in size and aspect that they can be used in a great many ways in garden decoration. Some of the fine small and broad-leafed species are admirably adapted for small rockeries, for pots and vases, while many of the larger growing kind are most beautiful for large rockeries, along walks, terraces and even as hedge plants. They are also well adapted for large vases in large gardens, and can even be used in many ways in connection with the new and now so fashionable Spanish architecture.

These plants, coming from dry, arid or even desert regions where they have a hard struggle for existence, can be grown with little or no care, but they respond very quickly to good treatment. The species are propagated in various ways—by seed, offsets, and young plants that are produced in immense numbers on the tops of the tall flower-scapes, where they finally get detached and drop to the ground where they immediately form roots and grow vigorously. They are also raised easily from seed, but it requires a long time before they are large enough to form impressive objects. Most all of the large growing Agaves do well near the beach, but they will not succeed in moist, rich soils. They are in reality dry land plants and fill as such a most important gap, growing as they do in places where nothing else will do.

It was a popular belief at not a very remote time that Agaves only flower once in a century,—hence the name Century-Plant. But this is an exploded idea. Agaves flower when they are large enough, in six, ten or fifteen years. I have in my Naples garden one or the other in bloom every year. Flower stems issue from the center of the leaf-rosette, attain a height of from 6 to 20 feet, according to the species, and are much branched at their tops. Mostly the flowers are of a yellowish-green color and quite inconspicuous.

The Agaves are very formal plants and are for this reason splendidly adapted for formal gardens and the new architecture so much in vogue now all over Florida. The leaves of the larger species are from 3 to 5 feet long, usually of a glaucous-green color, and each leaf has at its apex a very sharp blackish, heavy spine. The leaf edges are also usually provided with a short, though formidable armor of spines. After flowering and having ripened its seeds and tubercles, the stem gradually dies with the old plant, but usually numerous offsets are formed around the plant, which can be used for propagation.

We in Florida do not make the use of the Agaves in the various ways as the people in southern California do. In the south of Europe everyone knows that the Agaves, and particularly *Agave americana,* are acclimatized and live in the open air, growing as fast and as vigorously as they do in their native haunts in Mexico. The entire shores of the Mediterranean on both sides are planted with *Agave americana,* which attains a great size, flowers and gives out suckers by thousands.

Smaller plants should be set out in Florida,—preferably in November and during the winter months,—the large specimens being difficult to handle on account of the long, sharp spines. They are excellent on the dry sandy beaches, where scarcely anything grows, and they are not injured by the salt spray. In fact the finest plants I have found in Florida grew in the lovely Coconut Palm Garden, at Sea Villa, Naples. They all were planted by the owner, Mrs. W. B. Haldeman.

I have only about ten different species of Agaves in my Naples garden, including the native ones and the almost indigenous Sisal Plant. The common Century-Plant (*A. americana*) is found in many gardens in Florida, from Jacksonville southward. Its variegated form, *A. americana* 'Variegata' is particularly cherished.

Several years ago a northern horticulturist, and a good landscape gardener, visited my place at Naples. He was particularly struck by the beauty of two long rows of Agaves lining the path leading to the road. These consisted mostly of *Agave decipiens,*—our native species, and a beautiful one it is— and only a few *A. americana* and *A. atrovirens.* About 8 years ago I took with me from Palm Cottage Gardens about 100 young plants that had formed in the top of the flower panicle, and all grew wonderfully well.

4

Palms in Florida

Florida has been called the playground of the rich and the paradise of the poor. In reality it is the paradise of the man with ideals, of the nature lover and of the horticulturist. There are drawbacks, to be sure, but untouched Nature is perfect. There are thousands of charming plants, native and exotic, and there are Palms. Florida is indeed the land of Palms. This is evident when we board one of the steamers running up the St. Johns,—the Welaka of the Indians,—one of the most lovely and unique rivers in this country. On every side we see groups and groves of Cabbage palms, always impressive, always delightfully interesting and always charming. Very often they form forests by themselves, but frequently they are found in company of other evergreen forest trees, such as Magnolias and Live Oaks.

Symbol of the Tropics

In the highlands and low lands we find as the most common species the Saw Palmetto, a creeping palm and not very particular as to soil and moisture. In shady dells and glens of the moist woodlands we come upon congregations of the very attractive Needle-Palm, and in the flatwoods the ground is covered with the tiny Scrub-Palmetto [*Sabal minor*]. These are the indigenous palms of northern and central Florida. Entering the region of the Caloosahatchee and Biscayne Bay we are in tropical Florida, on the threshold of the most magnificent, the noblest species in existence,—the Royal Palm.

From Palm Beach and Punta Gorda southward the Coconut Palms are at their best. Seldom straight, the trunks of these imposing trees sweep upward from the poorest of sandy, shelly soils, provided only it be near the salt sea. The great swaying leaves seem to have a peculiarly undefinable unrest.

Thanks to the insinuating breezes, they are forever murmuring their languorous longings, reaching restlessly out to the beautiful blue sea. And then there are quite a number of smaller fan-leafed palms, very elegant and graceful,—four [2] species of *Thrinax* and two [1] species of *Coccothrinax,* tender tropical plants that will not thrive in the open even in the region of Lake Apopka and Lake Tohopekaliga in central Florida. The interesting Sargent Palm (*Pseudophoenix sargentii*) is found on the keys, while the two tufted species (*Acoelorrhaphe wrightii*), one known popularly as the Everglade Palm, is only found in dense wet hammocks in extreme south Florida. The other [*Serenoa repens*] is the Saw Palmetto. When well cared for it forms beautiful tufts.

These sixteen [11] different species of native palms teach us a lesson. They convince us that Florida is really a land of palms. They persuade us to enter the great and enchanting realm of palms, to enjoy their beauty, to study their habits and ways and to select the most lovely and majestic for our subtropical and tropical gardens. In addition to our native species we have a long list of exotic species to select from, though we scarcely have begun to accumulate collections to form real palm gardens.

Along the borders of the beautiful lakes in central Florida; in the high, hilly, healthy lake region; along our streams and bays; along our well built highways, beautiful winter homes will spring up everywhere, and wonderful tropical gardens, replete with palms and tropical trees, will be laid out. No other state offers such splendid possibilities along these lines. And though much attention will be paid to our native trees and shrubs, to the Chinese and Japanese evergreens, to the blue Jacaranda and the glowing Royal Poinciana, the appeal of the palm will be paramount. It will imbue these tropical gardens with an air of noble and refined beauty.

Florida is a large state, touching almost the Tropics. Many species, not hardy enough in the northern and central parts, can be grown successfully in the extreme south,—in places where the Mango, the Sapodilla and the Avocado ripen their fruit. I am of the opinion that we have scarcely entered the realm of palms. What a magnificent sight do the lines and masses of Coconut Palms present at Palm Beach and Miami and on the West Coast, where the glowing sheets of flowers of the Royal Poinciana and the scarcely less brilliant blossoms of the native *Cordia sebestena* (Geiger Tree) light up the landscape with the brilliancy of their glowing red flowers; where the leaves of the Traveler's Tree attain gigantic proportions; where the candela-bra-like heads of the Screw-Pine (*Pandanus utilis*) attract our attention and where thickets of resplendent Crotons abound in every good garden.

Beautiful Native Florida Palms

"The genus *Thrinax,* comprising fan-leaved, usually slender-stemmed palms, is represented in Florida by four [2] species, all of them living on the lower keys and the extreme southern part of the mainland. Until recently the species have been in much confusion, it having been believed that all of ours were West Indian forms. Not long ago Prof. C. S. Sargent discovered that three of these were new and bestowed new names on them and de-scribed them." (Simpson.)

These small slender palms are very handsome when well grown, and they look especially fine when grown in groups in the foreground of tall species. A collection of our native and the West Indian species of *Thrinax* and our two [1] *Coccothinax* growing all together in rather dense masses as is the case in Prof. Simpson's garden on Biscayne Bay, is an extremely beautiful sight. They ought to be grown extensively by all palm lovers. Unfortunately we find them very rarely in collections, not even at Fort Myers where fine palms are especially appreciated. They are, according to my own experience, very difficult to transplant from their native haunts. Pot-grown plants have to be resorted to in order to be successful.

"All the species of the *Thrinax* group," says Prof. Simpson, who has un-doubtedly the largest collection in the state, "that have come under my no-tice grow slowly at first, but all are beautiful either as pot plants or in the open where they are not subject to frost. They grow more rapidly when they attain to some size and are perfectly at home in partial shade or sunshine and in all soils from damp muck to high pineland."

I have found that here at Naples they will not grow on high dry pineland unless a good deal of muck is mixed with the sand. At Palm Cottage Gar-dens, I grew quite a number of species, especially from the West Indies, in a lath house among Ixoras, fancy-leaved Caladiums, Alocasias, Dracaenas and other tender plants. Within a few years they formed handsome little speci-mens, looking beautifully among their associates. In February, 1917, I lost almost all of them by a heavy freeze. I particularly valued a group of about a dozen species among some fine large *Cycas circinalis, Ceratozamia mexicana, Dioon spinulosum* and various Zamias. The contrast between the Cycads and these small palms was extremely unique, and very charming.

[*Thrinax morrisii*] is a native of the Florida Keys, having been reported from the Marquesas and Crab Keys. Mr. John Soar, whose name is indelibly on record in all matters concerning the botany of extreme south Florida as well as that of Prof. Chas. T. Simpson, found it also on Pumpkin Key. It grows luxuriantly in the evidently poor sandy soil, being fully exposed to the sun like all its congeners. It has full formed, large, thin fan-leaves, being dark [pale] green above and [whitish] underneath. The trunk is much stouter than in the preceding species, being sometimes from 12 to 14 inches in diameter. It grows about 25 feet tall and is raised on a base of thick-matted roots, sometimes 3 feet in height. It is evidently a rather common species in its habitat, but like all its allies, it is rarely seen in cultivation, never being offered in the trade.

According to Prof. Sargent, this "is a tree rarely more than 30 ft in height, with a trunk 8 to 10 inches in diameter, covered with smooth pale blue rind, flowering in the spring and ripening its fruit late in the autumn. The leaves are from 2 to 3 feet across. The color of the leaf is rather pale green on the surface silvery-white beneath and more or less tomentose when young." [The names *T. keyensis* and *T. microcarpa* used by Nehrling, Simpson, and Sargent, both refer to plants of *T. morrisii*.]

Our wide-awake nurserymen and plant collectors should make it their aim to introduce largely all the native and West Indian *Thrinax* species and their allied forms. These very lovely small palms, forming beautiful groups if set out properly, are indispensable in the decoration of large palm collections. They are of equal value among tropical trees and shrubs and should never be missed in parks and pleasure grounds. Though said to flourish in dry sandy soils and without fertilizer, I have found that they respond very rapidly to good applications of organic fertilizers and to good cultivation. They do particularly well if planted in well prepared soil. A deep hole should be dug, and this should be filled with rich compost, such as much mixed with stable manure and surface soil. Only well-grown pot plants should be set out. In the dry season watering is very beneficial. These rules apply to all these palms.

Thrinax microcarpa [also = *T. morrisii*] has a slender stem with the boots having a tendency to adhere. No matted roots at the base. Leaves glaucous green above, very thick, [whitish] beneath. Fruit much smaller than a pea; white. Our specimens are from 6 to 25 feet tall.

[*Thrinax radiata*] occurs from Cape Romano to Cape Sable, and is also found on several of the lower keys. It has been sold as *T. parviflora* from Jamaica, and also as *T. argentea*, a Cuban species. According to Prof. Simpson, "There are certainly four species of *Thrinax* [two] native of extreme south Florida, all of which are well worthy of cultivation and are perfectly at home without fertilizer in our poorest soil. One of them the writer brought to the attention of botanists recently, and though quite common, it has been overlooked or taken for something else. It is *T. wendlandiana* [= *T. radiata*]." It seems to be one of our most common forms on the lower keys and on parts of the south shores of the mainland, being the most common *Thrinax* palm in the Chokoloskee region, also abounding in the Deep Lake Hammock and in Royal Palm Hammock on the Tamiami Trail. It is the only member of the genus found in some of the gardens at Naples.

There are two very interesting specimens, about 18 feet high, in front of the Naples Hotel and there is another very fine specimen in General W. B. Haldeman's grounds, growing under the shade of some large Florida Banyan Trees, while those in the hotel grounds occupy a position in the full sun. The crown of leaves is quite dense. These leaves are deep green above, and somewhat duller green on the underside, not showing the silver color which is so much admired in almost all our other species. The flowers appear in April and May in large airy clusters among the leaves, standing quite upright, the fruit in large pendant clusters in September and October. The berries are white and very juicy, and they have a sweet, aromatic taste. I have been informed that small plants were brought to Naples from Chokoloskee by fishermen many years ago and were distributed over the gardens. Only three grew; the rest,—several dozen—died.

That it is quite difficult to transplant these woodland nymphs is shown in my own case. I planted young specimens repeatedly, and bestowed much care on them, but as yet I never succeeded to start them into growth. I am now resorting to growing them from seed. These small seedlings are transplanted into pots, and will be set out in groups as soon as they are large enough to stand the vicissitudes of the open ground. Like almost all other palms, they prefer shade and rich soil. In dry, poor sand they are of a very slow growth and always look stunted. All the *Thrinax* and *Coccothrinax* species, native and exotic, look most beautiful and effective in groups or masses in the foreground of other palms or of tropical trees and shrubs. Bamboos of the giant species or of the medium sized kinds such as *Bambusa argentea, B. gracilis* and *B. alphonse-karri,* all growing in clumps, also form a fine background for these palms.

[*Coccothrinax argentata*], Dwarf Silver Palm: "Mingled with *Sabal palmetto* and [*S. etonia*] is a dwarf fan-leaved palm of exquisite beauty, named for a dear botanist who explored and collected in south Florida. The upper sides of the leaves are glossy rich green; the under-surfaces are of the loveliest satiny or silvery color imaginable. It is rather a slow grower and never attains any great height. It is found only on the shores of Biscayne Bay." (Prof. Chas. T. Simpson in a letter to the author.) [*Coccothrinax argentata*]. This is the Dwarf Silver Palm of the Biscayne pineland region. Stem short, rarely more than 3 feet tall. Leaves dark green above, intensely silvery underneath, deeply cleft. Fruit as large as or larger than a pea, glossy purplish-black. Our specimens came from surrounding pine woods (small ones) and from below Homestead (taller ones).

The late R. D. Hoyt, an ardent plant lover, after speaking of the chain of reef keys and their border of *Thrinax* palms, says that "some ten miles to the eastward I found *T. argentea* [no doubt *Coccothrinax argentata*], the most beautiful of Florida palms, smaller than *T. parviflora* [*T. radiata*], but more graceful. The leaves are dark green above, the under surface glistening silvery white, with yellow petioles; and the sight of these leaves when turned up to the sunlight and waving in a stiff sea-breeze is something that one will never forget. If these only could be transplanted to some northern conservatory, but unfortunately they cannot, as every effort in that direction has proved a failure. They refuse to be moved from the ocean washed island that is their home."

This beautiful and dainty little gem grows best in shade and in rich soil under cultivation. It is rare in gardens, but should be largely grown.

I had several of these dainty and elegant palms in my lath house at Gotha for years. They grew in half-shade and in the rich moist soil among Alocasias, Spathiphyllums, Homalomenas, Agalonemas and other aroids, and among Marantas and dwarf specimens of Ixoras, *Palisota barteri* and fancy-leaved Caladiums. Chamaedoreas of half a dozen species grew in the same bed. The entire combination was very charming, and the *Coccothrinax* "gar-

beri" stood out very prominently among them all. A slight frost did not hurt the plants, but the heavy freeze early in February, 1917, killed many of these small palms, and this species was among the losses.

[*Coccothrinax argentata*], Silver Palm: This is another very elegant and beautiful native palm with fan-shaped leaves like the former, but it has a stem from 12 to 25 feet tall, while *C.* "*garberi*" has only very short trunks or none at all. I received a few small seedlings from my friend Mr. Simpson, who had grown them from seeds which he had gathered on Bahia Honda Key. He wrote me at the time: "'*C. garberi*' is a beauty, but '*C. jucunda*' is superb. Its glossy and very elegant leaves are deep green above and brilliantly silvery beneath. The stem is thin and slender, smooth, and of brownish-gray color. It is found in several of the lower keys." [*Coccothrinax* [*C. argentata*] has a smooth stem, no matted roots at base. Leaves bright green above, silvery beneath. Fruit small, black. Our specimens are from 12 to 20 feet tall. From Cape Sable and Big Pine Key. [*Coccothrinax garberi* and *C. jucunda* are both synonyms of *C. argentata*.]

About the transplanting of large specimens of the Thrinax palms Mr. R. F. Deckert writes me as follows: "Here at Mr. Chas. Deering's estate we have quite a number of large Thrinax specimens that were brought by boat from the keys and the Cape Sable region and were planted successfully in our pineland, also on and close to the shore of Biscayne Bay here at Buena Vista. They were taken up with a ball wrapped in wet burlap sacking and, of course, were defoliated, except the heart, and very few were lost." Mr. Deckert characterizes the six native species as follows:

In regard to the last species, Mrs. Marian A. McAdow of Punta Gorda writes me under date of Oct. 14, 1923: "This *Coccothrinax* whose seeds I sent you came from Reasoner Bros. in 1912 and it was listed as *C. garberi*. It is about 6 inches in diameter, closely wrapped with the cloth of its old leaf shields from the ground up. Has never lost even one single leaf. The bunch of seed was higher than my head. I reached it with a long clipper, so I should say the trunk is about 9 or 10 feet to where the leaves begin. These make the palm 6 to 7 feet taller." [The palm described was probably not a native of Florida but *C. barbadensis*, which was widely cultivated, fruits heavily, and is fast growing to some height.]

The Cabbage Palmetto

"To northern eyes,—yes, to the eyes of all who are really in sympathy with whatever is attractive in nature,—this strange tree is always wonderful. I can never pass it without turning to gaze at it with awe and admiration; it is so absolutely unlike anything that the dweller of the temperate zone is used to. Singly or in groups it is always attractive." (Chas. T. Simpson.)

The Cabbage Palmetto, Carolina Palmetto, and simply Palmetto, is the most common and popular palm of Florida. It is the northernmost of palms in this country, occurring as far north as North Carolina and thence southward into Florida, mostly near the coast or along streams and in the rich hammock woods around our large inland lakes. It prefers moist, rich ground, often even standing in water, though it will grow vigorously on high and dry pineland provided that it is planted in deep holes filled with rich soil. Being a gregarious palm it is, as a rule, always found in large groups or in masses, many thousands often standing close together.

In northern and central Florida it is undoubtedly the most impressive, the most tropical looking, the most interesting of our native forest trees, forming a most characteristic feature along all our water courses and in the rich hammock woods throughout the greater part of the state. To see the first noble palmetto growing wild on the bank of a river is an event in one's life, but to behold groups and forests of them is like a miracle. They form pictures of enchanting scenery in the soul of the lover of nature which are indelibly impressed as long as life lasts. When I first saw single specimens, and a little later groups, and finally forests of Cabbage Palmettos on the banks of the St. Johns I was overwhelmed with their beauty and grandeur. A single well developed specimen with its massive trunk and dense leaf-crown is a most beautiful object, but far more effective are groups and masses of a hundred and more. They simply defy description. Though growing usually gregariously in moist, rich soil, they are frequently found among other forest trees, such as *Magnolia grandiflora* and Live Oaks on high, hilly, hammock soil.

Here in my Palmetum and Tropical Gardens of Naples are dozens of Cabbage Palms, old and time-worn, but extremely effective, imparting to the entire place an air of dignity and charm. Nature, as if not satisfied with the beautiful individuality allotted them, decorates the trunks and even the crowns with epiphytal plants and climbers.

Young Cabbage palms are always surrounded with the bases of the dead leaf-stalks, usually called "boot-jacks" by the natives. They encircle the entire trunks, imparting to them a massiveness and picturesqueness not found in the old and taller specimens, which have dropped the old leaf-stems, and which, for this reason, look very smooth and slender. In the pockets of these half-rotten leaf-bases, close to the trunk, humus accumulates as time passes on, and numerous ferns find a foot-hold, soon forming conspicuous associations around the entire trunk. The most common, and at the same time the most charming, fern growing on the trunks of these palms is the Golden Polypody—the Palmetto Fern as it is often known by the plain people of the woods—the [*Phlebodium aureum*], which forms wreath-like circles just underneath the crown of fan-leaves. In the mountain woods north of Canton in China, the stately *Caryota ochlandra,* one of the Fish-tail Palms, is similarly embellished by an allied fern, the beautiful [*Aglaomorpha coronans*] (*P. conjugatum* [?]). Then we often meet with clusters of the dainty Resurrection Fern and here in my hammock the Sword Fern or Boston Fern (*Nephrolepis exaltata*) is also often seen on the trunks of these palms, often in company of orchids especially [*Encyclia tampensis*], masses of [*Encyclia cochleata*] and *Epidendrum nocturnum*. The leafless succulent roots of [*Polyradicion* or *Polyrrhiza lindenii*] adhere closely to the smooth trunk. I have added large clumps of Bee-Swarm Orchid (*Cyrtopodium punctatum*), many *Rhipsalis* species and numerous bromeliads and climbing aroids, such as *Monstera deliciosa,* [*Epipremnum aureum*], [*Syngonium podophyllum*], *Philodendron* and [*Epipremnum merrillii?*], vigorously climbing up the trunks, decorating them with beautiful foliage.

On the East Coast many of the palms are covered with *Selenicereus boechmanii* [probably *Cereus pteranthus*] and *Hylocereus triangularis* [*Cereus undatus*], and I also have these and other climbing cacti on my palm trunks. Now and then we find the palms, especially on the St. Johns, covered with the rampant masses of Moonflower [*Ipomoea alba*], a perfect white sheet when the silvery light of the moon falls upon them. Their delicately delightful perfume fills the night air everywhere. We never should plant the Moonflower out in our gardens, as it soon will cover every bush and tree with its rampant growth, and it is almost impossible to eradicate it.

Much more charming are the palms when covered with the graceful festoons of the Carolina Jessamine (*Gelsemium sempervirens*) in January. The rather large vivid yellow, deliciously fragrant flower-trumpets are so lavishly produced that the whole crown appears like one solid sheet of yellow. In this way nature points out to us how we can adorn these princes of the plant world either with an air-garden or orchids, bromeliads and ferns, or with attractive climbers. I never tire of my groups of fine old Cabbage palms and their trunks, covered with epiphytal growth, afford an additional charm. Such exquisite scenes will remain to cheer the minds of men when now notorious events and personalities have passed into oblivion.

Almost all palms are rather slow growers, and the Cabbage palm is no exception. In rich soil, however, it will soon form very stately specimens. Seedlings that were planted out ten years ago at Palm Cottage Gardens on high pineland have not yet started to form a trunk, while others set out in deep rich soil in the same year have grown trunks 5 to 6 feet high and formed magnificent leaf-crowns. Though avenues of Palmettos are wonderfully charming, I prefer natural groves or groups as we find them in our woodlands. Wherever they are found they should be carefully preserved. Frequently we come upon large assemblages of Palmettos, forming large forests by themselves with no other tree among them and with scarcely any underwood. Their leaves meet overhead, the light is obscured, and when we look upwards it seems as if we had entered a dome or a cathedral. Now and then Live Oaks, Magnolias and numerous small shrubs are found in their company. As a rule these palm forests are confined to the banks of rivers and lakes. Along the railroads they are rarely seen. In fact, one may travel for miles and miles without perceiving a single specimen.

There is scarcely a place in Florida where Cabbage palms will not grow well. If the holes are dug deep and filled with rich soil they will grow as well on high and rolling pineland and on the rich moist banks of our watercourses. The reason why they are not found among the pines on high land is chiefly due to the annually occurring forest fires which consume every particle of humus in the soil, leaving behind them a bare sandy waste. Were it not for these devastating conflagrations our woodlands would be dotted with Cabbage palms everywhere. This is amply demonstrated on my place where young palmettos, *Magnolia grandiflora* and young Florida Cedars come up everywhere in the surrounding woodlands, which have not been struck by fires for the last twenty-five years.

For immediate effects, large heavy specimens may be transplanted from the woods. In selecting Cabbage palms for planting the small ones without a trunk or only with a short trunk should not be chosen. While they are comparatively easily removed from their wildwood environments, they will, in most cases, not start afresh. The best and most satisfactory results are obtained by picking out specimens with massive trunks six to eight feet, or even ten to twelve feet high. The places which they are intended to occupy in their future life need some preparation beforehand. Very frequently all the roots and leaves are cut off in transplanting. If done in the right season, this procedure is quite successful.

The color of the widely spreading leaves is a deep lustrous green, often with a slight glaucous hue. In well fertilized, cultivated specimens the colors are much more intense than in those from the woodland. The leaves are from three to four feet in diameter. The immense flower-cluster appears in the center of the crown among the axils of the leaves, hanging down in graceful curves from all sides. Isolated flower-clusters may appear as early as May, but the main flowering period is the months of July and August. The individual flowers are small and of a greenish-white color, but they appear in such enormous masses that during the blooming time the Palmetto has an additional charm. The flowers are sought by swarms of bees. The large clusters of shining black berries ripen in winter. Each berry is about as large as a pea. Though rather dry, they are relished by numerous birds, particularly wild turkeys, and by mammals, such as raccoons, opossums and bears. The small nutlet, which is surrounded by a sweet, thin, fleshy coat, is dropped by the birds, everywhere, and young plants spring up even in cultivated grounds by the thousands. The berried clusters must be cut as soon as the fruit is ripe, or the weevils will soon destroy every seed. The seeds also should be sown immediately after they have been harvested.

I have often heard the remark that our Cabbage Palm is a valueless plant, because it is claimed that it has no useful properties. Life has taught me a most important lesson—the lesson that the ideal, the beautiful, the noble, the elevating, is as valuable, only more so, as the useful. It would be an extremely sordid, gloomy, uninteresting life if beauty, charm, idealism were missing. The practical side of life, the chase after the dollar—mercenary accomplishments—has often killed all elevating interests even in men who want to be known as possessing culture and refinement. Nothing shows the highest culture of mankind more plainly than ornamental horticulture.

Though palms are known to belong to the most useful of plants, many of them are mainly famous for their beauty and magnificence. The Cabbage palm belongs in the last category. In its beauty lies its usefulness mainly. A background of large Magnolias, Live Oaks and other tall evergreens heightens their effect in a most charming way.

Though the main value of our Palmetto lies in its beauty, it is by no means entirely without economical importance. The first settlers named it Cabbage Palm on account of the heart which they cut out and ate like cabbage. Every plant which is deprived of this "Cabbage" (the heart of the plant)—invariably dies. While wandering one day around in the Big Cypress Swamp in Lee County, I came upon a group of young Palmettos which had at their top a very ragged appearance. A close examination revealed the fact that no human beings had climbed the palms for the heart. The surrounding leaves of a harder texture seemed as if they had been chewed, not cut. The heart of quite a number had been pulled out after the surrounding leaves had been chewed and twisted off. A little later I found another group with battered leaves, and here I found the fresh tracks of the culprits. They were bear tracks. Hunters told me later that it is not at all a rare occurrence to find that the black bear relishes the heart of the Cabbage Palm, as he is also a lover of its fruit.

The leaves are used for thatching, and hats and fans are made from them. Fort Ripley, a stronghold in the rear of Fort Sumter, is almost entirely built of Cabbage palm trunks, which afford an excellent material for this purpose, as cannon balls soon lose their force in the spongy fractures, and detach no dangerous splinters. Palmetto logs are also used for constructing wharves or other works under water, as they are never injured by the toredo worms.

In conclusion I quote the following notes from the pen of Prof. C. S. Sargent:

> Of the tree palms of our country the best known is the Cabbage Palmetto of the coast region of the southeastern states, where in the immediate neighborhood of the sea it ranges from an island off the mouth of Cape Fear River in North Carolina to southern Florida, and along the Gulf coast to the Apalachicola. This tree is interesting to botanical geographers as the most northern arborescent palm in the world; and probably nothing so delights and instructs northern travelers in the South as their first introduction to a grove of these plants.
>
> The large terminal leaf-bud of this tree and of many other palms is cooked as a vegetable—a fact to which it owes its common name. The

custom is an extravagant one as the removal of the bud, which is n̶ ̶ ̶
replaced, kills the trees, and as young vigorous trees produce the most
succulent buds it is rather remarkable that the species has escaped extermination. But if it has survived the vegetarian, it will not long survive the
maker of scrubbing-brushes, who now uses the fibers of the sheaths of
the young leaves in his industry. To obtain his material, the top of a
young plant with its bud is cut off, trimmed down to a disk of about 8
inches in length, and then, after the soft edible core has been removed,
boiled to separate the fibers. The removal of the top kills the plant, as we
have already said, and as one concern in Jacksonville, Florida, alone con-
sumes 7,500 buds a week, the time is not very far distant when the *Sabal
palmetto* will become a rare tree. The buds, which are now mostly pro-
cured from the West Coast of Florida, where the palm is most abundant,
are worth at the mill only 6 or 7 cents each, and it is not probable that the
extravagance and wastefulness of this brush industry is exceeded by that
of any other in the United States.

The genus *Sabal* consists of pigmies and giants. Our small [*Sabal minor*]
never makes a trunk. Our Cabbage palm appears small at the side of the
gigantic [*Sabal jamaicensis*] of Jamaica. There are perhaps 14 to 15 species,
all different, spread over southern Texas, northern Mexico, Bermuda and the
West Indies. One species is common in Trinidad, occurs also in northern
South America. This is the fine and distinct *Sabal mauritiaeformis*. All are
hardy in Florida.

[*Sabal minor*] is a low-growing palm. The Dwarf Palmetto is found in
low grounds along streams, in pine barrens and flatwoods from Louisiana to
Florida and northward to South Carolina. It is stemless and never grows
higher than 2 or 3 feet. A novice at first glance might mistake it for the Saw
Palmetto, but its leaf-stems are free from spines, the leaves are usually of a
deeper green than those of the Saw Palmetto, and though it will grow on
rather high land, it is naturally always found in swamps and low ground. In
low hammocks where there is a rich deposit of leaf-mold, one often finds
whole colonies of it. The short stem is always buried in the ground, and the
dark-green, fan-shaped leaves, with slender, erect flower spikes rising high
above them, make it one of the most beautiful of dwarf Fan Palms. The
seeds are small, about as large as a pea, and round. This palm has long been
in cultivation in other countries and is a favorite, both for pot-culture and
open-air planting in countries where the temperature does not often fall

below 10°F. I have never seen it in cultivation in Florida except in my own garden. I think that the very dwarf Fan palm of the Florida flatwoods is a distinct species.

[*Sabal etonia*] is another low-growing species with creeping stems. It is extremely common in many parts of peninsular Florida, growing often together in dense masses in the way of the Saw Palmetto, with which it is often mingled. In clearing it is well to leave specimens occasionally, as they make fine clumps when given a chance. I have never seen it cultivated.

Sabal Palms

All the Sabals belong to our most beautiful and valuable garden palms. All are very hardy and even grow well on high, dry, pineland soil. Our native Cabbage Palm assumes its greatest dimensions and its most refined beauty on rather low rich soils. Around Sanford all the woodlands are dotted with these palms and they are found in all stages of growth from the tiny seedling to the tall, slender giant. They evidently grow most luxuriantly here where flowing wells of sulphur water occur.

Oct. 9, 1915, was one of the events of my life. A lady friend of mine, Mrs. Susan B. Wight, took me out along the Sanford and Geneva highway towards the upper St. John's to show me the masses of flowering *Coreopsis*. The land is low and exceedingly rich. Flowing springs of sulphur water are found everywhere. The woods were sprinkled with Cabbage Palms which quite often showed a deep bluish-green hue. About five miles from Sanford towards the east the flat prairie, at the time a golden sheet of flowering Coreopsis was before us. This grand picture of bright yellow was framed on all sides by forests of Cabbage palms—all tall, all of the same height and scarcely any young ones among them. There was no underwood. High above in the sky their crowns met, casting a solemn shade. I was fascinated, spell-bound. The miles and miles of flowers exhaling a peculiarly aromatic odor—a sea of yellow unbroken by trees or shrubs, and all around the magnificent frame, a deep green forest of tall palms. The true lover of the beautiful is always delighted when he sees these palms scattered through the dense forest, but to see them in masses—many thousands of them, in forests all by themselves—the view is awe-inspiring, sublime. To walk among such masses of towering, slender palms creates a very peculiar and strange feeling,—a feeling as if we walk in a sacred spot, in an immense Gothic cathedral.

I have several fine specimens of *Sabal mexicana* (*S. texana*). It reminds one much of our native Cabbage Palmetto, but the leaf-stalks are longer and the color of the leaves is more bluish-green. Prof. O. F. Cook, our American Palm specialist, discovered not long ago a very fine and highly ornamental new species in a garden of Victoria, Texas. He had the kindness to send me several fine seedlings. This is *S. exul* [= *S. mexicana*]. I also have a promising specimen of the Porto Rican *S. causiarum,* used so extensively in its native home in the manufacture of hats. It is a beautiful Palm and perfectly hardy here as are all the Sabals. [*S. bermudana*] is represented in my garden by several fine specimens. The large fan-leaves are carried on long petioles. It is a rapid grower if well fertilized, and its leaf-crown attains an immense size. My plants were raised from seed received from Bermuda.

A still more impressive, distinct and very massive species in my garden is [*S. jamaicensis*]. Many years ago Sir Daniel Morris published a very interesting article about this species in the *Gardener's Chronicle.* This fascinating description of the forests of these palms in the savannas of Jamaica created in me the desire to add it to my collection, and Mr. W. Fawcett, Director of Public Gardens and Plantations of Jamaica, was kind enough to send me seeds. The leaves of this species are very large, hard to the touch, not so much plaited as in other species and carried on comparatively short petioles. Nevertheless the crown is immense. Even the inexperienced observer is attracted by its distinctive and massive appearance.

Leaf Stalks Impart Character to Sabal Palms: All of the Sabals retain their old leaf-stalks close to the trunk for many years. They impart character and massiveness to these fine palms. These leaf-stems, usually called "bootjacks" by the old inhabitants, should never be removed until they rot away naturally. It is a mistake and a sin against good taste and common sense to scrape them off in order to get a smooth surface. Unfortunately this is done in many gardens, and thus the characteristic beauty of the Sabals is destroyed. Of course all dead leaves must be cut off close to the trunk, but a remnant of the clasping end part should be left intact. These leaf stems gather humus in their pockets in which the spores of the Golden Polypody find a foothold. In their native wilds most all of the cabbage Palmettos bear wreaths of these fine large ferns just underneath their crown. Several trunks of Sabals and many of the hardy Coconut Palms [no doubt referring to *Syagrus* spp.] in my garden are adorned with dense masses of various ferns.

Our wide-awake nurserymen and plant collectors should make it their aim to introduce largely all the native and West Indian *Thrinax* species and their allied forms. These very lovely small palms, forming beautiful groups if set out properly, are indispensable in the decoration of large palm collections. They are of equal value among tropical trees and shrubs and should never be missed in parks and pleasure grounds. Though said to flourish in dry sandy soils and without fertilizer, I have found that they respond very rapidly to good applications of organic fertilizers and to good cultivation. They do particularly well if planted in well prepared soil. A deep hole should be dug, and this should be filled with rich compost, such as mulch mixed with stable manure and surface soil. Only well-grown pot plants should be set out. In the dry season watering is very beneficial. These rules apply to all these palms.

Pseudophoenix Palms

This new genus of palms consists of only one species and is native of several of the keys of southern Florida. It was established by Hermann Wendland, the late celebrated palm specialist of Herrenhausen in Germany, and its specific name was given in honor of Prof. C. S. Sargent of Harvard University, and director of the Arnold Arboretum at Jamaica Plain, near Boston. Prof. Sargent is the author of the monumental work, *Sylva of North America,* and other famous books, among them one on the trees and shrubs of Japan. For about ten years he published *Garden and Forest,* the best horticultural periodical ever issued in this country. Unfortunately this first-class publication had to be discontinued on account of lack of interest. The American people lingered too far back in culture to appreciate a refined, high-class horticultural journal. Those who are fortunate enough to possess a complete set of the volumes have a wealth of reliable and valuable information close at hand.

Pseudophoenix sargentii, Sargent's Palm, Buccaneer Palm: On this highly interesting palm and its discovery Prof. Sargent writes as follows in *Garden and Forest* (Vol. I, p. 352):

On the 19th of April, 1886, in company with Mr. C. E. Faxon, Mr. A. H.

Curtiss, and Lieut. Hubbard of the U.S. Navy, I landed from the Lighthouse Tender "Laurel" near the eastern end of Elliott's Key, one of the larger Florida Reef Keys, at the house and pineapple plantation of Mr. Henry Filer. Our attention was at once directed to a solitary plant, a small pinnate-leaved palm left standing in the clearing, which at first sight was mistaken for an *Oreodoxa* [= *Roystonea*], but the large orange-scarlet fruit at once showed that we had stumbled upon a tree unknown before in the North American Flora, quite unlike any of the species of palms known to us. Specimens of the fruit, which was not, unfortunately fully ripe, were sent to Dr. Wendland of Hannover, who provisionally pronounced our palm to be representative of a new genus for which he proposed the name *Pseudophoenix*. A short account of this discovery, with the announcement of Dr. Wendland's new genus, but without characters, was published in the issue of the *Botanical Gazette* for November, 1886, but it was not until a year later that I received through Mr. Curtiss ripe seeds of the *Pseudophoenix* which was sent to Dr. Wendland, who has drawn up from it generic characters.

Pseudophoenix sargentii is a slender, low tree, 20 to 25 feet high, with a trunk 10 to 12 inches in diameter, and abruptly pinnate leaves 4 to 5 feet long; the pinnae are lanceolate-acuminate, 12 to 16 inches long, bright green above and glaucous on the lower surface. The branching spadix appears from among the leaves, it is (the only specimen seen by me) 36 inches long by 30 inches broad, the main and secondary branches light yellow-green.... The three-lobed fruit,—often one or two-lobed by abortion,—is a half to three-quarters of an inch in diameter, bright orange scarlet and very showy....

A few individuals were discovered scattered through the woods in the neighborhood of Mr. Filer's plantation, and late in the same year a grove of them was discovered near the east end of Long Key by a gentleman from Bay Biscayne. There are about 200 plants, large and small in this grove. These are the only stations where *Pseudophoenix* is now known, but as the flora of the Florida Reef Keys is Bahaman in its constitution, and probably in its origin, it would be a singular fact if this tree was not found in some of the Bahama groups, the plants of which are still imperfectly known.

As far as I know, almost all the original groups and plants of Sargent's palm have been destroyed by the settlers. The uneducated, uncultured American has never had reverence and love for the rare and the beautiful. His savage tendency to kill and destroy all that is beautiful in nature is really shocking. Several of these palms were dug up and planted at Miami. Prof. Sargent's supposition has proved to be correct. It has been found to be abundant in some of the Bahama Islands.

When I saw my first specimen, about 9 or 10 feet high, in the grounds of the Royal Palm Hotel at Miami I mistook it for a young plant of the Royal Palm. This was early in May, and it bore a fine bunch of very glossy orange-colored ripe fruit—a very beautiful and striking object. From some of these berries I raised a number of seedlings at Palm Cottage Gardens, but they all were killed by a heavy freeze. Later I saw a fine group of small specimens, each about 8 feet high, in a garden at Palm Beach. Planted out in groups of a dozen or more, and not too far apart, these palms look very effective and make fine landscape pictures. It grows well in our sandy soils, but it does much better in half shade and in rather moist soil. A little fertilizer of organic origin and good cultivation help it along wonderfully. It grows quite fast if well cared for, though in its native haunts it is said to be a very slow grower. Years ago Reasoner Bros. listed it in their catalogues.

A second species has been discovered lately in the Island of Haiti, which has been named [*Pseudophoenix vinifera*]. It is described as being much larger and much more beautiful than Sargent's Palm. Prof. O. F. Cook has sent me a dozen fresh seeds of this new palm for my Naples Garden.

Royal Palms

Single tall Royal Palms are sublime. Groups, masses, avenues of it defy description. They are simply the most charming, the most lovely, the grandest pictures Nature is able to form. There is nothing like it, not even among palms. Every plant lover in south Florida is able to use it in the formation of ideal gardens. Only a little good taste is necessary. They should never be mixed in with other trees or even with other palms. Their beauty and magnificence demand a free open position not obstructed by other vegetation. But the effect of their wonderful form is brought more vividly before us if there is a fine background of dense, tall, tropical trees.

[*Roystonea*] is the undisputed queen among palms. This name was given to it by Humboldt, signifying "glory of the mountains." Everywhere in the tropics where palms are planted for ornament, the Royal Palm—the Palma Real of Cuba—take the lead. It is undoubtedly the most beautiful and the most lovely of all the members of this royal family. In stateliness, grandeur, dignity and majesty no other palm can rival it. Only good qualities are its attributes. Perfection is its banner. It glossy, deep green, plumy leaves, its great white flower trusses, its gigantic cluster of bright deep crimson berries, its smooth, silvery-gray, massive trunk and its easy growth in the right kind of soil combine to make it the ideal among palms.

The genus "*Oreodoxa*" [*Roystonea*] consists only of a few species. The very tall and slender West Indian Cabbage Palm (*Roystonea oleracea*) and the Porto Rico Royal Palm (*R. borinquena*) are well established in extreme south Florida. There are, perhaps, two more species, being confined to the mountains of northern South America, of which *Oreodoxa sancona* from Ecuador is probably the best known [this palm belongs to a different genus, *Syagrus*].

The Royal Palm is the pride of Florida in the same sense as the Sequoia is the pride of California. There were at one time large Royal Palm forests in extreme south Florida. In order to get really familiar with these palms, to admire them in all their glory, majesty and nobility one must visit the several Royal Palm hammocks still left. The wonderful grandeur once predominant, where hundreds and perhaps thousands of these lofty palms over-towered the dense tropical forest has, for the most part, vanished. Hundreds of the centuries old giants have been ruthlessly destroyed by scoundrels who wanted the seeds. But we are still overwhelmed when we look at the remnants of these once so glorious Royal Palm hammocks.

Fortunately the Royal Palm is easily cultivated. Fort Myers really is the "City of Royal Palms." Miami, Coconut Grove and Palm Beach closely follow. Even the man with sordid views of life, and the one whose main existence seems to find its goal in the accumulation of filthy lucre cannot help to be struck by the beauty and nobility of a fine, large specimen of the Royal Palm. Though always very distinguished when seen in single specimens, it reveals its charm and its entire glory most effectively when planted in groups and avenues. Nothing can be more imposing, more captivating than the avenues and groups of Royal Palms as seen in Fort Myers, Miami, Palm Beach and other places of south Florida. It is the favorite palm for avenue and group planting in all tropical countries, sharing honors only with its close relative, [*Roystonea*] *oleracea* and to some extent, with [*R.*] *borinquena*. In Honolulu, Peradenyia, Buitenzorg, in many places of India and Australia, in Cairo and Alexandria, in all the West Indies, in British Guiana, Brazil and Peru, wherever we may travel in the tropics, this native Floridian,—our

Royal Palm,—is everywhere the leading species in the decoration of parks, gardens, streets and highways.

I have called the Royal Palm a native Floridian. This is a fact, though it was first discovered and is most abundant in Cuba. Florida and Cuba share the honor of calling it their own. [*Roystonea "elata"* was, in fact, first described by Wm. Bartram in his "Travels . . ." (F. Harper, 1946).] "This majestic tree," says Dr. John Gifford, "reaches its optimal growth in Cuba, of which country it is emblematic; it adorns the Cuban Two-cent postage stamp and coat-of-arms and its rich berries fatten many swine for their Christmas festivities. It is extensively planted in south Florida and appears to be indigenous in several patches in the neighborhood of the Everglades."

There cannot be the least doubt that it is a native species. Being a strictly tropical palm, it is confined only to the shores of Bay Biscayne and the Keys and several hammocks of the interior in extreme south Florida where the vegetation is purely tropical. Its home is at present more restricted than it has been,—in several hammocks of the Everglades; one in Dade County, at present known as the Royal Palm State Park, and formerly as Paradise Key, and another one in Collier County, back of Cape Romano. There are quite a number of trees in these localities that must be at least a hundred feet in height.

After speaking in high terms of the West Indian Cabbage Palm or Palmiste [*Roystonea oleracea*], Prof. C. S. Sargent refers to the subject of this sketch as follows:

Another West Indian species, "*Oreodoxa*" *regia,* the Royal Palm, is a tree often 100 feet high, with a trunk which is often largest near the middle, but otherwise generally resembles the Cabbage Palm (*R. oleracea*), and is equally graceful and beautiful. This species which is common in Cuba, extends into southern Florida where it inhabits two or three hammocks on Rogue's River, about 20 miles east of Caxambas Bay on the West Coast; Paradise Key and the shores of Bay Biscayne near the mouth of Little River.

The presence of a lofty palm in southern Florida was hinted at more than sixty years ago, and the fact is mentioned in Nuttall's *North American Sylva,* but it was not until 1859 that this palm was known to be [*Roystonea regia*]. In that year Dr. Cooper found it on Bay Biscayne, and twenty years later Mr. A. H. Curtiss established the fact of its presence on Rogue's River and Paradise key.

The palms referred to are the Royal Palm and its congener, the Royal Cabbage Palm. The great peculiarity of these palms is that there rises upon the whitish trunk a grass-green, smooth, thinner shaft like a column placed upon a column, and from this the leaf-stalk springs. The leaves are from 20 to 25 feet long and from 5 to 6 feet broad, arranged in a beautiful crown, and all are gracefully arching to all sides. Its tall white stem and the fine head of leaves make this palm a particular favorite in gardens.

It is a delight to observe that settlers who have a taste for the poetry and beauty of Nature everywhere plant Royal Palms. Usually they are set out in avenues, along garden walks, on streets and highways, but now and then we notice the attempt to form smaller or larger groups in a natural way. In a few years hence Fort Myers will look as if placed in a Royal Palm park. The romantic Tamiami Trail will be studded with these princes among plants. The entire region of south Florida, wherever it is possible, will reveal to the tourists landscapes of beauty and distinction that will remind one rather of a dreamland than a land of reality. The Royal palm never palls; it is always intensely interesting. It will and must be the predominant figure in all south Florida landscape views. In fine Italian pictures the Italian Cypress is scarcely ever absent, and in most of the Cuban views the two Royal Palms are usually well represented. It should never be missing in any of our landscape illustrations pretending to be characteristic of the region.

Prof. Chas. T. Simpson speaks in the following way of our Royal palm:

If the Coconut Palm is a marvel of titanic grace, the Royal Palm may be called a marvel of titanic majesty. I know of no tree on earth to which the term majestic can be more appropriately applied.... I never look at one of these lordly trees but I am thankful that I live in a land where it not only grows, but is native. Mr. O. F. Cook, of Washington, believes that the Florida form is distinct from the Cuban, but other authorities differ from him and believe it to be [*Roystonea regia*]. Certain it is that I have never seen any of the royal Palms in Cuba attain either the height or dimensions that wild or cultivated specimens reach in Florida. At the Royal Palm Hammock back of Cape Romano, and on Paradise Key in the southern part of Dade County, are many trees which must be over 100 feet in height. I never see one of these majestic palms but what I feel as though mortals ought to fall on their knees before it and worship with bowed, bared head. The Royal Palm is most at home in low, rich hammocks, but does well in salt marshes if not too wet and salty. As a rule, it does not do well on high pineland, but it may be helped by liberal mulching, by digging in muck and by fertilizing, Quite a number of them growing wild in the swamp just north of me were destroyed since I came here.

I supplement these notes of Prof. Simpson from a letter he wrote me March 20, 1914:

The great Royal Palm Hammock lies about six miles from Cape Romano, and contained when I was there about 500 trees. It probably is still in existence, as it is almost inaccessible. It is magnificent, but not so fine as Paradise Key in the glades at the extreme southeast part of the state,—a glorious hammock with hundreds of splendid Royal Palms rising far above it. I agree with you that they both should be saved. Some of these palms have a considerable swelling in the center of the trunk; in some it is above the center and rarely below it, while many have no swelling at all.

On July 12th, 1918, I had the great pleasure to visit Paradise Key, now Royal Palm State park, in company of Prof. Simpson. It is situated about 40 miles from Miami and 12 miles from Homestead. The drive was an exceedingly interesting one. When we were still miles away from the park I saw in the far distance the lofty crowns of many of the Royal Palms waving their leaves high above the dense hammock. All were sharply defined against the clear blue sky, giving an appearance of lightness and cheerfulness which was most exhilarating.

When we entered the place, formerly known by the beautiful and appropriate name of Paradise Key, we met Mr. Chas. Mosier, a kindred spirit who was at that time the warden of the park. I was amazed when I perceived the immense broad Live-Oaks covered all over with Tillansias, Catopsis and Guzmanias, with numerous Epiphytal Ferns, and such Orchids in big masses as [*Oncidium undulatum*] and [*O. floridana* or *ensatum*], besides many species of Epidendrums. Ten miles of paths have been hewn out of the dense forest by Mr. Mosier,—broad, smooth and winding,—leading to the finest and tallest of these giant Royal palms. This wonderful and most enchanting Royal Palm Park, replete with many hundreds of rare tropical trees and shrubs, indigenous here, rests on a foundation of limestone rock. The soil is a thick rich vegetable mold and very productive. There were a number of greedy tomato growers who already had laid their hands on this beauty spot when the State Federation of Woman's Clubs rescued it from their clutches.

One of the most ardent plant hunters I have ever met is Judge E. G. Wilkinson of Naples. In his younger days he often accompanied the late botanist and collector, A. H. Curtiss, in his excursions through the primeval forests of Florida. In this way he has become a real woodsman. These rambles have made him a lover of all that is rare, unique and beautiful among the wild plants. Several years ago he invited me to accompany him to a so called Pop Ash and Pond-Apple swamp. I have alluded to this interesting excursion in another place. In July, 1921, he—then county commissioner and promoter of the famous Tamiami Trail—had contemplated to surprise me with a new picture of wild forest scenery. He told me that we would motor along the Tamiami Trail for a distance of about 30 miles. We went through forests and glades, through Cypress swamps and over grassy prairies, studded with the pure white fragrant flowers of *Crinum americanum*. The bushes were covered with a lovely climber, *Rhabdothamnus biflora*, also with fragrant white blossoms. The trip was so intensely interesting that the time passed very quickly.

Finally we halted in a dense hammock. Judge Wilkinson had told me that he had a surprise for me in store. Here the surprise came. He led me through a rough path hewn out of a dense forest growth, and finally he stopped at a more open place. "Look around," he said, "feast your eyes." And a most wonderful picture presented itself to my dazzled eyes—dozens of lofty Royal Palms overtowering the forest everywhere around them. There must have been at least a hundred of these sublime giants scattered over a large area. The sight was as majestic and enchanting as it was beautiful and unique. Never before had I seen such an untouched tropical forest containing so many Royal Palms, so impressive and grand. I was simply overwhelmed by a sensation of grandeur. This day will always be remembered as a red letter day of my life. It was full of new pictures and impressions and real adventures.

On our way home Mr. Wilkinson led me through a Cypress swamp, partly under water, to a pond-like depression surrounded by old mossy and gnarled Pond-Apple trees (*Annona glabra*), loaded from top to bottom with air plants and other epiphytes. The Royal Palms I had left only a short while ago displayed many [*Polyradicion* or *Polyrrhiza*] *lindenii* specimens, their dense network of succulent gray roots harmonizing wonderfully with the silvery gray color of the palm trunks, closely hugging their support.

Prof. C. S. Sargent has said that this wonderful Royal Palm hammock is situated on Rogue's River,—an ominous name, when we consider that only a short while ago more than twenty-five of these century-old giants have been ruthlessly destroyed by some rogues and rascals who should be sent for at least 25 years behind iron bars. This palm hammock is now owned by a wide-awake man, a man of visions and ideals,—Mr. Barron G. Collier,— who intends to create here a state park for the benefit and education of future generations. I entertain the sincere hope that the remnants of these wonderfully beautiful specimens may be saved and preserved for all time. "Three noble Royal Palms once stood on Cape Sable, visible eighteen miles out at sea, but were destroyed by the gale of 1872."—Pliny W. Reasoner.

Mr. J. E. Hendry Jr., of Everglades Nursery, a passionate lover of all palms, and particularly of Royal Palms, is well supplied with a large stock of pot-grown plants ready to set out now or almost at any time during the year. These young plants were raised from seeds coming from the finest and most majestic specimens I have ever seen in cultivation—from the grounds of the Royal Palm Hotel at Fort Myers.

The Royal Palm, like the Coconut Palms, is strictly tropical. A frost of only a few degrees will kill young plants outright and will injure even larger specimens. Mr. Ralph Robinson has quite a number on his place at Terra Ceia, and there are some fine specimens at Bradenton. On the East coast I have seen a few as far north as Fort Pierce. Its real home begins from Palm Beach and Punta Gorda southward. It is largely planted in Miami and Coconut Grove. There are magnificent avenues, groups and single specimens everywhere on the lower East Coast. But the finest, the most beautiful, the grandest are only seen at Fort Myers. There are many specimens that are really without a rival. At present miles and miles of royal Palms are planted along McGregor Boulevard leading from Fort Myers to Punta Rassa. Within a few years the entire length of this tropical highway will be a magnificent avenue of Royal Palms, 20 miles long. For about five or six years a fine group of these palms could be seen in one of the gardens of Orlando. They grew rapidly and had attained a height of about 12 feet, when they were destroyed by the freeze early in February, 1917. The lofty Royal Palms at Fort Myers, of Miami and Coconut Grove are too well known to require special notice.

Palms in Peninsular Florida Gardens

Washingtonia filifera [California], [*W. robusta*, Mexico], *W. robusta* [Baja California], [*W. filifera*, Arizona]—all these Washingtonias are present in the gardens of the southwest Coast, but *W. robusta* is the most common. *W. filifera* is not much planted. They all form a feature in the landscape and are easily grown in rich moist soil.

Archontophoenix cunninghamiana thrives splendidly in Thomas A. Edison's garden and also in several other places at Fort Myers; there are even a few good specimens at Bradenton. *Ptychosperma elegans* thrives with *Livistona rotundifolia* and [*L. chinensis*] luxuriantly in the writer's Tropical Gardens and Arboretum at Naples. *Ptychosperma elegans, Elaeis guineensis, Dictyosperma* [*D. album*], [*Syagrus romanzoffiana*] and *Caryota rumphiana*, and quite a number of other tropical palms, are objects of grace and beauty in Mrs. Marian A. McAdow's garden at Punta Gorda, where many of them flower and fruit. The Sugar Palm [*Arenga pinnata*], *Archontophoenix alexandrae*, the dainty and slender *Hydriastele wendlandiana*, the clumps of dense Arecas (*Chrysalidocarpus lutescens*) [recently referred to the genus *Dypsis*; Dransfield (1995)], of [*Syagrus romanzoffiana* and *S. flexuosa*], of [*Aiphanes caryotaefolia*], of *Pritchardia pacifica* and *P. thurstonii*, of *Latania loddigesii, L. verschaffeltii, L. commersonii* [= *L. lontaroides*], not to mention the tropical *Sabal* species in the gardens of Miami and Fort Myers, fill every lover of these royal plants with a feeling of wonder, exaltation and surprise.

Mr. E. N. Reasoner of the Royal Palm Nurseries at Oneco, Fla., deserves the credit for having introduced and disseminated these and many, many other still rarer species. The late Mr. E. H. Hart must never be forgotten by coming generations. One of the pioneers of orange culture and ornamental gardening in Florida, he had most beautiful specimens of [*Polyandrococos caudescens*] and [*Allagoptera campestris*] of southern Brazil, of *Livistona* [*L. saribus*], [*L. chinensis*] and the splendid *L. rotundifolia*, all from Java, for many years in the garden at Federal Point, until they were completely destroyed by the freeze in February, 1895. He wrote me that all the Livistonas,

L. chinensis and *L. australis* included, need shade and very rich moist soil to grow them successfully. The pygmies of the family, the dainty and graceful Chamaedoreas, Geonomas, several Pinangas, etc., thrive only when planted out in covered and enclosed lath houses from which frost can be excluded. Leaf mold, muck and a little old cow manure, water and shade are what they require.

I cannot refrain from mentioning in this connection, as a matter of fact, that the Fan Palm, *Washingtonia robusta,* and *W. sonorae* [= *W. robusta*] is more luxuriant and grows faster in Florida than in California. They are very fine for avenue planting in rich, moist soil, doing well from Jacksonville and St. Augustine to Miami, though they are much inferior in this respect to the Royal Palm as well as to [*Syagrus romanzoffiana*], *S. flexuosa* and [*Syagrus romanzoffiana*]. They do not grow well on high pine land. The avenue of *Washingtonia robusta* in the grounds of the Royal Palm Hotel at Miami, facing Biscayne Bay, is a grand sight with their coats of old pendant dry leaves covering the trunk just underneath the leaf-crowns. The effect is heightened by the many Royal Palms and Coconut Palms growing in the same grounds.

"Repetition is the mother of vision." For this reason I again urge my readers to plant palms,—as single specimens where room is limited, in avenues, in groups and in masses. Nothing in the whole plant world can lend such an air of dignity, nobility and beauty to the landscape.

Mrs. Marian A. McAdow has a very fine specimen [of *Coccothrinax barbadensis*] which bore bunches of ripe glossy black berries, the size of a very large pea, in September and October of this year (1923). Mrs. McAdow's plant is about 15 to 17 feet high.

The very massive Canary Island Date Palm and the Wild or Indian Date Palm (*Phoenix canariensis* and *P. sylvestris*), the latter with bluish-green leaves, look more beautiful on a large lawn as isolated specimens, the former often having a spread of 30 feet in diameter. Groups of the various grayish or glaucous green hardy *Cocos* (*Butia*) species are very handsome and particularly when the background consists of large clumps of feathery bamboos, *Magnolia grandiflora*, Live Oak, Holly, etc.

Small palms of the common species are very cheap. Rare palms are of course, more expensive, and larger, more fully developed specimens of all species, grown in pots, are cheaper in this state than anywhere else. Only pot-grown, good-sized specimens should be set out. There is little risk of losing them if properly planted and cared for. All palms require from the very start a rich soil and plenty of water in dry weather. With a comparatively small outlay the most charming landscape pictures can be created. Yet how barren and desolate do many of our small towns and villages usually look!

Every community in Florida, every town and city should not only embellish the streets and gardens, but should also supply the means to employ educated gardeners to lay out interesting and beautiful public places where people can rest and dream and enjoy the alluring surroundings.

Large and well laid-out parks are an absolute necessity for every community, not only in an educational sense for the resident, but primarily to attract the winter sojourners. Such men as the late H. B. Plant and Henry M. Flagler were well aware of these facts. They immediately employed landscape gardeners to proceed with the work of landscape ornamentation. Thousands upon thousands every winter are drawn to the East Coast, to St. Augustine, Ormond, Palm Beach, Miami and Coconut Grove because these places have a world-wide fame as beauty spots. And this beauty mainly consists in the art of the landscape gardener. Especially the palms, so lavishly planted around the great hotels, in connection with other tropical plants, are the foundation of this fame.

The palm is a formal tree. No other plant can be used so advantageously in connection with fine architecture. While some of the large, feathery bamboos, formal too, in outline, serve particularly to hide unsightly spots, the proud and majestic palms always heighten the effect of beautiful architecture.

The preparation of the soil, preceding the planting, is the most important point in the cultivation of palms everywhere, but particularly so in Florida, where the sandy soil is very deficient in plant food. Undoubtedly some palms will grow in rather poorly prepared soil, but they have to keep up a constant struggle for existence, growing either very slowly or being at a standstill for an indefinite period. Such specimens never will reveal their full beauty and they are mostly a pitiful sight. [Preparation of the holes and soil is discussed later.]

Our open air palms, if well cared for and kept in good health by proper fertilizing, are rarely troubled with insects. Now and then scale insects infest them, but they are easily eradicated by spraying, using the same remedies that are in vogue for orange trees. The hardy species of Butias are now and then troubled with blight. A spray of Bordeaux mixture will be necessary in this case.

Small palms are usually quite tender, but they are easily protected from frost. Bottomless barrels put over them, or pine needles and bunches of Spanish-Moss, or Cedar boughs are usually a very efficient protection. The hardy [*Butia*] palms, all the Date Palms and the Sabals never need any protection at all; neither do the Washingtonias.

What can be done with palms, even in the northern part of the state, has been demonstrated by the late Mr. Edward H. Hart of Federal Point, 18 miles north of Palatka on the east side of the St. John's River. A list which he sent me Jan. 1, 1891, may be useful to many palm lovers in the upper part of the state. This pioneer in palm culture had at that time a beautiful and large collection. [Names and sizes are in the first edition.]

All my large specimens succumbed to the four days continued freezing in January, 1886. The soil is wet flatwoods, clay bottom and artificially drained. I think most of the palms not sub-aquatic will grow on high pineland if irrigated. Palms can hardly be fertilized too much. The more fertilizer and water they get, the faster they grow. They will thrive under applications of strong manure that would kill almost any other tree.

Mr. Hart, one of the noblest and best educated men that ever came to Florida, concluded one of his palm articles in the *Florida Dispatch* (June 25, 1888) as follows:

> Dr. Bennett says of an avenue half a mile long of Livistonas, *Chamaerops humilis* and *Dracaena draco* in the Jardin d'Essai of Algiers, that the effect was perfectly magical. Try it, Floridians! Plant avenues through your grounds of such characteristic forms as majestic palms, noble Agaves, Yuccas, Cacti, Dasylirions, Cycads and Bonaparteas, and it will do more to create an enthusiasm among your northern visitors and to bring them back again, than all the brandishments of your immigration societies and land agents. The baits thrown out by the latter appeal mostly to the sordid appetite for filthy lucre, and draw a class whose thoughts do not rise above mercenary considerations, but by changing the monotonous pine barrens into gardens of the most exquisite natural forms, people of refined tastes and aspirations are tempted to cast in their lot among us, and come to Florida to "live the gentle life."

Mr. Theodore L. Mead of Lake Charm, another pioneer, a man of culture and a scientist, has written a good deal about the palms that could and should be planted in Florida. I quote the following lines from one of his articles:

> The few palms native of our warm temperate climate, perhaps more than any other feature of the landscape, persuade us that though we may not really have reached the tropics, that fabled region of perpetual bloom and growth cannot be far away. And yet in point of fact the climate of upper south Florida,—say between the 28th and 29th degree,—is far from tropical. Frosts,—light indeed, but still frosts,—may occur at any time during five months of the year, and the wonder is rather that so many tender plants should flourish here than that we cannot persuade the equatorial species to endure our climate. But as the most enduring and persisting weeds of temperate latitudes are almost always tropical species or species of tropical origin which are in some way constitutionally able to endure some frost, so we should not despair in naturalizing even equatorial palms until the experiment has been faithfully tried with each species in varied aspects and exposures. The failures must be put on record as well as the successes, and enough in this way has already been done during the past forty years to serve as an important guide to the cultivator. Some noble and striking species have been found to be thoroughly at home with us and others are shown to be available for more or less sheltered spots, while of course, for the lower extremity of the peninsula the list might be almost indefinitely extended.
>
> It may be of interest to mention that in my place at Lake Charm I had over 80 species of palms growing out of doors without artificial protection this winter (1889). A thermometer at the house has registered 20 to 28°F two or three times at intervals during the winter, yet I find but one or two individuals killed outright, and ten species more or less burned in leaf, while 70 species are uninjured. Most of these were fully exposed. A few, believed to be somewhat tender, were planted in shady, moist forest land near a running stream.

In conclusion let me quote from another pioneer of Florida horticulture, an enthusiast and in every respect an exceptional man,—the late Pliny W. Reasoner: *The Pompous Palms of Florida* and of these palms dear old Bartram wrote more than a hundred years ago, as he floated along the sea islands of Georgia and Florida and up the majestic St. Johns River, having

observed on the way many curious vegetable productions, particularly
Corypha Palms (our great Cabbage palmetto). And then the dear old chap
would run off into rhapsodies on the beauties of nature and the palms and
magnolias, in poetical monologues that it refreshes one to read in these de-
generate days when everything must be practical."

In the following I shall enumerate the species that were successful in my
garden at Gotha, in Orange County, on high, dry pineland. Only towards
little Lake Audubon is a strip of moist land which I found well adapted for
the moisture loving kinds. All my palms were raised from seeds which I
mostly received from Blumenau, Brazil, from Argentina, from the Jamaica
Botanical Gardens and from the Canary Islands. Many also came from
Haage & Schmidt, Erfurt, Germany. They all were grown from seedlings
raised in my greenhouse in Milwaukee from 1890 to 1897. They were sent to
Gotha always in November and planted out by myself.

Chamaerops humilis and [*C. humilis* var. *elatior*], and a few varieties of
the first: These are the European Fan Palms. There are fine large specimens
in the garden, flowering and fruiting every year. *Cocos* of the new genus
Butia all have thorny leaf-stems, bluish-green leaves and most juicy, aromatic edible fruits in heavy bunches. This is the so-called [*Butia capitata*]
group.

The next group consists of species of the "*Cocos plumosa*" type, all fast
growing and very beautiful plumy palms, taking the place of the Royal Palm
in the orange belt. They are not thoroughly hardy. *Syagrus coronata, S.
flexuosa,* very dense and beautiful palms. [*Syagrus romanzoffiana*], a specimen about 15 years old is over 30 feet high. All need rich soil and good care.
The true [*Syagrus romanzoffiana* var. *australe*], a fine species, is the hardiest.

Acrocomia totai, from Paraguay, is a very beautiful palm, reminding one
of "*Cocos plumosa,*" if seen from a distance. Armed with long, sharp spines
on the trunk and leaves; grows well on high pineland if planted in very rich
soil and occasionally watered.

The *Phoenix* species, or Date Palms, are the next most important feature
of Palm Cottage Gardens. The nomenclature is in much confusion. All are
very vigorous and all are provided on their leaf stems with long, sharp dangerous spines. [Many cultivated plants are hybrids; Nehrling cited 13 species
of *Phoenix.*]

Though there are many fine specimens of *Livistona chinensis,* the Chinese Fan palm, in the gardens of Orlando, I could grow this species only

near the lake in rich, moist soil and in shade. The same holds true of *Livistona australis, L. humilis,* and [*L. chinensis*].

Among Fan palms all the species of the genus *Sabal* are available. I have many fine specimens of the native *Sabal palmetto,* the Cabbage Palm, all raised from seed. [*S. minor*] is a stemless native species. All these palms do well on high pineland, and they grow rapidly if put in very rich soil when set out. *Nannorrhops ritchiana,* from Afghanistan, etc., and *Trithrinax braziliensis,* from southern Brazil, also did well.

In my Caladium lath house among Alocasias, Ixoras, Marantas and many other plants, I had large dense specimens of the Bamboo Palm *Rhapis flabelliformis* [= *R. excelsa*] and *R. humilis,* both from Japan and China, and perfectly hardy in moist, half-shady places. [*Microcoelum weddelliana*]; *Chrysalidocarpus lutescens; Geonoma gracilis; Chamaedorea arenbergiana; C. elatior; C. elegans; C. ernesti-augustii; C. fragrans; C. glaucifolia; C. martiana; C. tepejilote; Synecanthus fibrosus,* and several other species of which I had no names, were all doing well in an enclosed lath house in rich, moist, well-drained soil under shade. In cold winters all of them needed protection, which I supplied by cedar branches, pine needles and Spanish-Moss.

Along the lower West Coast, from Punta Gorda southward, and especially at Fort Myers, the following palms are grown successfully in the open:

Acoelorrhaphe wrightii (*Paurotis wrightii*), City Park, Fort Myers—A fine tufted specimen with stems about 12 feet high. *Acrocomia aculeata* (*A. media*) from Porto Rico—I have quite a number of young specimens raised from seed. Took four years before germination. *Acrocomia sclerocarpa* from Brazil—Seeds collected by Dorsett, Popenoe and Shamel. *A. totai,* Paraguay—I have a group of these beautiful palms, one fruiting. *Archontophoenix cunninghamiana,* Australia—Quite a number of young plants in my garden; large fruiting specimens in Thomas Edison's garden at Fort Myers. *A. alexandrae*—Fine large specimen in Mr. Burroughs' garden of Palms, and in the grounds of Royal Palm Hotel, Fort Myers. *Areca alicae,* Queensland, Australia—Grows well in rich, moist, well-drained shaded soil. *A. singaporensis* [?]—In my collection. Needs further study when in flower and fruit. *Arenga* [*pinnata*], Sugar Palm, Southern India—A magnificent specimen in old garden at Fort Myers. Young specimens in Mr. Burroughs' and my collection. *A. tremula*—Grows in tufts, Philippines. In my collection. *Attalea cohune,* Central America—A number of young plants in my collection. A tall and most exquisite specimen in Commodore Munroe's place at Coconut Grove. *A. gomphococca*—Mrs. McAdow pointed out to me, some time ago, a young plant in high school grounds, Punta Gorda. Introduced by E. N. Reasoner.

Bactris major: Two very fine specimens, one in Mrs. McAdow's garden, Punta Gorda, and one in Mr. Ewald Stulpner's garden, Fort Myers. Identification doubtful.

Caryota mitis—Small plant in my collection. *C. rumphiana*, India and North Australia—One of the grandest palms imaginable; very dense, fronds drooping. There was a tall specimen in Mrs. Marian A. McAdow's garden at Punta Gorda. It died after flowering and fruiting. [*C. mitis*]—Several fine tufted specimens in my garden. Seeds came from Buitenzorg, Java. *C. urens* from India, the common Fishtail Palm—Many specimens, large and small, at Fort Myers. *Chamaedorea elatior, C. ernesti-augusti, C. glaucifolia* and *C. tepejilote*, all from Mexico and Central America—Do well only in shade, in deep, moist, but well-drained humus soil. *Chrysalidocarpus lutescens* (*Areca lutescens*)—A most lovely, rather common tufted garden palm from Madagascar. [*Cocos australis* [probably *Butia capitata* var. *capitata*; Nehrling gave *Butia* as an alternate genus for all up to *C. yatay*, reflecting taxonomic uncertainty of the time], *C. blumenavii, C. campestris* [probably also *B. capitata*], *C. datil* [= *Syagrus romanzoffiana* var. *datil*], *C. eriospatha* [= *B. eriospatha*], *C. gaertneri* [= *B. bonnetii*], *C. lapidea* [?], *C. nehrlingiana* [= *B. capitata* var. *nehrlingiana*], *C. yatay* [= *B. yatay*]—All in my collection at Palm Cottage Gardens and Naples; highland palms. True *C. australis* belongs to [*Syagrus romanzoffiana*] group, Brazil. [*Syagrus coronata*], Brazil—In my collection. *C. flexuosa* [may be *Syagrus flexuosa* but much horticultural material at that time may have been *S. romanzoffiana*], Brazil—In my collection. [*Syagrus romanzoffiana*], Brazil. [*Syagrus romanzoffiana*], Brazil—In Mrs. McAdow's collection; I have fine young plants. [*Microcoelum weddellianum*], Brazil—Grows well in shady, rich moist, well-drained soil. *Cocos nucifera*—Common all along the coast, from Punta Gorda southward. *Cocos* sp.—Introduced by E. N. Reasoner. Very distinct. Two good specimens in the gardens of Fort Myers. *Corypha elata* (*C. gebanga*), India—Grows well in rich, moist soil in my garden, a fine palm.

Dictyosperma album, D. rubrum [= *D. album*]—Both in my garden. A fine avenue of the latter has been planted in Fort Myers. Need some shade and a rich, well-drained moderately moist soil. [*Normanbya normanbyi*]—Two fine slender specimens in front of Mr. Geo. Kingston's home at Fort

Myers. Identification doubtful. Has been offered in the trade as *Balaka seemannii*. Introduced by E. N. Reasoner. *Dypsis madagascariensis*—A large specimen in Mr. Burroughs' collection. Identification doubtful. *Elaeis guineensis*—Fine fruiting specimen in Mrs. McAdow's garden, Punta Gorda, and Mr. J. E. Hendry's collection, Fort Myers. Hardy and fruiting at Orlando. *Erythea armata, E. edulis,* Guadeloupe Island, and *E. brandegeei*— All three of these grand palms grown by Mr. Geo. Dorner, Bokeelia, Pine Island, in rather moist black soil. Precarious under cultivation in Florida, Lower California.

Guilielma [*Bactris*], Costa Rica—A fine young specimen in my collection. *Howea belmoreana (Kentia belmoreana)*—Specimens in one of the gardens at Fort Myers. *H. forsteriana (Kentia forsteriana)*—A fine large and most beautiful specimen in Mr. Geo. Kingston's garden at Fort Myers. Both extremely rare in Florida, difficult to grow; right treatment not yet struck. *Hydriastele wendlandiana*—An exquisite palm. A fine fruiting specimen in Mrs. McAdow's collection, Punta Gorda. Fruit bunches glowing red. Have seedlings of it in my garden. *Hyophorbe amaricaulis*—Small plant in my collection. *H. verschaffeltii*—A slow growing, beautiful palm like the former. Not uncommon at Fort Myers. I have some fine specimens. Large avenues in Miami. *Hyphaene crinita* (*H. natalensis* [?]), one of the Dooum Palms— Only a small plant in my collection.

Iriartea sp.—Introduced by Bureau of Plant industry. A fine specimen in my collection. *Latania commersonii*, Mascarene Island, *Latania loddigesii*, Mauritius, *L. verschaffeltii*, Mauritius—Beautiful Fan palms. All raised by me from seed. Small specimens in my collection. Fine large specimens of the second one in Mr. J. E. Hendry's garden, and of the third one in Mr. Burroughs' collection at Fort Myers. [*Livistona rotundifolia*]—Two fine large specimens in Royal Palm Hotel grounds, Fort Myers. Many young ones in my collection. *L. australis*—In my collection; Australia. *L. chinensis*, Chinese Fan Palm, Southern China—Many fine specimens in various gardens. [*L. saribus*], Java—A beautiful palm for south Florida; in my collection. *L. humilis*—Small plant in my collection. *L. jenkinsiana*, Assam—Several small plants in my collection. *L. mariae*, Red-leaved Fan palm—A fine large specimen in Mrs. McAdow's garden. [*L. chinensis*]—Many fine young specimens in my collection. *L. rotundifolia*—A beautiful specimen in my collection.

[*Roystonea borinquena*], Porto Rico—Many specimens at Fort Myers and in my collection. [*Roystonea oleracea*]—Tallest Royal Palm in existence.

Common in the West Indies. Young plants look very similar to the next, and are difficult to distinguish. Specimens in Fort Myers and in my collection. [*Roystonea regia*]—Native of Florida and West Indies. Our finest and most common garden and avenue palm.

Phoenix acaulis, Stemless Date Palm of India—Grows in dense tufts, leaflets hard and spiny. In my collection. *Phoenix canariensis,* Canary Islands—Not as common in south Florida as in the orange belt. A most beautiful, massive and effective palm when afforded sufficient space and rich soil. Some fruiting specimens at Fort Myers, Punta Gorda, etc. *P. dactylifera,* Common Date palm—In many gardens; raised from seed. [*P. loureirii*]. India, Burma, southern China, rare—In my collection. *P. leonensis* [?], West Africa—Strong tufted and massive in growth; in my collection. [*P. loureirii*], India—Introduced by Bureau of Plant Industry. A fine small palm, resembling *P. humilis* and *P. hanceana* [both synonyms of *P. loureirii*]. *P. roebelenii,* Assam—The pygmy of the genus. Very beautiful and elegant. Fruited largely in Mr. J. E. Hendry's garden, Fort Myers. *P. rupicola,* Sikkim—The most beautiful of all Date Palms. Not common. Four fine specimens in city park of Lakeland. Small plants in my collection. [*P. reclinata*], Senegal region, West Africa—A dense tufted palm. A few small plants in my collection. [*P. reclinata*], tropical Africa—Grows much like *P. reclinata,* but leaves harder to the touch and each leaflet provided with a sharp spine. Common in gardens. Fine tufted specimens in Mrs. McAdow's collection. *P. sylvestris,* Sugar Date of India—Fine dense species with bluish-green leaves. Rare. In my collection. [*P. pusila*], Blue Date Palm of Ceylon—Dense tufts of beautiful bluish-green leaves. Rare. In my collection. Most of the Date palms are very difficult to identify, as many of them are hybrids.

Pritchardia pacifica, Fiji Island Fan Palm—A most beautiful and elegant species. In Mr. J. E. Hendry's grounds. Finest specimen I ever saw grows in a shell mound in front of old hotel in Caxambas. *P. thurstonii,* Fiji Islands— Several fine fruiting specimens in Mr. Geo. Kingston's garden, Fort Myers. Identification somewhat doubtful.

The above list contains ca. 100 species, some of them of doubtful identification. It has taken a considerable amount of study and time to complete it. Quite a number of beautiful exotic palms,—almost 50 species,—have been introduced into my garden at Naples within the past five or six years, but they have not become sufficiently established to warrant their inclusion in the list I have given. It is impossible to determine at the present time those that may persist and those that may die out. The difficulty to import seeds of rare new palms is almost unsurmountable, and there are many other obstacles in the way of increasing our palm collections. I have been aided largely in my endeavors as a palm specialist by the Botanical Gardens of Buitenzorg, Java, by the Castleton Botanical Garden, Jamaica, and by the Calcutta Botanical Gardens. Seeds of palms I have also received from Dr. Elmer D. Merrill, Bureau of Science, Philippine Islands, and from the Porto Rico Department of Agriculture. Quite a number of the finest and rarest palms in my collection came from our Bureau of Plant Industry, Washington, D.C.

Pleasure Not a Luxury

Pleasure is not one of the luxuries of life; it is one of the necessities. And pleasure is not always what people mean to imply by the word. Real pleasure is not found in the rough commercialized sports of the day; not in boisterous, unbehaved gatherings—still remnants of barbarous, savage ages. Pleasure—real pleasure—is vividly brought before our minds in Sir John Lubbock's (Lord Avebury's) charming book *The Pleasures of Life*. This little volume should be in the bookcase of every refined and cultured family. It should be read; should be studied. Pleasure is found in the full enjoyment of good music, song and art, in enjoying the beauties of Nature, in strolling around in woodland and glen and by the water side. Pleasure is found in the song of the birds and in their habits.

Ornamental horticulture is one of the purest, one of the most elevating, one of the noblest and grandest pleasure of life. Only cultured people of refined tastes and lofty ideals are able to create earthly garden paradises. These thoughts came to me one day when I perceived a young fine specimen of [*Roystonea*] *oleracea* in a garden at Miami. It was surrounded by a number of tourists from the North, all raving about it and enjoying its noble form and beauty as children do a Christmas gift. And its owner, who had planted it and many other fine palms and trees, pointed out with pride all its characteristics and related its history. He told about its gigantic size in the West Indies and described the glorious avenue of these palms in the botanical gardens of Rio de Janeiro in Brazil.

Butia, the Hardiest of Palms with Edible Fruits

The most important and beautiful of all palms for high dry pineland culture are the hardy species of the genus *Butia* (*Cocos*), all natives of southern Brazil, Paraguay and Argentina. All of them are perfectly hardy as far north as Jacksonville. Usually their foliage is hard and leathery and its color is a beautiful glaucous green. *Cocos datil* is the largest and most massive of the genus. [Nehrling appears to have confused *Syagrus romanzoffiana* var. *australe,* which he called *C. datil,* and *Butia capitata,* which he also called *C. datil.* His meaning here appears to be *Butia capitata.*] Its trunk is of an immense size, and its leaves stand in straight perpendicular lines along the stem. The fruit-cluster weighs from 35 to 50 pounds. The fruit, very aromatic, juicy, as large as a plum, is closely packed together on small branches along the stem. [*Butia capitata*] also ripens four or five bunches of beautiful, edible, sweetly aromatic orange-yellow, juicy fruit each summer. The bunches weigh from 15 to 25 pounds. This is a beautiful silvery-green palm with very broad and densely clustered leaves.

[*Butia eriospatha*] is my especial favorite among the hardy "Cocos" species. Its beautiful recurved leaves are usually 6 to 7 feet long, glaucous, faintly suffused with dark green and the leaf-stems show a deep purplish violet tint. The flower spathe distinguishes it from all its congeners. This is covered with a dense soft felt-like wool of a beautiful chestnut-color. The fruit is as large as a good-sized cherry, yellowish-green in color, covered with innumerable gray dots, very juicy, not aromatic and of a most delicious plum-like taste. I have also fine bearing specimens of [*Butia yatay*].

The importance of these palms and their great economic value is as yet little understood in Florida. Their fruit can be used for preserves. It supplies a good jelly and an excellent wine, or by distillation a highly aromatic liquor. Chickens, turkeys and guineas are exceedingly fond of the fruit, and the oily seeds form an excellent feed for hogs. Their main importance from the standpoint of the plant lover lies in their great beauty and symmetry, their hardiness and easy cultivation. They look best planted in groups of a dozen or more specimens. Not adapted for low moist lands. I have several other distinct species of hardy glaucous-leaved *Cocos plumosa* (*Arecastrum romanzoffianum*) [= *Syagrus romanzoffiana*]. I now can point with much satisfaction to a fine *Cocos plumosa* which is 35 feet high, though only ten years old. It bears a magnificent crown of leaves with densely-set pinnae which reminds of gigantic ostrich plumes. All these Cocos palms are extremely elegant and beautiful, and all hardy in ordinary winters as far north as Sanford. Young plants must be protected during cold weather.

Phoenix Palms Fail to Come True from Seed

The Phoenix or Date Palm seeds all came from Haage & Schmidt, who obtained their supply from the Riviera. Their nomenclature is in a deplorable condition, many hybrids coming from the same lot of seeds. I planted an avenue of Canary Island Date Palms running from the house to the lake. The plants made a good growth, but scarcely one of them is true to name. They are all hybrids of *Phoenix canariensis* fertilized with the pollen of *P. sylvestris* and *P. dactylifera*. It was necessary to order the seeds from the Canary Islands directly, and I have now a number of young plants that show their true nature. The Canary Island Date Palm does not do very well on high pineland, where the Indian Sugar Date Palm (*P. sylvestris*), the elegant *P. rupicola* and the drooping-leaved *P. reclinata* thrive so well. It is one of the most magnificent palms in cultivation. Massive specimens of it can be found in all the best gardens of Orlando, Winter Park and Sanford and as far north as Jacksonville. On the south and north sides of the courthouse at Orlando four small plants were set out, one on each side of the walk, about fifteen years ago,—at present four immense massive and most beautiful specimens. Their trunks are about twelve feet high and each as thick as a water barrel. They begin to flower early in winter and the great clusters of orange-yellow fruits ripen in April and May.

On rich moist hammock and flatwood soil this palm is a fast grower and attains an immense size. The leaf stems have a decidedly yellowish tint, while the color of the big feathery leaves is a bright green. I have two very fine specimens of *P. sylvestris*. It grows well in my garden, and its massiveness strongly reminds me of *P. canariensis*. The leaves are over ten feet long and of a fine glaucous-green color. It is a very beautiful and distinct tall growing palm and excellent for large groups and for avenue planting. [*P. pumila*] grows in tufts, producing numerous suckers around the lower part of the trunk. These must be removed as soon as they appear if a specimen with a single stem is desired. There are a few single stemmed specimens in the Laughlin place at Zellwood which are pictures of elegance and beauty. The color of the foliage is almost as blue as that of the Colorado Blue Spruce.

Phoenix rupicola from the Sikkim Himalayas is an outstanding palm, one of the most refined and elegant of all the Date Palms. One of the specimens of this palm is featured in my garden, being about 15 feet high, with a trunk 8 feet high and with beautiful glossy green leaves each 10 to 12 feet long. Smaller specimens are extremely ornamental as pot plants. No other species has such delightfully soft green glossy leaves, reminding one, especially in small specimens, of some species of *Cycas*. The daintiest of all the Phoenix species is *P. roebelenii,* which is represented in several Florida gardens. It does not thrive on high pineland, but is most successfully grown in lath houses and in the moist soil of rich hammock lands in half-shady places. It excels most other small palms in grace, elegance and beauty. In the Abbot garden at Orlando there is a fine specimen about 5 feet high, a picture of loveliness, all its leaves being densely arranged around the slender stem and all recurving elegantly to all sides. On account of this trait it is popularly known as the Fountain Palm.

Washingtonia Palms among Most Rapid Growers

The Washingtonias cannot be successfully grown on high pineland. I planted dozens of seedlings of *Washingtonia filifera* [Calif.], *W. robusta* [Mex.], and [*W. filifera*] [Arizona], fine robust specimens, but all pined away. In localities where the clay subsoil is near the surface, in hammock and flatwood soil they are the most rapid growers of all our garden palms. In such soil they soon form fine objects all over the state from Jacksonville to Miami. No other species, not even the glorious Royal Palm, has found so much favor with the real estate men in South Florida as *W. robusta,* and none is so much used for avenue planting. It is a peculiar coincidence that these Washingtonias, known to grow in their native haunts, in California and Sonora only in very dry regions, should refuse to grow in Florida in dry soil, while they thrive admirably in moist, even mucky localities. [Where Washingtonias grow naturally the climate is dry, but they always have their feet in a water source.] The two Erytheas (*Erythea armata* and *E. edulis*), which naturally also grow in the dry regions of California and adjacent localities and which form such wonderful ornaments of the gardens of California, will neither grow in moist nor dry soil in Florida. I have planted several dozen at various times, but none ever started in growth.

Miscellaneous Palm Sketches

Among the Livistonas the Chinese Fan Palm (*Livistona chinensis*) is the most important for central Florida, and thence southward. In the fall of 1896 I set out quite a number of three and four year old seedlings. All soon died. I repeated the experiment and added *L. australis, L. humilis, L. mariae.* The result was the same. All these fine fan-leaved species require rich moist soil and shade while young. There are tall specimens of *L. chinensis* in the late Mr. E. H. Hart's garden at Federal Point, and many young specimens at Sanford, Orlando and many other places. These palms look particularly beautiful in regular groups, consisting of a dozen and more specimens.

Chamaerops humilis, the European Fan Palm, and its quite distinct varieties are perfectly adapted to our high pineland gardens. They grow in tufts or clusters forming most elegant specimens in the course of time. I received seeds of about four distinct varieties from Haage & Schmidt in 1893 and my seedlings were set out in 1896. Two of them, *C. humilis* and [*C. humilis* var. *elatior*], have at present main stems 6 to 7 feet high. They bloom profusely in February, filling the air with a peculiar, but pleasant odor. The flowers are densely clustered around the upper part of the trunk in the axils of the leaves, looking like yellow sponges fastened tightly to the trunk. These Chamaerops are pigmies compared with the Sabals, Washingtonias and Livistonas, but they are extremely graceful and very elegant. My largest two specimens form the foreground of a few large Magnolias. The European Fan Palm deserves to be largely planted in high and low lands. It is especially valuable for small gardens.

Trachycarpus excelsus, the most elegant Chinese Windmill Palm, one of the hardiest of all palms, has not been successful in the sandy soil of Florida. I have a very fine specimen near my study growing among *Camellia sasanqua,* Hollies and other shrubs. It is about 8 feet high and its trunk is constantly shaded from the sun. It is a most beautiful specimen. I raised it from seed in 1897 and planted it out in 1900. An abundant supply of water, shade and a fertilizer rich in ammonia, are what it requires. This is a fine palm for Tallahassee and other regions in northern Florida where the soil consists mostly of clay.

Acrocomia, a distinct and hardy palm, is one of the most distinct and stately palms, and hardy as far north as Federal Point in well protected localities, is *Acrocomia totai,* a native of Paraguay. Mr. Theodore L. Mead introduced it about thirty-five years ago. There are at present magnificent specimens in my gardens. Near the railroad station at Lake Alfred, in Polk Co., there are two fine young specimens, about ten feet high, which fill the heart of any lover of palms with rapture. They grow on high land in a heavy red clay soil. It does not do well in the elevated sand hills except special care is taken before planting to dig a large hole and fill this partly with clay, partly with old cow manure. I had two fine specimens near my house, but lost both in 1907 after I had transplanted them to a more favorable position. Not only the trunk of this species but also the leaf stems are provided with a dense armor of formidable spines. It is a most beautiful and elegant palm, almost as graceful as "*Cocos plumosa*," but of a deeper green. It looks best in groups of a dozen or more specimens and it should be planted largely where soil and climate favor its growth.

Jubaea spectabilis, the Coquito or Monkey Coconut of Chile, an exceedingly massive and, in its young state, a beautiful palm, was also planted. I had raised several good young plants from seeds. All grew, but only one of them formed a small healthy looking specimen. The *Jubaea* is only 2½ feet high. In California this species ranks among the most massive and beautiful of all garden palms. As it is very hardy it undoubtedly can be successfully grown in the clay soil of northwestern Florida.

Planting Palms

In order to succeed with palms and the other vigorous growing plants on high pineland a good deal of care is necessary before planting. The soil must be thoroughly worked and fertilized and the plants set out must be watered, shaded and mulched. I have found the following way the best for palms, especially for the strong growing species, such as Sabals, Washingtonias, Livistonas, Acrocomias, Date Palms and "Coconut" species: Put stakes in the places where the plants will find a permanent position. Then dig a hole from five to six feet deep and as wide. Fill this up to two thirds with stable manure, clay, bones, old tin cans, rotten wood, leaves and grass and other rubbish and finally fill the upper one-third with leaf mould and surface soil. After six months another filling up is needed. Surface soil is now advisable, but this must be mixed with one or two water buckets of cotton seed meal, castor pomace, sheep or cow manure. Stir frequently until the fertilizer is thoroughly mixed. After five or six weeks have elapsed the soil will be in condition to receive the plant. Select good, thrifty young specimens from 5- to 6-inch pots and about two or three feet high. Plant in such a way that a saucer-like depression is formed; water thoroughly and mulch with old leaves, weeds, pine needles, stable manure or rotten wood.

After the hole has been brought into the right condition, plant your palm in the center, fill in the soil and tread it down with the feet. Then apply water to settle the soil. Plants from pots are much easier to set out than those from the open ground. In this case it is only necessary to bury the entire ball without disturbing the roots. Large plants in wooden tubs may be buried just as they are. The tub will rot very soon and the roots will find their way into the surrounding soil. In every case the plants should stand in a saucer-like depression. This is important for watering purposes. A thick mulch of weeds, old grass, pine needles or rotten wood is the next procedure. Put the mulch thickly around the plant. This keeps the soil cool and moist. Later when the roots have taken hold of the soil and a vigorous growth has followed, a mulch of stable manure is of great help. When this rots it should be dug in around the plant.

Never burn old rotten wood, leaves, weeds or pine needles, but use them as a mulch and fertilizer. In order to keep up a vigorous and rapid growth and to obtain fine, imposing specimens, fertilizer and water are the most important factors. In the Riviera and in Italy large and healthy specimens of palms are the chief ornaments of all the best gardens. Frosts and poor rocky soil are always drawbacks there. Every spring each palm receives a one-horse cart of stable manure. In our light Florida soils two applications of fertilizer should be given,—one in May or June, consisting of a heavy mulch of stable manure. In October this manure should be dug in and an application of commercial fertilizer rich in phosphoric acid and potash should follow. This will harden the palms sufficiently to withstand our occasional cold spells.

When setting out small specimens of pot-grown plants from the nursery it is not necessary to prepare such large holes as recommended. These holes, however, must be filled with a rich compost. All the palms, when set out as seedlings or small plants, should be planted with their base as deep in the ground as is consistent with their nature. Otherwise they are apt to be blown over after they have made tall trunks. The proper way is to set each palm in the center of a basin-like depression a foot or even more in depth. Rains and material for mulch will fill this up gradually.

The Sabals or Palmettos, the Date Palms and the Acrocomias in germinating provide naturally for this deep setting, since the sprouting seed sends a strong growth downward for a considerable distance before beginning its upward start. The process of imbedding the trunk as deeply as possible continues for several years by an actual downward growth. Not until the plant has established itself thus firmly does the upward growth begin. In dry weather all newly planted palms must be thoroughly watered. Applications of manure water now and then have a very beneficial effect.

The above rules apply to our high pineland and high hammock lands. In rich moist soils it is not necessary to make such elaborate preparations. A hole three feet deep and three feet wide will suffice, but even in this case it must be filled with a mixture of well rotted stable manure, mulch, leaf mold and well aerated surface soil. Some of the hardy palms will not thrive on high pineland. I have never been able to induce the Washingtonias to grow well in such soils. All the Sabals, *Cocos* [Butias] and *Phoenix* species, the *Chamaerops*, *Rhapidophyllum* and *Serenoa* grow extremely well after they have been properly planted. On the other hand the *Cocos* (*Butia*) of the [*Butia capitata*] type do not grow well on flatwoods or low soil. They are pre-eminently the palms for high pineland gardens.

Always set out your plants in the rainy season, or preferably, in November and December—never in the dry season. About eight years ago I transplanted a number of small seedling Cabbage Palms. For one specimen I dug a large hole and filled this partly with night soil. All the others were planted in rather small holes and no manure was used, but they received strong applications of commercial fertilizer after they had been set out. The difference in growth is most remarkable. The specimen treated in the proper way is at present a large, massive and very beautiful plant and at least ten times larger than most of the others.

The species of the genus *Cocos* [= *Butia*], particularly all those with glaucous foliage, have a rather shallow root-system and the holes prepared for them need not be quite so deep. All my plants,—palms and bamboos included,—were only fertilized during the first three or four years after they had been set out. They subsist now entirely on the only leaves and rotten wood that accumulate around them, which at present consists of a heavy layer several inches thick. No leaves, old wood and weeds are burned. Everything is used as a mulch for my large specimen plants. The formerly dry, poor, white sand has been transformed into a fine rich hammock soil.

All the old palm leaves which are cut off are thrown on the compost heap and after thoroughly decomposed are used as a mulch. Chickens, guineas and turkeys do the cultivating and keep the soil free from injurious insects. All the dish-water, wash-water,—everything that contains plant food,—is used for the plants near the house. There is no doubt that all my palms and other plants would have grown much more rapidly if they could have been supplied with good applications of commercial fertilizer, but this was out of the question.

All of south Florida should be a paradise of Royal Palms, with such bright flowering trees as the Royal Poinciana, *Spathodea campanulata*, [*Lagerstroemia speciosa*], *Jacaranda* and the dense-growing *Ficus* or rubber tree in the background. And there are hundreds of others, though less effective. We grow three species of Royal Palms in our gardens, our native [*Roystonea regia*] being best of all. [*Roystonea borinquena*] of Porto Rico is better adapted for dry soils, but it is not quite as beautiful as the former. Its trunk, just as smooth, shows a rather brownish tint, instead of the grayish-white.

The so-called Cabbage Palm, Trinidad, is a Royal Palm,—[*Roystonea oleracea*]. It is the tallest of all, said to attain a height of almost 175 feet. The trunk is very slender, never bulged. The celebrated avenue in the botanical garden of Rio de Janeiro, Brazil, consists of this species. It is preferred in British Guiana for avenue planting. I have grown it from seed repeatedly, but I always lost the young plants as they are very tender. There may perhaps be good specimens at Miami and Coconut Grove. Prof. Charles T. Simpson, the best authority on all subjects pertaining to ornamental horticulture of Dade County, says that it does well in lower lands. It should be largely planted.

The Coconut Palm is not adapted for avenue planting, on account of its leaning, bending and crooked growth, but it is a magnificent tree for groups, groves and masses. As an ornamental palm it ranks right after the *Roystonea regia*. Here on the west coast it grows best along the seashore, but thrives almost equally as well on rather dry soils. In poor, thirsty ground it repays well for good care and some fertilizer.

Flowering of the Talipot Palm, *Corypha umbraculifera*

Dr. H. F. Macmillan, the Director of the Ceylon Botanical Garden, writes from Peradeniya:

In close proximity to the Cannon-ball Trees is a handsome specimen of the Talipot Palm (*Corypha umbraculifera*) in flower, and which has been found to be of the following dimensions: Height of trunk to inflorescence, 73 feet; height from this to top of inflorescence 30 feet; total height 103 feet; girth of trunk at base, 13 feet. The inflorescence, which tapers to the top, consists of 50 main branches, one of which has been found to measure 15 feet in length, having 26 branchlets, averaging 2 feet in length. The branch measured required three strong coolies to carry it; thus, making allowance for smaller branches at top, quite a hundred coolies would be required to carry the whole inflorescence. The Talipot flower collectively is therefore by far the largest in the vegetable kingdom. The individual flowers are inconspicuous, greenish-white, unpleasantly scented and are blown about by the wind, giving a snowy appearance to the ground underneath. Estimating by the number counted on one spike, the whole inflorescence contains 60,000,000 flowers.

Some Rare and Unusual Palms

The Double Coconut Palm

The genus *Lodoicea* consists of one species, *L. sechellarum,* Double Coconut or Coco de Mer. The only spot in the world where the nuts grew, in the year 1743, they were only known from having been found floating on the surface of the sea in the Indian Ocean, and near the Maldivian Islands. Even in the time of Rumphius the nuts were spoken of as the "mirum miraculum naturae, quod princeps est ominium marinarum rerum, quae rarae habentur."

The history of this celebrated Palm sounds like a fairy tale. The Malay and Chinese sailors used to tell people that this huge fruit was borne upon a tree deep under water, which was similar to a Coconut Palm, and was visible in placid water on the coast of Sumatra, but that it instantly disappeared if they attempted to dive for it. "The negro priests declared it grew near the island of Java, where its leaves and branches rose above the water, and in which a monstrous bird or griffin had its habitation, . . . furthermore, they avowed their ships were attracted by the waves which surrounded this tree, and there retained, the mariners falling a prey to this savage bird, so that the inhabitants of the Indian Archipelago always carefully avoided the spot" (Seemann).

With such and many more strange ideas respecting its place of growth and history, is it not wonderful that this nut should have been highly prized? In the Maldivian Islands it was death to any man to possess it. All nuts that were found became the immediate property of the king, who sold them at a very high price or offered them as the most precious regal gifts. They were also used in native medicines, and the shell was carved into many useful utensils. The discovery of the Seychelles Islands and the knowledge derived there that these nuts grow on Palm Trees, as other Coconuts, reduced their value considerably.

The Seychelles, or Mahe Islands, as they are sometimes called, lie to the northeast of Madagascar, in about 5°S. latitude and 55°E. longitude. It is in this group only that the Palm is found, and among them on no others than the Isles of Praslin and Curieuse and Round Island. These are within half a mile of each other and are mountainous and rocky. I quote here from a letter of Mr. R. W. Plant, written to Mr. John Smith, Curator at Kew. It gives a picture of the home of the Double Coconut.

> In the Seychelles I more nearly realized my preconceived ideals of tropical vegetation than at any other place;—the beach fringed with common Coconuts; the ravines and water-courses overhung with Bananas, Bamboos and three or four indigenous Palms; the open ground full of pineapples—many of them run wild; the tops of the mountains covered with forests of Ebony and Rosewood, interspersed with Tree Ferns of some 20 to 30 feet high; and then these glorious Lodoiceae, with their leaves of 15 to 20 feet span, and trunks reaching to the sky; to say nothing of groves of Cinnamon and Cloves and Breadfruit, all new to me in this their natural wildness and beauty. You may believe me that I enjoyed it,—so that I nearly forgot the errand that brought me there. We have many beautiful scenes in this country (Natal) . . . but it is altogether of a different character.

The foliage of the Double Coconut is used for thatch and even for the walls of houses and cabins. With a hundred leaves a convenient dwelling may be constructed, including even the partitions, the doors and windows. In the Isle of Praslin most of the cabins and warehouses are thus made. The down covering the leaves, serves as filling for mattresses and pillows. The leaf-stalks supply fiber for baskets and brooms and the young unexpanded foliage is an excellent material for hats. The nuts are used in many ways. When preserved whole the shell serves to carry water. Some of the nuts hold

3 to 4 quarts. Cups, plates and dishes are also formed of them. Their strength and durability makes them particularly valuable.

The Double Coconut Palm attains a height of from 80 to 90 feet and is surmounted by a beautiful crown of fan-shaped leaves. These leaves are of a large size, often reaching a length of 20 feet, and are 10 to 12 feet wide. In some cases they are 30 feet long, including the petiole which is of sufficient strength to bear the weight of a man. Male and female flowers are borne on separate trees, as this Palm is dioecious. The fruit is an olive-green color, and generally double, sometimes triple and even quadruple and frequently attains a length of 18 inches and a circumference of 3 feet, weighing sometimes from 40 to 50 pounds. It is in fact the largest fruit produced by any tree. "A remarkable circumstance connected with this tree is the length of time necessary to mature its fruit and the long duration of its bloom. It bears only one spadix in each year, and yet has often above ten in bloom at once; it has flowers and fruits of all ages at one time."

The fruit, when ripe, drops on the ground and is no longer fit to eat. In a few months, if not buried in the soil or exposed to the rays of the sun, the fallen nut begins to germinate and a new plant is formed. The immature fruit is regarded as a delicacy by the natives. It is easily cut with a knife, and is very tender and of an agreeable taste.

The Double Coconut Palm grows in all kinds of soil, from the sandy shore to the arid mountain top, but the finest trees are found in deep gorges, on damp platforms covered with vegetable soil. In such situations the great height and slender form of the trunk, and the length of its enormous leaves, produce a fine effect; though near the seashore, its leaves torn by the storm and hanging in strips, the effect is quite desolate. It is to be regretted that the peoples of those islands where it is at home do not cultivate it, and then the practice has prevailed of cutting it down in order to obtain the fruit and tender leaves. In fact, it is feared that the species ere long will be exterminated. Nuts have been sold for 10 Pounds apiece, but they seem to be much cheaper now. Good specimens are found in Kew Gardens and other botanical institutions in Europe and elsewhere. In the summer of 1890 two germinating nuts were sent to Kew from the Seychelles, and after growing successfully in a warm pit for two years, the stronger one was removed to the Victoria House, where it since has made extraordinary progress and is now to all appearance in perfect health. The plant is placed over the warm water of the tank, the bottom of the pot being for a few inches immersed. It now carries a fine bunch of leaves. There are fine specimens in the Peradenya Botanical Garden in Ceylon.

G. Marshall Woodrow in his *Gardening in the Tropics*, often having spoken of the shell of the fruit, cut in four and being used as a begging dish by fakirs in India, says:

> The nuts weigh 30 pounds and are frequently imported in Bombay and a few are found to grow in a moist atmosphere without extremes of temperature. One has grown at Peradenya, Ceylon for forty years. The seed should be placed on a bed of deep sandy soil and covered with wood-ashes (to keep away ants) and grass and kept moist. A shoot will appear and pass two or three feet along the surface and the end will turn upward; roots will appear at the lower side and leaves at the upper. There is at present a healthy plant at Kew. The wood-ash covering has to be renewed about every month, as the potash dissolves and it is believed this is the effective part of the wood-ash.

Our own Prof. Chas. T. Simpson has the following to say in his book *Ornamental Gardening in Florida*: "It is a wonderful tree with a trunk a foot in diameter and a hundred feet high; . . . It does not bear fruit until it is thirty years old; the nuts . . . require ten years to ripen. . . . The nuts require a long time to germinate, but they have been sprouted and are growing in Washington. They should be tried in lower Florida."

Last year (in March) I received three fine Double Coconuts from our Bureau of Plant Industry in Washington. These three nuts had a weight of 96 pounds, the light box included. I planted them at once and in holes that were specially prepared for them. These holes were 3 feet deep and as much wide and were filled with rich mucky soil. On top of the mulch I put a thick layer of good sandy soil and in this the nuts were planted, I covered them only lightly with sand and a good deal of fibery sphagnum moss and old grass. Up to this time (April 30, 1927) none of the seeds have sprouted, but I am still waiting for this event. Our common Coconut often requires over a year to show its first sprout and so the Double Coconut may still come up.

This palm has the following synonyms: *Lodoicea callipygo, L. maldivica, Borassus sonnerate,* and *Cocos maldivica.*

Palmyra Palms

This genus includes only one species, *Borassus flabelliformis,* the celebrated Palmyra Palm of India,—not only one of the most majestic and most impressive, but also one of the most useful of all Palms. [In fact there are two species, the second occurring in tropical Africa.] The Palmyra Palm is at present cultivated in all parts of tropical India, west to the Persian Gulf, extending to the 30° latitude north. Immense groves of it, apparently wild, but in fact planted by man, are found all over India, where it finds soil and climate congenial, mostly along the coast. It is found on the banks of the Irrawaddy in Burma, and in the Indian and Malayan Archipelago, including Java, Sumatra, Borneo, Ceram, Amboina and the Moluccas. It is also found in Ceylon up to an altitude of 2,400 feet. The Palmyra needs full sunshine and alluvial soil containing lime, for its best development. The low sandy plains, scarcely elevated above sea level, exposed to the burning sun and the force of the monsoons, are its home.

The trunk of the Palmyra is remarkably straight, often 70 feet high and 2 feet in diameter, and provided with the old leaf-stems. The fan-shaped leaves are usually over 6 feet in diameter and are borne on very strong spiny-edged petioles. The crown of leaves has a majestic appearance on top of the columnar trunk. It is very large and of fine form. The flowers are dioecious (male and female flowers produced on two different trees) appearing in the axils of the leaf-stalks. The large brown drupes also form a characteristic feature of the Palmyra.

In the following I follow more or less Dr. Berthold Seemann:

> The number of uses for which the Palmyra is employed may be said to be almost infinite. Indeed, one of the eastern languages, the Tamil, spoken in a portion of the region which is acknowledged as its native country, possesses a poem, entitled "Tala Vilasam," enumerating no fewer than 801 different purposes to which the Palmyra may be applied, and this poem by no means exhausts the catalogue. The roots are perhaps the only part to be regarded worthless in an economic sense, though their sap is used to cure sores, and also in cases of dysentery. The young plants two or three months old, are an article of food, and are cultivated for this purpose. If not eaten fresh they are deprived of their parchment-like covering and dried in the sun, and are then kept for future use.
>
> A full grown Palmyra is from 60 to 70 feet high. Its trunk at the bottom is about 5½ feet, at the top 2½ feet in circumference. Its wood is favor-

ably known in Ceylon and the maritime parts of India. Large quantities of it are exported from Point Pedro and other parts of Jaffna to Madras and Colombo. At certain seasons of the year the felling, splitting dressing and exporting of it give work to thousands of the Tamil people of the northern peninsula of Ceylon. The trees have to arrive at a considerable age before they are of use for timber. When a hundred years old they are excellent, but it is a well known fact, that the older they get, the harder and blacker does the wood become. Its durability has been well tested, there being doubtless many buildings in Ceylon which have rafters more than a century old. Its specific gravity is 65 pounds per cubic foot. Pillars and posts for verandas of the houses, well-sweeps, etc., are made of this timber.

In the sandy parts of Jaffna where water is found near the surface and where, from the strong winds and other causes, the wells are liable to be filled up, a hollowed part of the trunk of a Palmyra is inserted, and forms a well, from which many a thirsty traveler refreshes himself. Palmyra trunks split into halves, with the heart scooped out, are used as gutters for various purposes, especially under the eaves of the houses. The thick split parts of the trunk are generally taken for rafters, the thinner ones for laths. The trunks of young trees or the tops of the old ones are often cut into pieces, split, and placed where game is plentiful. The wild hogs and hares are very fond of the soft, white, spongy hearts of the logs, and in resorting to them are frequently shot by the natives.

The dark outside wood of very old trees is used to some extent in Europe and America for umbrella handles, walking canes, paper rulers, fancy boxes and other articles. The workman operating on this wood has to be extremely careful, as some of the wiry fibers get loose, and are apt to run under his nails of his fingers, or into the flesh of his hand. It is well known in India that the female tree produces the best and hardest timber, and that that of the male is considered so inferior that unless the tree is very old it is never used.

The trunk, as a rule, is simple, but occasionally it is more or less divided. We sometimes also notice here in Florida Cabbage Palmettos with two or more heads. Ferguson says: "The first of such trees I saw had four heads upon it, but with marks where three or four others had been. These divisions began about 25 or 30 feet from the ground. I noticed one near Oodooville with six heads on it. One of them grew nearly in a line with the body of the tree, while the other five formed a whorl, but bending somewhat outward before they could attain their upright posture. There were marks where other three had been."

The leaves on trees in the jungle, or at a distance from human habitations, will be found extending until the tree attains a height of 25 to 40 feet from bottom to top, the older ones displaying their stalks only, the blade or fan part having rotted away. The foliage is distributed on the trunk in spiral rows, beautifully ascending from right to left in some, and from left to right in others. The blade of the leaf has from seventy to eighty segments, forming nearly an entire circle. Each tree has from twenty-five to forty green leaves at a time, and of these the natives cut off twelve or fifteen annually, or a greater number once in two years to be used for various purposes, as well as to enable the fruit to ripen and increase in size. These leaves are used for thatch or for other purposes. In Jaffna, and doubtless also in India, the blades are put into the ground of the rice-fields until they rot and thus yield an excellent manure, adding a quality of siliceous and other matter to the soil. Mats are made of Palmyra leaves, and are used instead of carpets on floors, for ceilings, for drying coffee on them, etc. Bags, baskets, hats, caps, fan, umbrellas are also made of these leaves.

But one of the most singular purposes to which they are devoted is that of writing upon. The oldest Hindu author who mentions writing on ollahs is Panning-rishee. He lived, according to Hindu reckoning, about the year 790 of the Caliyugam, or about 4,225 years ago, and resided at Arittuwarum, near the source of the Ganges. Pliny says expressly that the most ancient way of writing was upon the leaves of Palms. The leaves of the Palmyra are not the only ones used for writing in India; those of the Coconut Palms and those of the Talipot (*Corypha umbraculifera*) serve the same purpose. Palm leaves, when they are prepared to receive the impression of the stylus, are called ollahs. The natives write letters on them, which neatly rolled up, pass through the post office. The Palmyra books are usually about two feet long and two inches broad. The statements respecting the age of Palmyra manuscript books are conflicting. Some authors say that they do not last longer than a century, while others claim that they may be preserved for four or five hundred years.

At the season when the inflorescence begins to appear and before the spathes have time to burst, the toddy drawer is at work in the Palmyra groves. His practiced eye soon singles out those trees fit for the scalping knife. After the spathes have been tied, they are beaten and crushed between wooden battens. This operation is repeated for three successive mornings on each, and the following fourth a thin slice is cut from the points of the spathes. All this is done to keep them from bursting and to encourage the flow of sap. On the eighth morning a clear, sweet liquor begins to flow from the wounded parts, which is indicated by the toddy-birds (*Artamus* sp.) and crows fighting and chattering among the trees. The toddy drawer then ascends again in the morning with toddy receivers in which he places the ends of the spathes and leaves them until evening, when they are found to contain a quantity of this liquor. It is said that a spathe continues to give toddy for five months. While it is seldom that three spathes are yielding toddy on the Coconut Palm, seven or eight will yield juice at once on the Palmyra. An expert climber can draw toddy from forty trees in a few hours. There is sweet toddy, the fresh mild champagne, others to cider and some to ginger beer.

Toddy serves extensively as yeast, and throughout Ceylon no other is used by the bakers. Large quantities are converted into vinegar, but the greatest quantity is boiled down for jagger or sugar. Both these words are derived from the Sanscrit sakar, whence also the Arabian shkar, the Latin saccharum, the German zuker, etc. It seems certain that the sugar from these Palms was used by the peoples of India at a very remote period of history.

Bismarckia nobilis is a very rare Palm, and has the reputation of being a difficult one to grow. Whatever it may be under ordinary methods of cultivation, it thrives exceedingly well in the Victoria House with its pot partly immersed in the tepid water, and is, in fact, in rugged health. This plant [related to the Palmyra Palm] is 4 to 5 feet high, its somewhat glaucous fan-shaped leaves measuring 3 feet across, the margins of the segments being furnished with a few white filaments. The species is a native of Madagascar. (A few years ago I received a fine seedling from the Bureau of Plant Industry, but as it was planted in too dry a spot at Palm Cottage Gardens and did not thrive.)

1. Palm Cottage Gardens, Gotha, November 1907. Visitor admiring tropical foliage in the lath house.

2. Palm Cottage Gardens, Gotha. Dr. Nehrling with *Alocasia odora.*

3. Dr. Nehrling in the library at Cornell University, ca. 1926.

4. Dr. Nehrling in his "Garden of Solitude," Naples, 1920s.

5. Nehrling family portrait, early 1900s. Left to right: Werner, Sophie, Bert, Henry, and Lydia.

6. Henry Nehrling's lath house with Caladiums and grandson (1920s?).

7. Nehrling homestead at Gotha.

Glimpse of a Florida Grove.

8. Postcard showing the view from Palm Cottage Gardens, overlooking Lake Audubon and a citrus grove.

9. Bert Nehrling, Henry's youngest son, with an ancient and frequently moved *Dioon spinulosum*.

5

Gymnosperms

After the palms the Cycads are the most beautiful and impressive ornaments of our south Florida gardens. Whether at home or abroad, choice bits of scenery may often be met with that are well worthy of imitation in our gardens, both out-of-doors and under glass. Such striking forms of vegetation could not fail to have a pleasing effect, specimens would be an inspiration and a revelation to the thousands of tourists who love and admire native and beautiful gardens.

Ancient Gymnosperms

Though Cycads to some extent resemble Palms, Pines and Ferns, yet they possess features which prevent them from being mistaken for any of these types of vegetation. Their headquarters may be considered to be Australia and South Africa, especially along the frontiers of Kaffirland. There are, however, numerous outlying members of the family scattered through Florida, Mexico, Central and South America, the West Indies, Asia, Madagascar and the South Sea Islands.

In bygone ages of the world Cycads formed a very considerable part of the vegetation. In fact, compared with these fossil forms, we must consider those still found at present only as remnants of a once magnificent and predominant plant association. In the geological history of plants Cycads appear to have occupied a prominent position among the very first of the dry land vegetation; that is, of the Devonian or Mesozoic age. They then appear to have been world-wide in their distribution, representatives of them having been found as far north as Greenland. They are said to be the remains of an otherwise extinct vegetation, and as Dr. Maxwell Masters has remarked, the existence of living representatives of Cycadaceae is quite as startling a fact in botany as living examples of Ichthyosaurus and Megatherium would be in zoology. It is no exaggeration to say that within the limits of the area in the southern Black Hills, between the forks of the Cheyenne River, now preserved as the "Cycad National Monument," there is a far richer representation of petrified Cycads than has ever been indicated by field observation or discovery elsewhere. In many other parts of the world fossil forms of Cycads have also been found and described. The Cycads of our present day have in some instances a grotesque and weird look. They have in general a simple, erect, stout cylindrical stem, bearing a most beautiful large crown of pinnate leaves which are very coriaceous in texture and quite hard to the touch. They produce large cones, male and female flowers being provided by separate plants; i.e., they are dioecious. The cones, as far as they have been produced in my collection, are long and rather cylindrical in the male plant and more rounded, dome-shaped and much shorter in the female plants. From this general description there are, however, a few exceptions as, for instance, in the case of *Bowenia spectabilis,* a plant from Rockingham Bay, North Australia, the foliage of which is bipinnate, i.e., twice divided, and it is the only species with [twice] compound leaves known to the Cycad family. Some old Cycads seem to become branched. I have about a dozen specimens of old so-called Sago palms (*Cycas revoluta*) which are branched at their tops. But these are always small plants. I never have seen a branched female specimen. In fact it is the most important and certain characteristic to distinguish the two sexes.

Prominent among the Cycads of the Amsterdam Botanic Gardens is a magnificent example of *Encephalartos caffer,* which has a straight stout stem 18 feet in height, at which point it divides into two equally strong crowns, each bearing a head of well-developed leaves. In the same garden, which is wonderfully rich in grand specimens of Cycads, may also be seen an example of *Cycas revoluta,* with a very stout stem, bearing five well-developed crowns, their stems being usually from 3 to 4 feet high, surrounded at their lower parts with several clusters of side shoots. The only other instance of a Cycad becoming branched was a fine large specimen of a *Cycas circinalis* which I saw in a garden at Palm Beach, and which had two beautiful crowns. It had a stem about 6 feet tall, and as it was in flower when I saw it (November) I could ascertain the fact that it also was a male plant. I may mention in this connection that the male cones of this species, as well as that of *Dioon edule*, emit a rather unpleasant musty odor. It may be added here, too, that some species of the Western hemisphere have quite slender stems, notably a few of the Zamias.

Cycads as a rule are of extremely slow growth. They must be allowed to grow when they please, and when they choose to be dormant for a season, which they frequently do, any attempt to force them into growth by bottom heat or other stimulants rarely ever has the desired effect, and the large and fine specimens which adorn many of the conservatories of our country and Europe, as well as a few gardens of California, must be of very great age. From observations taken respecting the progress of trunk-growth in *Encephalartos caffer*, under cultivation, it would seem that nearly twenty years are required to form one foot of stem or trunk, while a plant of *Macrozamia spiralis*, growing in the collection of the late Mr. E. H. Hart at Federal Point, Fla., had only a foot of stem, when I saw it in 1914, and it had been in cultivation for about thirty years. This peculiarly slow growth has its advantages as well as its disadvantages, for while those who have large specimens need have no fear of their outgrowing even limited accommodations, those on the other hand who have only small plants will feel dissatisfied because they cannot be made to quickly assume more noble proportions. I have a fine old specimen of *Dioon edule* in my collection. It flowers every two years and is a male plant. The trunk is about 3 feet high, quite rough and is adorned with a dense growth of the Resurrection Fern. This specimen has a very interesting history. It was bought, in 1867, by the late Alexander Mitchell in Edinburgh, Scotland, and he was told that it was at least 100 years old, a statement which was corroborated by the director of the Edinburgh Botanic Garden. It was sent with many other plants to his conservatories in Milwaukee. In 1895, when the glasshouses were discontinued, Mrs. T. D. Mitchell, his daughter-in-law, kindly offered me the specimen as a present. I had it for several years in my greenhouse and sent it in 1899 to my place at Gotha, Fla., where it was allotted a position in my sandy pineland garden, among Magnolias and Palms. Here it grew without any extra care and soon formed a most striking specimen, flowering every other year during September. It is a male plant, and the cylindrical, much pointed cone was usually from 12 to 18 inches long. The odor of this flowering cone was quite strong, musty and rather unpleasant.

There was a fine female plant of this species at Bishopstead, at Orlando. Though its trunk was only short, it flowered several times. The cone was shorter, broad and dome-shaped, and there was no odor. My old plant was sent to my Naples garden in 1918, with several other large Cycads. I planted it out near a fine *Ficus nympheifolia,* and it soon formed a new crown of leaves, very hard and almost metallic, with sharply pointed pinnae. Several offsets—the first ones since I obtained it—were formed, but unfortunately the finest of them were stolen by rambling, roving gardeners who make it their business to enrich their collections by stealing fine specimens and off-sets whenever they obtained the confidence of the proprietors to enter gardens.

My old *Dioon edule* has now a trunk about 3 feet tall, by 8 inches in diameter. When I moved this massive plant again last summer it had a weight of about 700 pounds. Owing to this naturally slow growth, and the plants in many places being subject to brush fires. Cycads are not found in their native habitats in such profusion as are Tree Ferns and other plants that grow up quickly and that therefore soon repair such damage. They are, however, by no means delicate in constitution, for the Australian species will thrive well in the open in the Riviera, Italy, Portugal, and California. As far as I know, these species have only now and then been tried in Florida and apparently, with good results. My collection is undoubtedly the largest in Florida, though it consists of less than two dozen species.

The importation of these heavy plants is very costly, and the restrictions placed on all such plants are unsurmountable for a man not blessed with this world's riches. The only way to obtain them in quantities rests with our wealthy plant lovers. An expedition could, perhaps, easily be arranged. Efficient collectors and plant hunters should be engaged and the localities in Australia and South Africa should be penetrated at the proper time, where are found most of the Macrozamias, several of the *Cycas* species and *Bowenia spectabilis,* and in Africa where the grand *Encephalartos* species and *Stangeria paradoxa* grow most abundantly. Though all of these plants can be raised from seeds, it requires at least twenty-five years for most of them to form a short stem. I had an *Encephalartos caffer,* one of the kaffir Bread species, which only formed a small thick stem two inches thick and three inches high, within twenty years. To import the dry trunks in various sizes is the only way to create grand effects in our tropical gardens in a very short time.

But only the man of means, who must be at the same time a passionate plant lover, is able to send out collectors and import the large trunks. The massive grandeur and noble proportions of the Cycads and the relatively little attention they require make me wonder that in our large tropical gardens they are not more grown than they are, and that we do not find masses of them and numerous single specimens. The species enumerated in the following essay comprise the majority of the Cycads in cultivation. Recently, however, several new forms have been introduced, with which I am not acquainted, but which will doubtless prove valuable as first-class ornamentals in our Florida gardens.

The most interesting species in my collection, the most conspicuous and beautiful, is *Dioon spinulosum,* which I received about ten years ago from the Missouri Botanical Garden. Up to now this plant was growing luxuriantly in my garden at Naples in rather moist mucky soil under a lath-roof. The fine bunch of leaves, about 4 feet long, consists of about 40 light glossy-green fronds, with rather dense pinnae each of which is covered along its edge with short rather soft spines. This species is really the queen among the Dioons. I removed my plant to Gotha, as attempts had been made by some scoundrels to dig it up and carry it away. In the following I shall give a short account of its history and its habitat in Mexico.

This wonderfully beautiful Cycad, a real gem for our south Florida gardens, but up to now exceedingly rare, grows wild in the ravines of Tuxtla, Vera Cruz. My dear old friend, Dr. C. A. Purpus, the celebrated botanist, knows where it can be found in quantities, but it requires days to get these over often dangerous mountain paths. According to Dr. L. H. Bailey, it grows from 6 to 50 feet high, and is one of the tallest of all Cycads, being only excelled by *Cycas media* of Queensland. My experiments have shown without a doubt that it is perfectly adapted to the soil and climate of south Florida, and that it does well in rich, moist, mucky positions and that it is entirely hardy. It is one of the most exquisite Cycads, outrivaling even the most elegant palms in beauty and easy growing. The large sturdy Cycads are most valuable plants for the adornment of our Florida tropical gardens. They are always good to look at, magnificent in every sense, and they are, as a rule, among the easiest plants to cultivate. Large stems of them may be sent long distances without suffering, most of the big specimens at Kew having been obtained from Australia and Africa by means of stems dug up and sent without any soil in the boxes. No packing material is used. Such species as *Encephalartos villosus, E. caffer,* and *E. altensteinii* ought to thrive in the open air all over south and central Florida, along the gulf coast and in California. But in spite of all their beauty and grandeur, the American gardening public is scarcely aware of the grand subjects at their disposal. Visitors to our botanical gardens and large conservatories are generally struck with the magnificence of these plants.

The collection of Cycads at Kew is the richest in existence, and many of the specimens are of large size and of great age. Species beautifully growing in my garden are: *Cycas revoluta, C. circinalis, C. pectinata, C. media, C. siamensis* (old); *Dioon edule, D. spinulosum, D. purpusii; Ceratozamia mexicana;* [*Lepidozamia peroffskyana*]; *Zamia furfuracea, Z. spartea, Z. umbrosa* and *Z. floridana* [both may equal *Z. integrifolia*]. I would have more if I had the means to import and experiment with them.

Propagation of Cycads from Cuttings

That excellent authority, Herr Neumann, in his standard manual *Die Kunst der Versnehrung,* etc. (3rd edition) says that the propagation of plants by means of sections of the stems is being practiced in most countries, and that he had made use of this method in propagating *Cycas circinalis,* a jewel of the highest value among plants, and still quite rare in gardens. There are two fine specimens of it in Dr. Stone's garden and a still larger one in Mr. J. E. Hendry's garden at Fort Myers. Neumann took cross sections of the stem 2 to 3½ inches thick after cutting off the crown, left them uncovered for 4 or 5 days to allow the surface to dry, and then planted them in pots of suitable size, placed them on bottom-heat, and covered each with a bell-glass. The scales soon formed roots, and shoots pushed forth between the scales. As soon as the shoots had reached a proper degree of development, they were detached and employed in the same way as cuttings, which now formed as erect, regular plants as the mother from which they were taken. The head of the Cycad which he had removed from the stem was exposed to the air for 3 weeks in the glasshouse before it was set in a pot, without his expecting any results, for it was a very young specimen. In the following years, however, he noticed that the crown had taken root, and growths were appearing between the scales, precisely as had occurred with the sections. These growths were employed as the others had been but they took almost a year to form roots.

Modern Gymnosperms

A few of the Araucarias form most beautiful objects in our south Florida gardens, though one of them, the Bunya-Bunya, is as hardy in Orlando as it is in Fort Myers, and in well-protected spots even in Jacksonville. The most generally grown, mostly as a pot plant, is the Norfolk Island Pine (*Araucaria excelsa*) [cultivated material under this name probably was *A. heterophylla*], which when fully developed will reach a height of 150 feet or more, and yet when not more than a foot high forms a beautifully symmetrical shaped specimen; hence it is very popular for table decoration. Owing to its popularity, considerable quantities of seed have been imported since many years, so that it can now be obtained at a cheaper rate. Small specimen seedlings are not much sought after, as they are not so well furnished at the base as plants raised from cuttings. The cuttings, of course, must not be formed of the side shoots, as they never will make a symmetrically shaped plant, the leading upright shoots only being chosen for this purpose. Where this *Araucaria* is propagated in quantity old stock plants are usually kept for the supply of cuttings; that is to say, plants that have become bare at the base or outgrow the space allotted to them. If the tops of these plants are cut off they will usually push out two or three or even more leaders, all of which that are firm enough may be taken as cuttings. The cuttings need to be put in small pots of sandy soil and placed in a closed propagating frame till well rooted. Given conditions favorable to growth and ample space, they will form equally symmetrical specimens, whether a couple of feet high or ten times that height.

The Bunya-Bunya (*Araucaria bidwillii*), also known as the Australian Monkey Puzzle, is a very beautiful and distinct species. While the former is a native of Norfolk Island, off the east coast of Australia, this species comes from the more northern parts of the Australian mainland. In the open ground, it often forms magnificent specimens. About ten years ago I was often delighted to see a large dense specimen in a garden of Orlando. It was at least 50 or 60 feet high, very dense, with rather drooping branches, and a spread of almost 40 feet in diameter near the ground. The lower branches brushed even the soil. This fine specimen was badly injured by a fire which burned the home nearby. The late Mr. Mills of Jacksonville also had a fine, but not so tall a specimen in his yard. At Fort Myers Mr. Ewald Stulpner, former gardener to Thomas A. Edison, also could point out a most wonderful specimen. Unfortunately the hurricane of 1926 broke off its top. The leaves of this species are lanceolate, very sharply pointed, and of a deep glossy-green color. It needs space in gardens. In dry pineland soil it always remains a pigmy.

Araucaria cunninghamii, one of the most useful timber trees of Queensland, has needle-like leaves as in the Norfolk Island Pine, but instead of the branches being arranged in a regular whorl or frond-like manner those of this species are more tufted and clustered, thus giving to the plant altogether a more irregular outline, which is maintained when the specimen attains tall-like dimensions. It is more effective in a young state when it is under that height.

Araucaria [*A. columnaris*], a native of New Caledonia, has the finest and softest foliage of any of the Araucarias, and it requires rather more care and attention than most of the others. The branches are numerous even on small plants, and well furnished with partially drooping branches, which in their turn are thickly clothed with short oval-shaped leaves. If this Araucaria is at all neglected, the foliage acquires a yellowish hue, and it is then very difficult to restore it to its normal tint.

Italian Cypress (*Cupressus sempervirens*): This beautiful upright Cypress is among evergreen trees what the Lombardy Poplar is among timber trees, a fine contrast to the more spreading and round-headed forms. It is a native of Greece and most parts of the Levant and was extensively employed by the Romans as an ornamental tree in their villa gardens. Owing to its fastigiate habit, it forms a suitable tree for planting near buildings where the prevailing architectural lines are horizontal. It succeeds best in a dry sheltered situation, but in this state, particularly in central Florida, even under the most favorable conditions, it rarely attains to more than 40 feet in height, although in its native country it reaches 80 feet and sometimes 100 feet, the famous specimen which Napoleon preserved when constructing his road over the Alps being 121 feet in height and 23 feet in girth of the stem. Its timber is of great durability, instances being on record of doors made of its wood having lasted for upwards of 1,000 years.

In 1897 I planted a dozen specimens at Palm Cottage Gardens. They all grew well for the first 5 or 6 years in the poor sandy pineland soil, and all were specimens of great beauty. Later, however, they gradually lost their lower branches and finally all died out. Only one specimen is now (1928) left and this is pining away. This Cypress is the wonder of all the finer Italian Gardens, and I think that it may thrive well in the heavier soils of Georgia and South Carolina. All the formerly fine specimens at Orlando and Winter Park are things of the past.

6

Florida, a Land to Treasure

Florida is a land of Flowers and tropical plants [but it's going fast]. Many years ago—in 1904—I sent my late friend, E. O. Painter, publisher and editor of the now extinct *Florida Agriculturist,* the following introduction to an account on our native shrubs and trees. I quote almost verbally:

Florida Is a Dreamland

No other region of our great country can compare with it. It is always alluring and full of enchantments in its natural state. There is nothing like it. Whenever you have gained a firm foothold its magic charm will not let you loose again. The nature-loving pioneer will pleasantly undergo all hardships, all inconveniences in order to enjoy the seasons, the truly fascinating landscapes. He is willing rather to live here in a shack than in the most comfortable home of the northland. The original Seminole Indians, who were hunted, robbed and finally forced to leave their beloved homeland, formed at one time the most picturesque and fitting ornament to the landscape.

In the sixties and seventies of the last century [1800s] a large number of highly cultured northerners and many intellectual Englishmen, attracted by the salubrious climate, the wild orange groves, the beauty of the forests, the lure of the lakes, rivers and mysterious springs; came to take possession of the land in order to lead the "gentle Life." The great beauty of nature and the mild sunny climate attracted many others who built congenial winter homes in the most attractive spots. These pioneers, as a rule, were a class of people of high ideals. Not a few selected sites for their homes among the Magnolias and Cabbage Palms, among the Live Oaks and Laurel Cherries on the banks of the St. Johns and other water courses or on the shores of one of the many placid clear water lakes, or even in the untouched pineland.

When I purchased my land in Orange County in 1885 and began to plant my garden there were wonderfully beautiful landscapes all around me. At present there are only remnants of the former beauty spots. The tall Long-leaf Pines are gone. The century old picturesque broad Live Oaks with their draperies and streamers of gray Spanish-Moss have vanished. The former flowery forest-floor is a thing of the past.

Fortunately not all of the natural beauty has been destroyed. It is high time, however, that steps be taken to preserve what still remains. The most beautiful and charming landscape pictures should be held sacred by a cultured and refined people. Many of our glorious dense hammocks surrounding our clear water lakes and bordering our dreamy water courses, should be kept intact for future generations. And this should be done now, before it is too late—before the axe of the woodsman destroys the beauty spots of a most alluring and enchanting subtropical landscape. Many of our dense Cypress swamps should never be destroyed by the grubbing hoe and the shovel of the ditch digger.

In years gone by it was only possible for the tourist to reach the central parts of the state by boarding one of the river steamers plying between Jacksonville and Lakes Monroe and Jessup. It was a wonderful trip—a trip full of romance, full of charms, and surprises, particularly where the river became narrow and full of bends. The banks, usually densely overgrown by trees, shrubs and climbers, seemed to be so close at hand that the conspicuous snowy-white blossoms of the powerfully fragrant Swamp Lily (*Crinum americanum*), or the masses of night-blooming Moonflower climbing over shrubs and trees, could almost be reached by hand. There was always something to see among the wild floral treasures. I inhaled the delicate odor of the yellow Jessamine (*Gelsemium sempervirens*)—the real odor of Florida—which was wafted by myriads of trumpet-flowers through the air. And then again, in March and April, the great noble clusters of *Magnolia grandiflora*—also most intensely fragrant—covered the glossy broad-leaved crowns of the trees with a most glorious array of white stars. In my younger days, in my native Wisconsin, I longed to live and die in a land where I could listen to the songs of the mocking-bird and the cardinal redbird. This dream of my youth has become true.

And again, our boat passes dense groups of water Magnolias (*Magnolia glauca* [= *M. virginiana*]) usually known by the name of Sweet Bay. The undersides of the leaves are silvery-white, and when the breezes turn up these undersides the color becomes almost snowy-white. The smaller, white flowers, appearing in the interior of the state at various times during the rainy season, exhale a strong tea-rose odor.

I made this trip quite often and at various times of the year. I found that the passengers at that time, with open eyes and with much enthusiasm, enjoyed this, to them, new world. The power of this wealth of charms is so strong, so lasting that no lover of the beautiful can resist it. When our steamer passed the first groups of tall Cabbage Palms there were always exclamations of enthusiastic delight. No human being of culture and refinement can look upon these noble masses of tropical growth without joy and emotion. They form one of Florida's outstanding and most valuable assets. Whenever we find these true aristocrats—the nobility of the plant world—they should be carefully preserved and properly protected from destruction.

Florida has become already the Mecca of thousands of nature lovers and pleasure seekers during the cold winter months, and the time is close at hand when hundreds of thousands will arrive from northern climes to enjoy the natural beauty of our landscapes, while other thousands are intent on owning and creating charming winter homes around our many fine lakes and along our rivers. It is this unique beauty and charm of our subtropical landscape that ever will hold the best class of our people enthralled. It is the most valuable asset Florida has. Without it the state would be a dreary and monotonous sand waste and the climate would be unbearable. Everyone who looks at our fine native scenery with open eyes and an understanding mind must feel convinced that it is high time to protect and preserve what is still left. It has taken nature centuries to create this beauty. After it has been destroyed no power in the world can bring it back. Of course we can plant artificially the most wonderful tropical garden paradises by using the wealth of exotic tender plant material, but the natural beauty of the Florida wilds gives the state its unique beauty and fame.

Though the foregoing lines were written a quarter of a century ago, they still hold true. My advice has not been heeded. Many of the most exquisite forest areas have been destroyed, and the destruction goes on unhindered by those who ought to know better. All the picturesque old Live Oaks between Gotha and Orlando have been sacrificed to the Moloch of filthy lucre. The tall Long-leaf Pines have almost completely vanished.

There were, not very long ago, quite a number of most interesting and extremely instructive Indian Mounds in my part of the Atlantic Coast, as well as along the Gulf Coast. All were covered with a very conspicuous and distinct plant growth and often even with larger trees. The aborigines of a remote period built these mounds, using mainly the shells they had used for food, pottery, stone-implements and even their own bodies. Hundreds of years probably were necessary to finish these very often large hill-like constructions. They undoubtedly had a special object in mind when they slowly accumulated these mounds. They intended to leave conspicuous memorials of their existence behind them, just as we do in building mausoleums and setting grave-stones in our cemeteries. They also undoubtedly considered them safe from those who would come after them. But alas! They did not imagine a degenerated civilization that would overrun the state and disgrace these memorials, as the one of our present generation.

What has become of most of these mounds? The following remarks will tell you. In 1906 my late friend, Mr. George A. Purdy, and I went on an exploring trip along the East Coast near Ormond. We found several of these shell mounds. All were covered with a dense growth of plants, mostly not found in the woods nearby. Several of them can now only be found in extreme south Florida. There were also quite a number of trees, even at their tips. The material consisted of many kinds of shells, bones, broken pottery and shades of black soil and ashes. When I again visited the locality a few years ago the shell mounds could not be found anywhere. They were gone. Nothing remained of the distinct plant associations. The road builders had hauled away the material for the foundations of the highways. These and many other shell mounds on both coasts are fast disappearing, a loss to our state and to our civilization and for coming generations that never can be repaired nor excused.

There were only a few years ago along the highway to Tampa and near Loughman venerable old Cypress Trees on the south side of the road. The undergrowth consisted of a dense mass of shrubbery. There were at least a dozen of these Cypress giants. But one day when I passed this highway again I found that most of them had disappeared and a straight line of woodland had been cut away and the big monarchs of the forest had been sacrificed. The case was clear enough. The telephone company was the culprit. In order to have a clear way to stretch the wires these trees had to go. I have heard many denouncing remarks, but it is now too late to prevent it. This was the most charming piece of woodland highway between Kissimmee and Tampa.

But the destruction still goes on. There was, not far from Fort Ogden, a group of medium sized and very fine Live Oaks close to the highway. There were about nineteen, a few quite small, but the rest perfect pictures of beauty. I particularly valued this group because the branches were covered with the finest specimens of Bromeliads (*Tillandsia utriculata*) I ever have seen, and there were many clumps of orchids [*Encyclia tampensis*] also. Many of the tourists enjoyed their lunches underneath these trees, which were known as the "picnic oaks." Beauty, however, does not seem to count with many people. Some road vandals cut almost all these trees down, leaving only one or two of them in a rather poor condition. There is no excuse whatsoever for such destruction. I hope sincerely that the time soon may come when all our public officials will be advanced far enough in their education to see the point and to prevent such misdemeanor.

The Palmetto, "State Tree"

Florida is the winter home of the most cultured class of this great country and Canada. The state has been made famous by its winter sojourners. Thousands upon thousands come and go like the migratory birds, seeking a congenial winter home where they can commune with nature in all her sympathetic and alleviate moods. For these ever increasing numbers of winter sojourners we must have natural attractions. The greatest allurements are found in our rivers and forests, in our lakes and ocean beaches and in our towns and cities made beautiful by judicious planting of ornamental trees and shrubs.

The Cabbage Palm is one of our most striking and valuable assets. It should take the lead everywhere in north and central Florida. Palmetto Avenue on Fort George Island at the mouth of the St. Johns is famous and unsurpassed in the state.

It is about one-third of a mile long. The trees were planted by a Mr. Houston, who was overseer on the island in 1813. They are quite uniform in height, being 40 to 50 feet high. Mr. Houston, with a keen eye for the beautiful, hoped to continue his avenue of palms to the plantation home, making it a mile long, but the unexpected return of the owner, a Mr. Kingsley, prevented it, who, upon finding the useless work, as he considered, in which Mr. Houston had employed his slaves, discharged him, yet leaving behind him a most beautiful memorial. Not far from

Palmetto Avenue stand some lofty old patriarchs of the palms, their long slender trunks reaching up 80 feet in the air; their round heads beautifully silhouetted against the sky. We cannot but have a feeling of awe in looking at the tall sentinels, having known, as far as we can reckon, fully three hundred years.

The foregoing lines came from J. F. Rollins, the mistress of the old plantation on Fort George Island.

Palmetto avenues and walks are unfortunately not often found in Florida, though they should form one of the attractions of every town, and should be enjoyed in every park, and besides being planted in groups and masses. I can remember only two such avenues, and both made an everlasting impression. Palmetto Avenue at Palm Beach was planted by Mr. W. Fremd, the gardener who laid out the beautiful grounds of the late Henry M. Flagler. It runs in a straight line across the island to the hotel, The Breakers, and is a mile long. It is a sensation to everyone who first visits Palm Beach. The Palmetto walk in the grounds of the Tampa Bay Hotel is also charmingly effective. It was planted by Mr. A. Fiske, the gardener to the late H. B. Plant, who also laid out and planted the hotel grounds.

Florida is the land of possibilities in ornamental horticulture. We are able to grow in the open air hundreds—and thousands—of species of exquisite tropical and subtropical plants which farther north can only be grown with much difficulty and with considerable trouble in expensive glasshouses. I have wandered through many parts of eastern North America in quest of birds and plants. I have sojourned amidst the primeval forests and untouched prairies of Texas, and made my home for a number of years in the Ozark region of southwestern Missouri. The fertile prairies of Illinois and their woodlands along the water courses are well known to me.

I have stood with admiration under the magnificent Magnolias and Live Oaks on the banks of the lower Mississippi, trying to understand the message which the mighty stream carries from the woodlands of Minnesota to the tropics of the West Indies and South America. The Cedar thickets of eastern Tennessee, and the masses of Azaleas, Mountain Laurels and Rhododendrons of the southern Alleghenies were a revelation to me. Most of the large gardens and parks in the North and East I have studied and admired. Nowhere, however, have I found such a wealth of beautiful native and exotic plants as in Florida, very aptly called the "land of flowers" and the "paradise of ornamental horticulture." Even if we were deprived of the exotic plants, we would be able to form wonderful gardens by using only the material found in our woodlands and along our water courses.

Florida Native Trees and Shrubs

Native plants should always form the foundation of every garden. Good material is close at hand and is easily obtained. Our southern forests and pine barrens are replete with the choicest ornamental plants, beautiful alike in form, foliage and flowers. Nature must be our teacher. She has lavishly spread out her beauties before our eyes, and she points out to us what is most refined and what is best adapted to our soil and climate.

There is no more beautiful evergreen tree in the whole plant world than our glorious evergreen *Magnolia grandiflora* bedecked with its noble lustrous foliage and embellished with its snowy-white, deliciously fragrant flower-chalices. How picturesque are our broad moss-festooned Live Oaks! I do not know of a more charmingly delicious perfume than that exhaled by our Swamp Magnolia or Sweet Bay. From April to September at intervals the air is literally saturated for miles with this sweet Tea-Rose fragrance, which is strongest and most lovely after a rain or in the evening. It is worth going far to see these trees in bloom and to inhale their perfume. The impressions will never fade from memory.

Scarcely any of the exotic trees can vie in beauty with our Loblolly Bay, with the American Holly and the Dahoon, with the Laurel Cherry and American Olive. All are broad-leaved evergreens of beautiful form and dense growth. The Florida Cedar is not only a very compact growing, handsome tree, but its wood is of great commercial value. Our native Palms are the princes of our forests, and always create effective landscape pictures. And how beautiful are our woodlands when the Carolina Jessamine is in bloom in February and March, or when the forest floor of the flatwoods is covered with numberless Zephyr Flowers or Catesby's Lilies! There is a constant procession of gorgeous and dainty wild flowers throughout the year. Suffice it to say that there is not a day without its wild blossoms.

It is always the greatest mistake to plant exclusively or even predominantly exotic species, as is usually done. In preparing a location for his home, the settler almost always removes the wonderfully picturesque old Live Oaks, the tall Magnolias, the towering Pines, and replaces them by

Camphor or the like. This is a grave mistake. Such a home always looks dreary and desolate, and it never can be made attractive by exotic forms. The native trees and shrubs, the almost endless list of herbs and flowers, beautiful in their form, their variation and their numerous hues and colors, and often enchantingly fragrant, always must be used as a foundation for every garden. And it is not advisable to plant only here and there a single specimen. Use them in groups, in masses as well as in isolated specimens. [Preserve them where they grow.]

A group of *Magnolia grandiflora,* each about 40 feet apart, forms a sight that cannot be rivaled by any other tree. In such groups every tree is a picture of perfect form with the lower branches almost resting on the ground. Live Oaks, Loblolly Bays, Hollies and particularly Cabbage Palms can be used very effectively in grouping. Evergreen ought to be preferred in our gardens, although there are a few most beautiful deciduous trees and shrubs that cannot be missed. In the following pages I shall give a list of our most ornamental native trees and shrubs. The palms are treated in a separate chapter.

Magnolia grandiflora, Laurel Magnolia: The great Magnolia is the "queen of beauty" among our native plants. It is one of the most beautiful trees in existence. Our great Magnolia is indeed a noble tree. From my childhood days the very name sounded in my ears like a poem. And the *Magnolia grandiflora* is really a live poem always and everywhere, be it in growth, foliage or flower. Even its seed cones, revealing the glossy brilliant red, extremely aromatic berries, are very beautiful. The very glossy, large leathery leaves impart such a marked tropical character to this noble denizen of our southland forests that one can scarcely believe that it is a native tree. The live poem is still more in evidence when the mocking-bird sings its varied melodies from the top of its crown and when numerous red cardinals flit through its dark-green branches. The fragrance of the large, milky-white flowers is so intense that it almost becomes intoxicating when the tree is in full bloom in April and May. There is nothing more charming than the unopened flower buds and the large white flowers among the dark green, shining, abundant leaves.

Like all other trees, the Magnolia assumes its full beauty only when standing alone. Isolated specimens, given sufficient room for development, having sufficient room to spread their branches to all sides are the most magnificent objects imaginable. Therefore it is a great mistake to remove the lower branches. In the woodland, where they have to keep up a constant struggle for existence with other rival trees, large specimens show a rather open, grotesque form, while in parks, gardens and fields they branch from the ground, forming strikingly beautiful, conical or pyramidal specimens. No other broad-leaved evergreen tree has such a noble form.

Gordonia lasianthus, Loblolly Bay: Next to *Magnolia grandiflora* and [*M. virginica*] I consider this the most beautiful evergreen flowering tree of our state. Though an inhabitant of the edges of swamps and bay-heads, it is not at all particular in its requirements, growing as well on high pineland as in more watery places. In my garden transplanted specimens from the bay-heads have formed fine tall trees in the course of years, provided with branches from the ground, and quite dense and of beautiful form.

A healthy specimen of the Loblolly Bay is a picture of refined beauty. The form of growth is pyramidal and rather dense. On account of its handsome foliage alone, which exhibits a very distinct and characteristic green, it should find a place in every good garden. The leaves are from 3 to 4 inches long 2 inches broad, oblong-lanceolate in form and somewhat lustrous on both sides. In winter and spring an additional charm is displayed, as many of the old leaves assume a brilliant red color, so that the whole tree appears as if flocks of cardinal redbirds had settled among the branches.

When in full bloom the Loblolly Bay is a most charming sight. Almost all the buds open at the same time and the large white, delicately fragrant cup-shaped flowers are densely scattered over the entire tree. The flowers immediately proclaim its close relationship to the Camellia and Tea-shrub. In my garden the trees begin to bloom late in May, lasting about a week in full beauty. Three or four more crops of flowers are produced during the season. When dropping, petals do not fall separately, but cling close together, and the ground underneath the trees appeared to be covered with the entire shells of pigeon's eggs. My first specimens were transplanted from the swamps in November, 1894. They are at present 40 feet high. Though they never received any fertilizer they have made a fine growth. A thick mulch of weeds, pine needles and fallen leaves enriched the soil around them in such a way that they made a very luxuriant growth.

Ilex opaca, American Holly: Our native American Holly is always a beauty when well grown. It is one of the most beloved and cherished trees of the South and should find a place in every garden. It is chiefly interesting on account of its dense spiny foliage, which is of a very beautiful rich glossy perennial green, but it is not less valuable for its very symmetrical dense growth and its vivid red berries, ripening at Christmas time and adding an indescribable charm to the dense foliage. Unfortunately our beautiful Holly becomes rarer from year to year in our dense forests on account of the senseless gathering of the berry-bearing branches for the Christmas market. In many localities it is already almost extinct.

Our native Florida Holly, which can be considered a distinct local form [*I. opaca* var. *arenicola*], has much less prickly leaves. In fact, they are almost free from spines and the berries are somewhat larger. My fine pyramidal specimen plants, provided with branches to the ground, were all raised from seeds which I gathered from branches bought at Christmas time in Milwaukee. These came originally from southern Alabama. In our Florida hammock woods beautiful small specimen plants are found that can be transplanted into our gardens. Such plants have to be cut back very severely, and if carefully dug up and replanted in November or December, they will soon become established.

The Holly is so beautiful, such an ideal tree, so full of poetry and sentiment, that no pains should be spared to make it at home in our ornamental plantations. It is worthy of all the care and attention requisite to its well doing. When well watered and cared for during the first few years after it has been set out it will do well even on high pineland, though it naturally prefers a rich and moist position. When well fertilized it soon forms very showy specimens, particularly beautiful at Christmas time when the entire tree is studded with the brilliant shining red berries. They are, however, hidden among the foliage, and we can only fully admire them in all their beauty when we occupy a place close by. As single specimens on lawns, or groups of three and more, planted about 12 to 15 feet apart, they make charming pictures of elegance and grace. A background of magnolias and Palms heightens the effect.

Ilex cassine, Dahoon Holly: The Dahoon is another fine evergreen holly common along creeks and on the edges of ravines, where fine dense specimens 20 to 25 feet high are sometimes met with. I have quite a number of large dense specimens near my little Lake Audubon. They were all raised from seeds which I gathered in 1895 along a ravine nearby. They assumed a height of about 15 feet and are quite as much in diameter, very dense and provided with branches from the ground to the top. The growth in its habitat is not as shapely and as dense as in the former species, but in good soil, and with some care and fertilizer, it becomes a very dense and spreading ornamental garden tree. The evergreen leaves are oblong, smooth, serrated on their edges, not prickly. The berries are rather small, glowing scarlet and so densely arranged in clusters along and around the branchlets that they can be seen from quite a distance. Sometimes the whole plant seems to be a sheet of brilliant red.

Another important point lies in the fact that the berries begin to color as early as September and that they last in full beauty to April. At this time they change to an orange yellow and soon drop. I am not acquainted with any other shrub or tree which holds its brilliant fruit for such a long time. The Dahoon is easily raised from seeds and is easily transplanted in November and December from its native wilds. The branches are also much used in Christmas decorations.

Ilex vomitoria, Yaupon Holly: Another beautiful native Holly is the Yaupon, Yupon, Cassine or Cassena Tea, *Ilex vomitoria.* When adorned with its masses of brilliant scarlet berries it reminds one somewhat of the Dahoon, but it is of an entirely different aspect, being of open straggling growth. In its haunts,—usually swampy places,—it attains a height of 8 to 25 feet, but it is much more frequently seen in bush form. The leaves are small, leathery, oblong, glossy evergreen. It is extremely common in northern Florida, and I have found it everywhere in swampy places in southern Georgia, Alabama and Louisiana, and very abundantly in southeastern Texas, where it is usually known under the name of Cassena Tea and Yupon.

"Cassine or Cassena is the name in the language of the Timucua Indians for an exhilarating beverage prepared from the leaves. The name seems to have been borrowed from the Muscogee word *assi,* (Leaves) modified by a prefix" (Alfred Rehder). Old settlers in Texas, as well as in Florida, told me that they used the leaves largely as a substitute for tea during the Civil War. When we consider that a closely allied species, *Ilex paraguariensis,* supplies the well known Paraguay Tea or Mate, so much used in South America, we can easily understand that the Yaupon, and very likely also the Dahoon, have similar properties. The berries appearing so abundantly along the branches, retain their brilliancy for several months and are much used for Christmas decorations. This fine shrub is an excellent object for gardens and parks and is easily transplanted. All the Hollies have inconspicuous greenish-white flowers of no ornamental value.

Ilex myrtifolia, Myrtle Holly: This Holly has small glabrous foliage less than an inch in length. It is a low straggling shrub or small tree with crooked

1. *Amherstia nobilis,* from Burma, of difficult culture.

2. *Cattleya* hybrid in tree, Naples, Florida.

3. *Ficus pumila* on building near Four Corners, Naples.

4. *Brunfelsia latifolia,* Yesterday, Today and Tomorrow.

5. *Lagerstroemia speciosa,* Queen's Crape Myrtle, from India.

6. *Lagerstroemia speciosa,* Queen's Crape Myrtle, from India.

7. *Roystonea oleracea,* Mountain-Cabbage, in Rio Botanic Garden, Rio de Janeiro, Brazil.

8. Palms in Botanical Garden, Rio de Janerio.

9. *Cycas circinalis*, branched specimen in national park, Sri Lanka (Ceylon).

10. *Spathodea campanulata*, African Tulip-Tree.

11. *Nicolaia elatior*, Torch-Ginger, from Southeast Asia.

12. *Dracaena goldieana*, a rare and tender plant from Africa.

13. *Jacaranda acutifolia*, "Glory of the Garden," from Peru.

14. *Jacaranda mimosifolia*, "Jacaranda," from Argentina.

15. *Camellia sasanqua*, "Susan Kuwa," in Japan.

branches. Systematic botanists consider it as a local form of the Dahoon, but it is quite distinct horticulturally. While in Pensacola in November, 1894, I saw fine groups of it in a garden studded with brilliant red berries.

Ilex glabra, Gallberry: Also known as Inkberry and Winterberry, the Gallberry is a common evergreen shrub in our flatwoods. It is usually only a few feet high, but now and then specimens 6 to 8 feet are found. The leaves are small, deep green, and the exceedingly bitter berries are deep black. It is easily transplanted and can be grown into a fine dense specimen 5 to 6 feet high.

Ilex verticillata, Winterberry: The Red Winterberry, also known as the Black Alder, is one of the most inspiring and delightful shrubs of our swamps, being particularly common in north Florida and in Georgia. It is the only deciduous native species. The glowing red berries, produced in the greatest abundance, imbue the swamps with a peculiar charm, particularly when seen among the native bamboos or canes and other evergreen plants. It grows well in gardens, but it requires a rich moist soil. Planted in groups near the water, it is especially effective. The brilliant berries remain on the branches until midwinter, and are rarely eaten by birds.

Quercus virginiana, Live Oak: When we speak of our native broad-leaved evergreens we must not assign an unimportant position to our picturesque Live Oak, *Quercus virginiana,* the monarch of our high pineland and hammock woods,—one of the most beautiful and magnificent trees in existence. It ranks in beauty, stateliness and massiveness right after *Magnolia grandiflora.* In the high pine woods, on the highway to Orlando, I have admired for many years the beautiful old picturesque Live Oaks, standing together in scattered groups among the tall Long-leaved Pines and densely festooned with garlands and streamers of Spanish-Moss. Some of these monarchs of the forest are hundreds of years old, and when destroyed and cut down by people who know nothing of beauty and grandeur, who only look for filthy lucre, nothing in the world can recall them; nothing can take their place.

It is true that young Live Oaks grow quite fast. When I planted my garden a number of young specimens came up. They were carefully preserved and they have attained a height of about 40 feet within 30 years. But only old veterans show their full beauty. Scarcely one of these old trees has a straight trunk. All are bent, curved, knotty, massive, covered with a whitish-gray deeply furrowed bark and all are beautifully picturesque. There is nothing like it in the plant world. These monuments of nature should be carefully preserved, and the new comer should build his cottage or bungalow among them. Not one of them should be cut down. These old picturesque aristo-crats are very much admired by the intelligent tourist. Young specimens grow in the way of other trees, and it must take hundreds of years before they assume their bent and massive form. No other tree is so free from dis-eases and is so rarely troubled by insects. Its beauty, its rapid growth and its healthy nature entitle the Live Oak to the first place as an avenue tree and as a shade tree along highways. It is the perfect tree for this purpose, being easily transplanted and easily kept in good condition, and I know of no bet-ter tree for cemeteries.

Quercus laurifolia, Laurel Oak [often called water oak]: This is a tree from 60 to occasionally 100 feet in height, with many slender branches forming a dense round-topped head. The leaves are linear-oblong, dark shining green above and from 2 to 6 inches long. They are evergreen here. This handsome Oak is much planted all over Florida as an avenue tree and is straight and dense; rapid growth adapts it admirably for city street planting. There is no better avenue tree as far as dense growth is concerned. In ornamental plantings and where space is limited it should not find a place, as it soon crowds out all other plants in its neighborhood. All along highways and in gardens the Live Oak should be preferred.

Quercus nigra, Water Oak: The Water Oak, *Q. nigra* (or *Quercus aqua-tica*), is another dense round-topped fast growing tree well adapted for av-enue planting and it is much used for this purpose, especially in north Flor-ida. Its deciduous leaves are from 1½ to 3 inches long, obovate, three-lobed at the apex, dull bluish-green above, paler beneath.

Quercus phelos, Willow Oak: This Oak comes up spontaneously where the Pines have been cut down. Is rather short-lived, but beautiful; young leaves beautifully pink and red. It sheds its old leaves late in December and the new ones appear in my garden early in March.

Prunus caroliniana, Laurel Cherry: In the Laurel Cherry or Evergreen Cherry, we have a very noble and beautiful native evergreen, an ideal street and avenue tree, a fast and dense grower of spreading form and provided with masses of medium-sized glossy foliage. The flowers appear in creamy-white racemes in February and March, followed the next winter by black cherry-like fruits which are abundantly scattered among the dense foliage. The cherries are not edible and the seeds contain a large amount of prussic acid. Though the Laurel Cherry thrives in rich, rather moist soil I can point with pride to a number of very beautiful specimen trees in my high pineland garden.

So distinctly handsome are these trees that they always attract the attention of the plant lover. I grow two very distinct varieties in my collection. One is of broad, dense, spreading growth, flowering late in January. The second variety is a dense upright grower, and has the shape of a Lombardy Poplar when young, and of more spreading form when older. It is a much denser, much more beautiful tree than the preceding and it flowers fully a month later. This tree is also known as the Wild Orange and Mock Orange,—both misnomers. It is easily raised from seed and is easily transplanted from the wild woods.

Prunus [*myrtifolia*], West Indian Laurel-Cherry: A still more beautiful species is this native of extreme south Florida and the West Indies, where it attains a height of from 40 to 50 feet and a spread of about 30 feet. Its leaves, flowers, form and fruit all combine to make it an ideal ornamental tree. Unfortunately it is not hardy here. I had fine small specimens 8 to 10 feet high, but they were cut down by the heavy freeze early in February, 1917. Though they sprouted again from the roots, they never assumed the beautiful form of previous years. I have planted a small specimen in a pot and sent it to my new place at Naples-on-the-Gulf, where it is doing well in rich moist soil. This tender species promises to be a very valuable shade and avenue tree in south Florida.

Persea borbonia, Red Bay: Another attractive evergreen of our woodlands is our Red Bay. Being closely related to the famous European Laurel of ancient poetical lore, its leaves are much like Laurel leaves and almost fully as aromatic. I have quite a number of dense tall specimens on my place which I raised from seeds gathered by me in the grounds of the Ponce de Leon Hotel in St. Augustine in November, 1895. One specimen has attained a height of 45 feet with a dense spreading crown and provided with branches to the ground. The bluish-black, aromatic, cherry-like fruits are relished by many birds, especially mocking-birds; in fact the birds have spread the seeds all over the grounds and thrifty young plants are coming up everywhere. This is also known as the Laurel Bay, Tisswood and Red Bay.

There are a few other species closely allied to the former and well worthy of a place in the garden, namely the Florida Bay or Swamp Bay, *Persea palustris*], a fine densely evergreen tree, and the Scrub Bay, *Persea humilis,* a common shrub in all our scrub lands. It is a handsome evergreen and its leaves are used in the same way as those of the European Laurel for seasoning. It is difficult to transplant, but easily raised from seeds.

Ocotea [coriacea], Lancewood: This is another beautiful evergreen of the Laurel family, being found from Ormond to extreme south Florida and assuming, in good soil, a height of over 30 feet. Its dense growth, its beautiful, strangely fragrant Laurel-like leaves and the dark blue smooth fruits, which are abundantly produced by large plants, combine to make this a most conspicuous evergreen tree. It grows well in gardens, but requires a good rich soil. In ordinary winters it proves hardy as far north as Sanford. Near Miami it is very conspicuous among the many beautiful tropical evergreens.

Osmanthus americana, American Olive: The American Olive or Devil Wood, is one of our most elegant broad-leaved evergreens, being common in all dry hammocks and even in scrub lands. It is easily transplanted during the late fall and early winter months and it thrives to perfection on high and dry pineland, needing very little care and attention. The leaves are large,—4 to 5 inches long,—broad, lanceolate-elliptic, of a delightfully green color, smooth and shiny. The flowers appear early in January in axillary clusters. They are small of a greenish-white color, and exhale a rather strong spicy odor. The fruit ripens in November. It is black in color with a bluish bloom, and looks in shape and size precisely like a true Olive, to which it is closely related, being however, inedible on account of its bitter taste.

In form and growth, in foliage, flower and fruit our Wild Olive is an extremely ornamental bush tree. Isolated specimens in my garden are very dense and symmetrical. They were planted twenty-five years ago and have assumed a height of from 25 to 30 feet with a crown diameter of 20 feet and are provided with limbs from the ground to the top. Like so many of our choice evergreens, the American Olive should never be planted in crowded positions. Such specimens invariably lose their individuality. Singly or in groups,—each specimen allotted a space of at least twenty-five feet in diameter—it looks best, being much more effective than many of the expensive exotics. Among our native trees it must be classed in the first rank with our *Magnolia grandiflora*, the Loblolly Bay, the Sweet Bay, the American Holly, the Laurel Cherry and the Live Oak. For landscape work it is indispensable. The wood of this tree is fine-grained, hard, and when dry, very difficult to split. Hence its name Devil Wood.

Myrica cerifera, Bayberry or Wax Myrtle: What a fine and distinct tree or large bushy shrub is our native Bayberry or Wax Myrtle. The large globose masses, all springing from one common rootstalk, 20 to 30 feet in diameter and 20 feet high, from very conspicuous and beautiful objects in our landscapes. Usually five or six strong tree-like shoots form a cluster, provided with dense branches and foliage to the ground. It forms a most delightful contrast to the deep glossy foliage of the Magnolia, to the lighter green of the Sweet Bay with its silvery color of the underside of the leaves. The green of the Wax Myrtle is very distinct and very different, having a slight, but very conspicuous brown tint in its green color. In landscape work this splendid bushy tree is indispensable, being one of the most ornamental, and of the most characteristic form and growth. Indeed, I know of no other tree, native or exotic, that grows in the same effective way. The dense evergreen, serrated small foliage exhales a very spicy and extremely pleasant odor when we touch the branches in passing by. This aromatic fragrance is quite strong after each rain and during the night. On account of this perfume alone I would not like to miss the Bayberry in my Garden. I have largely planted it, and the dense bushy masses contribute their share to the beauty of the place.

The male and female flowers are borne on different plants. That is, one individual bears only male catkins, the other only female ones. There appear independent catkins in March that are of yellowish green color. Swarms of bees and other insects invade the flowering Wax Myrtles in search of pollen. In fact, this species is a most valuable bee plant. In winter the female specimens are covered with masses of small black berries (or rather nutlets), appearing white on account of their silvery bloom. These nutlets are surrounded by a thin powdery wax-like substance which in bygone days, was largely used in the manufacture of candles, particularly for churches, on account of their fine incense-like odor. Birds are very fond of these berries. My specimens swarm with numerous northern immigrants, especially myrtle warblers, coming from high northern latitudes. In fact, these interesting birds, which usually appear in large swarm just before a cold wave sets in, derived their common name from their fondness for Wax Myrtle berries.

The most beautiful specimens of Wax Myrtles are always found on low moist lands, but it grows well on high pineland after it has been well established. Unfortunately this picturesque and handsome evergreen is only short-lived. My old specimens, having been planted in 1894, are now dying out, though numerous young shoots come up in dense masses. From the tendency of forming several strong trunks close together and curving or leaning to the outside it soon spreads over quite a large space. For this reason it needs considerable room in order to develop its unique beauty. On account of this dense and characteristic growth it is invaluable for parks and large gardens, as landscape effects can thus be obtained which are otherwise impossible. Tree or shrub assuming a maximum height of about 30 feet, has straight stems.

Chionanthus virginica, Finger Tree or Old Man's Beard: Strictly speaking, the Finger Tree, Old Man's Beard, White lady or Sunflower Tree, is deciduous, but in my garden it is almost evergreen. It sheds its large, glossy, leathery leaves just before flowering. When in full bloom early in March, just before the new foliage appears, it forms a magnificent sight—a sheet of pure white color from top to bottom, looking enchantingly beautiful on our glorious moonlight nights. This singular shrub or small tree is so showy when in flower that I cannot recommend it too highly. It grows abundantly in all our high hammocks as an underbrush, usually from 6 to 8 feet in height, but occasionally assuming the size of a small tree from 15 to 32 feet in height. My specimens were gathered in one of the hammocks nearby. In our woodland the Finger Tree often looks stunted and scraggy, but where sufficient space is given to it and when well cared for it soon forms dense well-shaped specimens, provided with branches from the ground to the top. Not being particular in its requirements, it grows to perfection on high pineland. Late in August the bluish-black juicy fruits are abundantly provided. They are as large as an olive and quite ornamental. The plants are easily transplanted when dormant.

Illicium floridanum, Anise Tree or Star Anise: Among the low growing evergreens I have had the native Anise Tree or Star Anise in two species, *Illicium floridanum* and *I. parviflorum* in my garden. Both require moist soil. They did not thrive on high pineland. Both are very handsome and interesting. The first one grows about 10 feet high and has large beautiful foliage. The flowers are nodding and brownish-purple. I found it along the Wekiwa in marshy soil. The other species grows from 3 to 6 feet high and its flowers are yellowish.

Magnolia virginiana (M. glauca), Sweet Bay, White Bay, Beaver Tree: Among our native trees this is a gem. It is one of our most abundant evergreen trees, usually growing together in dense masses in all our bayheads and swamps. The pretty evergreen foliage is bright green above and silvery-white beneath. It is not as large nor as thick and leathery as in *Magnolia grandiflora,* being rather thin and papery. A large mass of these Sweet Bays in the foreground of a swamp look often like a sheet of white flowers when the wind or a stray breeze blows against the foliage, so that the silvery-white underside is turned upward. The individual trees in such groups are rather tall and slender, and the crowns are narrow, the branches only being crowded together in the uppermost part of the trees.

The pure white cup-shaped flowers are produced abundantly among the foliage from March to September. They are about 5 inches in diameter. In places where these Magnolias are abundant the air is pervaded with the delicious perfume, one of the most charming odors a bountiful Providence has created for our delight and pleasure. It is one of the most exquisite perfumes in existence, reminding one strongly of that of the tea rose, but having an individuality entirely its own. Particularly after one of our summer rains this sweet fragrance, exhaled by many thousands of dainty-white chalices, is wafted over wide areas and we also inhale it during our cool and lovely evenings. So strong and so delicious is this odor that we never forget it after having become familiar with its charm.

This jewel among our native evergreen trees, far superior to most all of the exotic species and one of the choicest gifts that nature has bestowed upon us, is never found in our Florida gardens. With the exception of my own, I have never seen it as a garden ornament. Here in my garden at Naples I found three stunted specimens on the edge of my Cypress hammock. They had been cut down repeatedly by land clearers, and forest fires had injured them quite often. I immediately took care of them, removed all the weeds in their neighborhood and kept down the encroaching climbers and ambitious coarse shrubs. This was about six years ago. One of the specimens is at present 25 feet high and at least 20 feet in diameter, very dense, and provided with branches from the ground up. It is a magnificent specimen, an ideal of thrift and beauty and is almost always in bloom from March to September. The air is constantly pervaded with the sweet perfume all through the rainy season.

With a little attention and care it grows well even on higher ground, though it prefers the moister soil of the hammocks and flatwoods. In good soil they soon develop into fine broad trees,—much taller, much denser, much more ornamental than in its native wilds. If well cared for and well watered and fertilized it also forms ideal specimens on high pineland. It is easily raised from seeds, which should be sown immediately after the cells in the small cones have burst and reveal the red, oily, aromatic seeds. It is transplanted from its native haunts with some difficulty. Only young or small specimens should be dug up. These have to be cut back to a short stump, and this stump must be planted, preferably in November and December, in rich moist soil. Should the soil have a tendency to dry out, watering has to be resorted to. In the succeeding spring the stump will push up strong sprouts which will form the future specimen. The Sweet Bay is a common tree from Boston, Mass., to Miami and Naples, Fla.

[*Juniperus virginiana*], Pencil Cedar: This is the celebrated Florida Cedar, a Pencil Cedar, so common and so beautiful in its native wilds and in the parks and gardens of north and central Florida. We in this incomparably beautiful state do not have an opportunity to enjoy the grace and loveliness of the Spruces and Firs. They adorn northern woodlands and landscapes, and serve as Christmas trees in many households. Here in Florida our most inspiring Pencil Cedar very properly takes their places. A dense, well-shaped specimen is a strikingly beautiful tree, being provided with leafy branches from the ground up to the apex, and showing a fine pyramidal form.

While at St. Augustine, in November, 1895, I came upon a whole avenue of Florida Cedars, with dense dark green crowns, but the lower branches had been cut off. In the grounds of the Ponce de Leon Hotel I found specimens fully 40 to 50 feet high, with dense rounded crowns and branched to the ground. Many of them carried a most abundant crop of the small black berries, covered with a fine glaucous hue. I collected a lot of these berries and succeeded in raising hundreds of fine young plants. These Florida Cedars form at present a most striking feature at Palm Cottage Gardens. They were planted in a row along the main entrance, and some along the highway—at the time when I set them out not even a forest path, and now a most substantial concrete road. They are at least 30 feet high and furnished with dense branches down to the ground. I also grew a number of Red Cedars, so common in many rather dry places in Wisconsin (Elkhart Lake), and elsewhere, but they cannot compare in beauty with our Florida species.

Seedlings of Florida Cedars come up all around my place, and in some instances several miles away. The berries ripen in winter, and many birds are very fond of them, particularly cedar birds, these rovers among our avifauna. The seeds are disseminated by them in their excrements and germinate surely and quickly. In the neighboring orange groves they come up by the thousands and in a neglected grove that had not been worked for three or four years many people at Christmas time came and obtained very beautiful dense Cedars, for Christmas Trees.

The growth of this Cedar or Juniper, is very dense, very symmetrical and gracefully pyramidal. It is one of the most elegant coniferous trees I know. The color of the leaves is a deep pleasing steel-green, and the glaucous berries, growing often in dense masses along the branches, add an interesting feature. As these Cedars can bear the pruning shears very well, they can be trimmed various ways to suit the taste. It is a fine plant—one of the best for cemetery ornament. In the North these branches are largely sold for Christmas decoration.

"Some years ago," says Dr. John Gifford, "forests of Cedar and Live Oak were reserved in Florida and elsewhere on the coast to insure a future supply of these valuable timbers for our navy. These were, of course, abandoned when steel replaced wood for this purpose. These, however were our first national reserves." For many years this Cedar was the main source of the pencil manufacturer; hence the name Pencil Cedar. The well-known firm of the Faber's at Nurnberg, Germany, had for many years a special post stationed at Cedar Keys and elsewhere to buy up Cedar logs. One of the most valuable timber trees, this Cedar should be largely used in reforestation. There are thousands of acres of rich moist land in central and north Florida that are available for this purpose. The very light and extremely durable wood is intensely and pleasantly fragrant, insect-proof and easily worked. Our cedar chests are largely made of the wood of this species.

Naturally this Cedar grows most luxuriantly in moist low places in the northern and central parts of the state. I have never seen it in its wild state south of Bartow. It grows most rapidly in its moist native haunts, but it does very well, indeed, in high pineland, as my specimens at Gotha show. I am unable to fully establish it at Naples. It thrives, but its growth is slow, open and rather unsatisfactory. While quite young and small it is easily transplanted from the field or swamp if some care is taken to lift it as a ball of soil. Its use for wind-breaks is by no means inconsiderable. It makes a most splendid and effective wind-break.

Tetrazygia bicolor, Tetrazygia: A very beautifully flowering small tree or vigorous shrub—one of the jewels of our native flora—occurring only in the flatwoods of the Homestead region in the southern part of Dade County. It is a member of the Melastomaceae or Meadow Beauty family and covers extensive areas in the flatwoods country, being loaded in winter and spring with its great clusters of white or pinkish flowers, much in the way of a white Rhododendron. I never have seen the species in flower, but I have admired the handsome and quite dense bushes along the highway toward Royal Palm State Park. There is an excellent illustration of it made from a photograph taken by Dr. J. K. Small in Simpson's book, *In Lower Florida Wilds.* Simpson remarks: "There are a number of plants found in the Homestead country in Dade County not known from any other part of the United States. Among them is the beautiful *Tetrazygia bicolor,* a shrub of the fire-swept pine-woods, but becoming a small tree in the protected hammock. It belongs to the Melastomaceae, a family which has its metropolis in the American tropics, but is feebly represented with us. When covered with its great heads of white blossoms it is one of the finest ornamentals."

It is a very handsome shrub even when not in flower, being densely clothed with characteristic thrice-veined green leaves, lanceolate to oblong-lanceolate in form, and silvery beneath. The purplish-black berries are abundantly produced.

The best descriptive account comes from my friend, Mr. Richard F. Deckert, and is found in a letter to the writer, dated September 3, 1923: "In the Homestead region, along the Ingraham Highway, a charming shrub is quite plentiful. It is *Tetrazygia bicolor.* I took up several small plants, cut them back severely, and potted them at home. They are now beginning to send out new leaves. The flowers are in upright spikes or panicles. The individual flowers are quite small, white with a delicate rosy sheen. A large bush of the Tetrazygia in bloom is a sight not easily forgotten." It never is found wild in acid or sour soils, and I could not induce it to grow in my Naples garden, but it did quite well at Palm Cottage Gardens, where it, however, succumbed to the heavy freeze early in February, 1917.

The Tetrazygia is not in the trade, but Dr. David Fairchild was so impressed with its unique beauty that he requested Mr. Chas. Mosier, another kindred spirit of the lower east coast, to collect a lot of seeds for the Bureau of Plant Industry. I think several hundred young plants were distributed all over the United States a few years ago.

"I scarcely find anything to add to the above account of this beautiful shrub," writes Mr. R. F. Deckert, except that I have found it in bloom during April and May, but it may begin to bloom much earlier. The berries are ripe in July, but sometimes remain on the shrub for months. They germinate quite readily in a mixture of coarse sand and a little clay-marl. In setting out plants put them in pineland soil, as this is usually well drained, and keep them watered until established. As the region where this Tetrazygia grows wild has very little soil—only small pockets of a red clay among the limestone rock—it would be advisable perhaps to mix a little lime in some form with your apparently acid soil."

Rapanea guianensis, Myrsine floridana [= *M. punctata* or *cubana*], Rapanea, Myrsine: "God has created all men equal." This is what we often hear in these days of so-called democracy. A childish illusion! God has created all men different, different in their blood, their wishes and ideals, their characteristics, their gifts—different in a thousand ways. So it is in all nature. Among trees and among plants in general there are, as among humans, "high and low-brows"—patricians and plebeians; there is a nobility and a cultured and dignified middle class; there are aristocrats and proletarians. These thoughts came to me when I strolled through my garden, coming in contact not only with such trees and plants that elated me and delighted my heart,—the plant nobility—but also with nettles and sandspurs, with poison ivy and other riff-raff of the plant world.

When I cleared my land here I found near the edge of the Cypress hammock a most lovely and distinct, dense, broad-leaved evergreen tree, a picture of health and beauty and one of the jewels of my wild garden—a real aristocrat. In order not to have it crowded out by its numerous ranker and coarser neighbors I made a clearing around it, but constant watchfulness on my part is necessary. The plebeians and the proletarians of the plant world are constantly encroaching upon it. The tree was new to me. I saw at once that it was something very distinct, very different from all other trees I knew, being very elegant and of a very dense and graceful growth.

Last summer (1924) I had the honor of a visit from Dr. J. K. Small, the great authority on our southern plants, and I showed him my treasure. He at once recognized it as [*Myrsine punctata* or *cubana*], the Myrsine, a strictly tropical dense evergreen tree, with laurel-like shining green leaves and rather curious and insignificant flowers. There is another larger and still finer specimen on the east side of the hammock, being 20 feet high and almost as much in diameter. It is not an abundant species, being limited to rich moist hammock. Near Ormond and Daytona in Volusia County, it occurs with the Florida-Myrtle, and the Marlberry. This is its northern limit. On the hammock islands in the Everglades and on the Florida Keys and thence southward to Guiana and Brazil, it has been traced as an indigenous tree. The most peculiar flower clusters, very insignificant, are scattered along the branches; berries small, black and ripening in winter, My plants grow wild. I have never made an attempt to transplant even some of the small ones that I found for fear that I might lose them. It is a first-class ornamental.

Sapindus saponaria, Soapberry: An interesting, but not a particularly handsome tree. I have had it for years in my garden at Gotha, and have received lots of ripe berries from a lady plant lover at Longwood, Fla. With me it is an evergreen. It refuses to grow on high pineland and demands for its well-being a rich moist soil. It is a native of extreme south Florida, and perhaps also of other tropical countries. Leaves are pinnate. In rubbing the seed in water they make a foam like soap, and in some countries are used like soap. The hard seed are also said to be used for making rosaries, necklaces, bracelets, etc. *Sapindus marginatus* is of botanical and economic interest only, but all would make good and interesting highway trees.

[*Mastichodendron foetidissimum*], Mastic: A beautiful evergreen tree, becoming about 80 feet high, with thin, leathery leaves, oblong to oval in form and quite smooth on the upper surface. Dr. John Gifford, one of the best authorities on forest trees and forestry we have in this country, says: "Valuable forest tree of southern Florida. Grows to be large and is quite common, shedding an abundance of yellow fruits which are edible in case one likes the flavor. Mastic would probably make a satisfactory shade tree."

Swietenia mahagani, Madeira, Mahogany: On account of its fine wood, perhaps, the most valuable tree we have in south Florida. It is the king of all woods, according to Dr. Gifford. Common on the keys and parts of the southern mainland. "Something ought to be done to encourage the perpetuation of this, our choicest native hardwood in the only part of the mainland of the United States where it can possibly grow" (Gifford). An old gnarly, broad and picturesque Mahogany Tree reminds one somewhat of a veteran Live Oak. Its crown is rather open, its side limbs sometimes immense and its foliage not very dense. In good rich soil it makes a fast growth, but the wood is inferior. The best wood is obtained from trees in drier soils and when the tree made only a slow growth. It is an interesting tree for parks and pleasure grounds and should be planted for educational purposes along our tropical highways. There is a fine large tree, close to a Cannonball Tree, in the grounds of the Royal Palm Hotel at Fort Myers. It grows easily from seed, and grows well under cultivation. The Madeira Hammock in south Florida is named for the abundance of the Mahogany growing there. Dr. John Gifford has a long and interesting essay on this tree in his little book *The Everglades of South Florida.*

Chiococca alba, Tropical Snowberry: I know this only as a spreading climber common in the hammocks of south Florida. It deserves attention in gardens for its exquisite bell-shaped flowers, which are honey-scented and appear during summer in great abundance. It has always been one of my special favorites. One of our foremost tropical gardeners, Mr. T. B. Donnelly, of Palm Beach, speaks of it thus: "This plant when growing in the jungle is a climber on trees, but when in the open and cut back a couple of times it makes a nice shrub that is covered with white berries, which remain on it all winter." It adds a certain atmosphere, so to speak, to our landscape gardens and parks where it should not be missed.

Chrysobalanus icaco, Coco Plum: This beautiful dense evergreen tree [shrub], sometimes about 30 feet high, is mostly a spreading large shrub near the coast. There is a fine large specimen in the grounds of the Naples Hotel which is about 10 feet high and 15 feet through and very dense. I have grown a large number of seedlings from this plant. It fruits in July and the oblong plums are of a dingy-white color. Children are very fond of them. It is excellent for parks and large gardens, where it can get enough room to spread.

Chrysobalanus icaco var. *pellocarpus* is similar, but the fruit is smaller, sweeter and of a purplish color. I have seen this variety only in hammocks on the east coast.

Chrysophyllum oliviforme, Satinleaf: One of our most beautiful evergreen tropical native trees, belonging to the Sapodilla family and growing abundantly on all the shell mounds from Estero to Chokoloskee and along the eastern coast also, being found scarcely less abundantly in the hammocks of the Everglades keys and the Florida Keys. It attains a height of about 30 feet and is very dense and of the finest form, when sufficient room is available for its development. It only grows in very well-drained and often quite dry soils, as the specimens on the shell mounds show.

I found my first Satinleaf Trees on a large and fine shell mound on the beach nearby, and I was struck with their beauty and unique dignity. They grew in company of Marlberry bushes, large specimens of Gumbo Limbo, Live Oak, Papayas and other forms of minor value. There were fine dense trees about 25 feet high, and many specimens in bush form. The twigs are pubescent. Leaves are oblong, elliptic-oval, quite large, deep glossy green above and satiny or velvety coppery-brown beneath. The fine form of these leaves and their exquisite color, especially the coppery red underneath, is so conspicuous that even the general observer cannot help but be delighted and surprised.

I have collected quite a number of smaller specimens on this shell mound and transplanted them to my garden, but none of them grew. Unfortunately this large and beautifully formed mound—a monument of a race of people that left many centuries before our money-mad destructive generation— has been almost entirely destroyed by the road builder who hauled the shells, bones and skeletons, of humans included, and many remnants of pottery, to the highway. There is no earthly excuse for such vandalism. Another highly interesting shell mound near Gordon's Pass fared the same fate. This also was a repository of the rarest and most beautiful plants.

The dark purple fruit appears at various seasons. They are small and of no economic use. This most beautiful and distinct tree should find room in every good garden. It can be easily raised from seed.

Citharexylum [*spinosum*], Fiddlewood: A member of a most interesting and important tropical American genus of trees belonging to the Verbena family. The flowers of many of the species are very fragrant and the abundantly provided, mostly red berries are much relished by many of the small birds. There are a few most exquisite specimens of a species of Fiddlewood in some of the streets of Punta Gorda. These trees are very dense, of fine form and highly ornamental, and are wonderfully adapted for avenue planting.

I never had an opportunity to see our native species. It appears to be rare and little known. Simpson in his excellent volume *Ornamental Gardening in Florida*, does not mention it. Dr. J. K. Small, in his *Florida Trees*, says: "The Fiddlewood grows in hammocks and pineland along the southern half of the eastern coast of Florida, on the Everglade Keys and the Florida Keys. The light red heart-wood is close-grained, heavy and very hard." I have two tropical species in my Naples garden—very fine and distinct—and the native Fiddlewood may also turn out to be valuable as an ornamental. A spe-

cies in British Guiana, closely allied to our native form, "is commonly cultivated for its deliciously scented white flowers, the perfume of which is
diffused for long distances in the evening" (Rodway).

Coccoloba uvifera, Sea Grape, Shore Grape: The Sea Grape and the Geiger
Tree are my special favorites among our native tropical Florida trees. Both
occupy a first rank as garden ornaments on account of their distinct and
singular beauty. The Sea Grape is particularly abundant along the beach
near my present home at Naples. Seen in the very poor sea sand, often growing together gregariously, it is mostly a broad and large-leaved stunted and
scraggy bush. Seen, however, in protected localities, in richer soil and where
it has room to grow and spread it is one of the most exquisite, dense and
charming large-leaved evergreens among all our trees. There is an excellent
large Sea Grape in the hotel grounds at Punta Gorda, near the railroad station. It is about 30 or 35 feet high, very dense, provided with masses of its
large characteristic leaves and covered in October with its grape-like clusters
of deep purplish fruits. In March, or even earlier, the not very conspicuous
racemes of small creamy-white flowers appear.

It is the large and distinct foliage which attracts the attention of even
those who show little interest in plant life, because of the form of these
leaves, being considerably broader than they are long. A leaf before me is 6
inches long and 9 inches broad, notched where the petiole joins the blade,
and slightly less long in the center, where it measures 5 inches. The form is
oblong round. In texture these leaves are very thick and leathery. Their color
is a fine, rather deep and glossy green and the midrib and veins are bright
and very conspicuously red. This red color is even more pronounced on the
underside of the leaves which is of a somewhat lighter green. Before falling,
the entire blade is suffused with various tints of bright red. In shady places
there is often not a trace of the bright red ribs visible. It needs full sunshine
to show its bright colors.

The fallen leaves lie flat on the ground and appear in substance and color
like brown tanned leather. The young leaves also show a most lovely red in
various shades, which adds largely to the beauty of the tree. It is this fine,
large beautifully colored and unique foliage which constitutes the real
charm of the Sea Grape. The flowers are of minor importance, appearing
early in spring—here as early as February. Individually they are small and of
a creamy white color. The fruit appears in grape-like clusters and is of a deep

purplish black color, sub-acid, juicy and is much used in making a well-flavored jelly. On account of the considerably large seed there is not much flesh present. A good and peculiarly flavored wine can also be made from these grapes, which ripen in abundance during the month of October. Wild turkeys are very fond of these fruits, but they form for a long time the main diet of the still very numerous raccoons, from which reason it is often called by the trappers of these mammals the Raccoon Grape.

I have quite a number of small seedlings growing in my garden, all raised from fruits which I collected on the beach. These small specimens grow very thriftily and assume a fine form, very different from the stunted, scraggy bushes near the shore of the gulf. Large trees and shrubs of it in gardens and pleasure grounds, having sufficient room to develop, are indescribably beautiful at all times of the year. Good cultivation and now and then a little fertilizer soon induce the plants to grow vigorously into most effective, dense and beautiful specimens. How far inland from seashore this tree will succeed I am not prepared to say. The Sea Grape is a strictly tropical tree, being found in Florida from Punta Gorda and Palm Beach southward, and also in the West Indies.

Coccoloba [*diversifolia*], Pigeon Plum: This is also a most charming evergreen native tropical tree, though quite different from the former. Its leaves are not as leathery, not as large and not marked with red. It is quite common in the hammocks around Miami, where I gathered many fruits during November. These fruits do not appear in grape-like clusters. Those I picked were found spread over the tree on single short stems. They are round-oval, of a deep purplish color and very juicy and quite sweet. In size they reminded me of large cherries. They are relished by many birds, but, as far as I could learn, are not used in the way Sea Grapes are used. The leaves are not as conspicuously beautiful as those of the Sea Grape, but they are also quite large, oblong to ovate, longer than wide and of a beautiful deep green color. This species grows more upright and dense, being not found near the seashore. In the dense hammocks, where it is usually found, it is well protected from the sun as well as from stormy winds. It is a beautiful compact tree where it has not to combat with encroaching neighbors. The finest specimens I found in the hammocks along Snapper Creek (Dade County), but I have not seen taller specimens than 15 feet. I have received fruits from some of the hammocks in the Big Cypress Swamp not far from here.

I never have seen the Pigeon Plum under cultivation, though its rare beauty entitles it to a place in every good garden and park. It is like the Sea Grape, well adapted for tropical landscape gardens and for city parks, where it would make a distinct show if planted in groups or in the foreground of large trees in parks. A well developed tree would also make a fine and distinct ornament on any lawn.

Jacquinia keyensis, Joe-wood: One beautiful morning, early in April, 1916, I was trolling along the eastern beach of beautiful Pine Island. After having passed a rather large and conspicuous shell mound I came in sight of some dense thickets of evergreen shrubs, some of them entirely new to me. Particularly one of them attracted my immediate attention—a most densely-leaved species, almost Pittosporum-like in appearance, with fine, thick, glossy deep green leaves. The leaves are cuneate-spatulate, or oblong-ovate. It made a most charming picture on this beautiful seashore. Its form was most beautiful. Its dense shining masses of leaves enchanted me. But I had not yet seen its flowers. I approached more closely, and now I had a new surprise. I found numerous corymbs of pure white blossoms, intensely and deliciously fragrant—so fragrant that the air all around seemed to be saturated with this perfume.

I was highly elated and deeply moved about all this beauty and fragrance before me and the impression never faded from memory. In fact, this extremely beautiful and fragrant shrub has ever since haunted me in my dreams. I wanted it in my garden where I always would have the pleasure to admire it. I have tried to raise it from seed, but failed for some reason or other, and plants were nowhere available. It seems to be strictly littoral, only growing in rather dry soil in the reach of the salt spray. These bushes I had found here were pictures of perfect health. Could they be transplanted and coaxed to grow in our south Florida gardens they would form enchanting ornaments. Though I only saw it in bush form, 5 to 6 feet in height, it is not infrequently found as a small tree, 12 to 15 feet tall. It promises to be of great importance as a garden shrub or tree along our tropical beaches, where the ordinary ornamental trees do not succeed on account of the salt spray.

I have been frequently asked by beach-lot owners for lists of littoral trees and for exceptionally fine and dense species that could be best used as ornamentals for seaside planting, and I do not hesitate to point to our native *Jacquinia* as one of the densest in foliage, and one of the most fragrant when in flower. It would create a wonderful effect if planted in groups and masses along the very front of such lots. The beautiful Sea Grape, also a littoral tree, can be used to advantage in combination with it. As the *Jacquinia* flowers and fruits more or less all the year round, it is particularly adapted for all places where high-class ornamentals are appreciated.

The Joe-wood is an inhabitant of our Florida tropical west coast, being very abundant along the shores of all the islands from Pine Island southward to the Florida Keys. It only grows in well-drained soil, even in pure white sea-sand. Undoubtedly it will respond to good cultivation in the same way as the Sea Grape does. It belongs to the Theophrastaceae (Joe-wood family), a most interesting and valuable group of tropical plants, trees and shrubs.

Calycanthus floridus (*Butneria florida*), Strawberry Shrub, Sweet-Scented Shrub: A very popular shrub in the lower South, especially in the Carolinas, Georgia, Alabama and North Florida. The deciduous leaves are quite aromatic. They are from 2 to 3 inches long. The flowers appear in April. Their color is a rather deep brownish-purple and they are intensely and delicately fragrant. This fine native shrub is usually 4 or 5 feet high, but sometimes specimens are met that reach a height of 8 feet. We usually find it in woodlands, along the banks of streams and brooks. It is often taken from the woodlands by southern plant lovers and planted in their gardens, where it grows without much care, though it prefers a shady spot.

I have had specimens in my garden at Gotha where they flowered in profusion for quite a number of years. On account of its strong perfume alone it should be found in every garden of the South. There are three additional species, but none can vie in beauty and fragrance with the one just described. It is also known as Carolina Allspice.

Heaths and Huckleberries

The beautiful and very interesting Heath family (Ericaceae), to which the charming Indian *Azalea* and the *Rhododendron* belong, is represented in Florida by a large number of fine species. These plants need a special soil free from lime and constantly moist, but not marshy. Along rivers and brooks, woodland streams and in hammocks around our lakes they are— almost all of them—perfectly at home. A few grow in our piney woods, among them the very dainty evergreen Upland Huckleberry, with very small glossy greenish red leaves and rosy-red bell-shaped flowers.

The Heath family (Ericaceae) contains many of the most showy and floriferous members, such as the Azaleas, Rhododendrons, the true Heaths or Heather (*Erica*), the Mountain Laurels (*Kalmia*) and others. In Florida it is represented by a large number of species, most all of them unusually attractive.

Befaria racemosa [Tarflower]: This is the pride of our flatwoods in May, often flowering abundantly even as early as April. It is one of the showiest shrubs we have, growing from 3 to 6 feet high and producing its pinkish-white clammy flowers in dense terminal corymbs. I never have seen it under cultivation, but I believe that it will grow well with native Azaleas and Andromedas in our gardens.

Azalea nudiflora [= *Rhododendron periclymenoides*], the Wild Honeysuckle of the early settlers can be easily transplanted from the moist borders of our hammock woods into our gardens. It requires acid soil free from lime, as do all the members of the Heath family. The flowers appear in terminal clusters and are of a white color, often suffused slightly with pink. It blooms early in spring and is very attractive. *Azalea viscosa* [= *Rhododendron viscosa*], the Swamp Honeysuckle, flowers in July and August. It is similar to the former. I only found it in Cypress swamps, where it assumes a height of from 3 to 9 feet. In the wet hammocks of Lake County a third species,—*Azalea serrulata* [= *Rhodendron viscosum* var. *serrulatum*]—is found. This species grows from 6 to 12 feet high and has also showy white flowers. The hardy deciduous Azaleas are very aristocratic and most beautiful garden ornaments in many a northern locality. Our native species should be used by the hybridizer, so that new and vivid colored forms are produced.

Leucothoe axillaris [Dog Hobble]: This is a handsome evergreen shrub, from 3 to 6 feet in height, and covered in spring with waxy-white bell-like dainty flower racemes. It grows in damp woods and swamps. *Leucothoe* [*populifolia*], also a fine evergreen shrub, is a little larger, and specimens 10 to 12 feet high are sometimes met with, but it flowers profusely in a much smaller state. Flowers appear in March and April. They are pure white. Also found in marshy thickets and woodlands. *Leucothoe racemosa* grows beautifully in my Gotha garden in fairly moist soil, though it is only found wild in moist marshy localities, usually on the edge of woods and thickets. The waxy-white flowers have a delicate odor of honey. An excellent plant for cut flowers. Blooms about Easter time.

[*Lyonia lucida*]: It grows abundantly along the small brooks and sandy bogs near my Gotha home. It is a dense and very beautiful evergreen shrub, and it is almost always in flower. The flowers are white and pink and sometimes bright red, and seem to appear all the year round, but most abundantly in spring. I have transplanted quite a number of fine bushy specimens from their original habitat and all grew well. It grows about 2 to 6 feet high. People around Gotha call it the "Lily-of-the-Valley Shrub," as the waxy blossoms remind one in form of those of that plant.

[*Lyonia ferruginea*]: A most beautiful and attractive dense evergreen shrub or small tree, being found in great abundance in our dry scrub lands, and imbuing them with a most dreamy charm, when in full bloom in April, or even in March. The small leaves are crowded densely along the branches. They are deep emerald green above, and rusty brown beneath. Usually the plant forms a small slender tree, with fissured bark, 12 to 15 feet high. The flowers are small, bell-shaped, waxy white and exhale a delicious honey odor. My attempts to transplant them into my garden were a failure, but there is no doubt that they can be moved if small plants are chosen. It would make a fine garden ornament if set out in groups.

[*Lyonia ligustrina*]: This is another charming species, usually known as *Andromeda paniculata* var. *foliosiflora*. Growing mostly in dense bush form, 5 to 6 feet high, we now and then find specimens 10 to 12 feet tall. It is not evergreen, but we cannot call it strictly deciduous as I always have found some leaves on its branches. It blooms in April and May near Gotha. The flowers remind one of those of the Huckleberry, being small, white, waxy and are hidden more or less among the foliage. The plant usually grows in a dense clump and can easily be taken up and transplanted in the garden. A moist spot is essential as it always grows near creeks and swamps in the low pinelands. [*Lyonia ligustrina*] is a handsome, densely branching shrub, 3 to 10 feet high, with more or less dense pubescent foliage. It also grows in swamps but I never found it near Gotha.

The Huckleberry family (Vacciniaceae) formerly included among the Heaths, and very closely allied to them, is well represented by many fine species in Florida. Besides their ornamental value, many of them supply very delicious fruits and are planted largely for this purpose. One of them, a dense, dainty, dwarf species, forming very fine clumps and covered with thick, evergreen, glossy foliage, is everywhere common in high pinewoods. It is as abundant on my place at Gotha as it is here in Naples. The berries ripen in May. They are dry and of shining black color; often used by the natives for preserves. This is of the true huckleberries. We have the following species here: *Gaylussacia dumosa, G. hirtella, G. nana, G. tomentosa, G. frondosa* (known as the Tangleberry, Dangleberry or Blue Tangle). All are lovely little plants, though the last named species attains a height of from 3 to 10 feet, and is spread by underground stems.

In northern Florida, in the hammock woods around Jacksonville, I often was delighted to see the Sparkleberry or Farkleberry, *Vaccinium arboreum,* a much branched shrub or small tree, with campanulate white or purplish flowers. The black berries are abundantly produced, but they are scarcely edible. I have seen very beautiful specimens of this species in the wild woods which would have made superb ornaments for any garden or park.

The genus [*Vaccinium*] includes the so-called Blueberry, Squaw huckleberry or Deerberry, and the fruits are green or yellowish and not in demand, being usually mawkish.

The true Blueberries are all included in the old Linnean genus *Vaccinium,* and this is well represented in Florida by very fine species. *Vaccinium myrsinites* and *V. tenellum* are low growing shrubs, and are found in rather dry pineland, while *V. elliottii* forms a shrub 3 to 6 feet high. The most valuable of all our species appears to be [*Vaccinium corymbosum*], which is much planted for its excellent berries. It is a fine, dense shrub, 3 to 10 feet in height and a heavy bearer. Mr. E. N. Reasoner, who lists it in his catalogue, says: "This is the fruit that, while attaining prominence in the horticulture of the state only recently, is unquestionably one of the most valuable brought forward in many years. While in reality a shrub, it attains a height of 10 to 12 feet, and is planted in rows 15 to 20 feet apart, and 10 to 12 ft. apart in the rows, and cultivated like orchard fruit. The berries average ¼ to ⅜ inch in diameter, blue-black in color, and in quality equal to the best New England blueberries from which they are scarcely distinguishable. The season lasts from May to August. It prefers a moderately moist soil—good corn land, and one at least slightly acid." He calls it Orchard Blueberry.

Ceratiola ericoides, Rosemary: In the dry scrub lands we often find an attractive dense upright shrub, evergreen, aromatic, and in winter studded with small white berries along the branches. This is what our educated English settlers delighted to call Florida Heather while the Cracker element coined the inappropriate name "Rosemary." The botanical name is *Ceratiola ericoides,* and it should be called by every educated person *Ceratiola.* It belongs to the family Empetraceae (Cowberry family) and it grows well in high pineland gardens.

[*Styrax americanum* var. *pulverulentum*]: While rambling around in the moist woods near Kissimmee I found in July not only numerous *Azalea viscosa* in flower, but also another shrub, new to me and highly attractive, of a rather fine ornamental habit, and with pure white intensely fragrant flowers. It reaches a height of from 3 to 12 feet, and when in full bloom it is one of our most showy and beautiful deciduous shrubs or small trees. Why it never has been brought under cultivation is difficult to understand. Many shrubs, especially exotic ones, have found a place in the gardens of the flower lover.

Strictly Tropical

All the preceding plants are best adapted to the gardens, parks and pleasure grounds of north and central Florida. There are many trees and shrubs being found wild in south Florida, of a strictly tropical nature, which only can be used as ornaments in tropical gardens. As the list of available species is quite a long one I shall confine myself only to the most beautiful and interesting ones.

Amyris elemifera, Torchwood: According to Prof. Chas. T. Simpson, this is "a delicately beautiful little tropical tree which inhabits only the lower end of the state, with trifoliate leaves and hard, resinous wood. It is found in hammocks and would probably do best in rich ground in partial shade."

Annona glabra, Pond Apple, Custard Apple: Not a very handsome tree, but exceptionally interesting when growing around ponds and bending over the water, with its trunk covered with most wonderful air gardens. It is very common around my new home at Naples. Here at Naples is also the home of Judge E. G. Wilkinson, an enthusiastic plant lover and an exceedingly good woodsman, having as a young man often accompanied the late botanical collector, A. H. Curtiss, in his expeditions through unknown primeval forests. He called my attention to an exceptionally fine old stand of this Annona, being found about five miles from Gordon Bay eastward surrounding in dense masses a shallow pond of considerable size. One fine day in August, 1921, he called on me to show me many surprises. When we reached the pond I perceived in the distance dense masses of old, moss-covered Pond Apple Trees, all curved and hanging over the water.

I was spellbound, but at least 300 feet of shallow water were between me and this interesting group. Without much thought I waded through the water, which was scarcely more than 2 or 3 feet deep. But it was quite deceptive. I suddenly struck a deep hole, 5 to 6 feet and more deep, and I went up to my neck into it. It was only with difficulty that I succeeded to get out of it. I had struck an alligator hole—a deep depression in the water—but none of the saurians seemed to be at home, or I would not have been able to crawl out alive.

I finally reached the trees without another mishap and I was abundantly repaid for all the trouble and excitement I had encountered just a few minutes ago. The old trunks, leaning gracefully over the water, were thick and solid and covered entirely with dense masses of epiphytes. The leafy crowns of the trees were quite dense. Here I found most beautiful specimens of such orchids as *Epidendrum nocturnum,* [*E. difforme*], *E. anceps,* [*Encyclia cochleata*], [*E. tampensis*], the purple *Bletia* [*purpurea*], masses of *Cyrtopodium punctatum,* the leafless and highly interesting white-flowering [*Polyrrhiza* or *Polyradicion lindenii*], and dense clumps of noble ferns, among which the Florida Bird's-Nest Fern (*Asplenium serratum*) and the Strap-leaved fern (*Campyloneurum phyllitidis*) were the most conspicuous. The air was pervaded with the delicious fragrance of hundreds of flowering *Crinum americanum*—"lilies," as they are called by the natives. These grew in dense patches underneath the Custard Apple trees. Air plants, or Tillandsias were found in great numbers among the orchids and ferns on the tree trunks; in fact I never before have seen such large specimens of *Tillandsia utriculata* and *T. fasciculata* as I found here. Three or four of the small species were also in evidence. No one not a lover of nature, an admirer of all that is noble, lovely and elevating, can imagine the intense and lasting delight such excursions afford.

In our moist rich woods and along ponds the Custard Apple reaches a height of from 25 to 45 feet. It has spreading branches, and fine large Ficus-like leathery, dark green glossy leaves, and white or cream-colored nodding, fleshy, fragrant flowers. The fruits, as big as a large peach, are pointed toward the apex. They are quite rough and of a green color, ripening here in August and September. They are very fragrant, edible, but insipid and full of seeds.

The Annona is easily transplanted from the woods. I have several fine specimens along the edge of my Cypress Hammock, and one nice plant on high dry pineland. All are doing well, and when well grown they are quite dense and ornamental. Easily raised from seeds.

Bursera simaruba, Gumbo Limbo: A very interesting and conspicuous tree of our well-drained hammocks in south Florida. In Mr. John Hackmeister's beautiful hammock on Gordon Bay it grows together with grand old Live Oaks, the American Mulberry, Red Maple, Marlberry bushes and many other tropical plants, and it is always conspicuous. It is nowhere a strikingly beautiful tree, as its leaf-crown consists only of a few tortuous branches not densely provided with foliage. The trunk is the most noticeable part of the tree, being of a light smooth reddish-brown color and covered with thin papery, glossy bark, which easily peels off like that of a Birch. It is easily propagated by large cuttings. Even large limbs stuck in the ground will easily grow. I have seen big trees at least 60 feet tall. The balsamic resinous sap supplies the gum elm of the druggists. The greenish berries are eaten by many birds. Would be a valuable tree and of interest to the tourists.

Canella winterana, Wild Cinnamon or White Wood: This is a very fine tree, small and dense, with thick shining leaves of oval form. Leaves and wood and bark emit a cinnamon odor. I have had a closely allied species from the West Indies,—*Canella alba,*—in my garden at Gotha for quite a number of years. Its flowers are violet-blue and deliciously fragrant. It is very tender. Our native Canella is very beautiful. It grows from 15 to 20 feet high.

Colubrina [*arborescens*], Wild Coffee Tree: This evergreen and very interesting native tree of the Florida tropics, has been in cultivation in Mr. Charles Deering's place at Buena Vista near Miami. Mr. R. F. Deckert sent me seeds from there, but they never germinated.

Conocarpus erecta, Buttonwood: A very interesting and handsome tropical evergreen tree when growing upright, but a very strange object when seen prostrate on the ground, which is very often the case when the tree gets old and heavy. This falling over does not seem to check its growth or vitality. I have seen many of these old trees near Naples in dense hammocks and even in the woods near the beach. A fine erect specimen, fully 35 feet high, appeared to me as an object of rare beauty. The berry-like fruit seems to ripen at various times of the year. The leaves are evergreen, oval and rather glossy and of a fine silky texture. The very heavy wood is much in demand for fuel, since it makes a great heat and almost no smoke. I have tried to transplant young specimens, without success. There is a classical account of this tree in Simpson's *In the South Florida Wilds* (pp. 263–271).

Cordia sebestena (*Sebestena sebestena*), Geiger Tree: This is one of the glories among tropical evergreen trees. Though it cannot be compared in gigantic growth, in massive brilliancy and in the most wonderful green of foliage with the Royal Poinciana, the small size makes it particularly valuable for small gardens, for lawns and along highways, where the former is out of place on account of its large proportions. Its flaming flower clusters, with which almost every shoot is terminated, vie in their dazzling effect with those of the unrivaled Royal Poinciana. They are, however, only spots—no clouds of color among the leaves. These flower clusters are about 5 to 6 inches broad and consist of a number of small individual blossoms.

The tree, when loaded with its glorious heads of orange-scarlet crimped flowers, makes a magnificent show. They usually are at their best in late June and during July. I shall never forget my first acquaintance with the Geiger Tree in full bloom. Prof. Simpson and the writer strolled around in the then small hamlet of Coconut Grove.

That excursion, in company of a kindred spirit, has been one of the events of my life. In one of the streets Prof. Simpson pointed out to me a most wonderful sight—a Geiger Tree in full bloom. Its flower bunches were so brilliant, so dazzling that I stood before it spellbound. I scarcely trusted my eyes whether this scintillating color was real or whether it belonged to fairyland. The tree stood alone in front of a large lawn. Only a few Coconut Palms were in the background, which heightened the effect considerably. It was about 15 feet high with a round, rather open crown and with numerous leaves along its branches. Each branch seemed to carry one of these brilliant flower clusters. Prof. Simpson called it the most dazzling red flower of all our native tropical trees, and no doubt he is correct.

The Cordia, named in honor of an early German botanist, Valerius Cordus, is popularly known all over south Florida, as the Geiger Tree. It is quite often planted for garden ornament along Biscayne Bay and as far north as Palm Beach. On the west coast I have only seen one fine specimen in the grounds of the Naples Hotel, growing on land that was formerly dry and poor. It flowers every year most brilliantly and most profusely.

Since Mr. Peter P. Schutt has taken charge of the hotel he has taken great pains to make the surroundings as beautiful as the circumstances allow.

Good soil has been hauled in. Fertilizer is abundantly supplied and thorough cultivation is given. The effect is very marked, and our Geiger Tree is now a picture of health and thrift and when in bloom it forms a wonderful sight. It is about 15 feet tall and almost as much through. The leaves are hairy, quite rough to the touch, broad ovate, irregularly serrated and of a beautiful shade of green with a slight touch of gray. The fruits are white, rather long and remind one in form of a date. They are quite fragrant, having a banana-like odor and ripen during the autumn months. The color of its flowers is so glowing, so extremely brilliant, so exceedingly impressive that it should find tender hands and minds in every garden to care for it. It is easily transplanted and is easily grown into good specimens. It is not a rapid grower, and as far as I know, it scarcely ever exceeds a height of 15 feet. The soil in which it is planted must be well drained and rather dry. In wet soils it does not even make an attempt to start into growth. It is a native of extreme south Florida, occurs abundantly in Cuba and other West Indian Islands.

[*Sideroxylon salicifolia*], Bustic, Cassada: An evergreen tree becoming about 50 feet high, but mostly seen as a tall shrub in the hammocks of south Florida. Its berries, oval in form, are much relished by our winter birds. Though quite an attractive small tree when seen at its best, it is comparatively little known and, so far, it has not been used as an ornamental. Belongs to the Sapodilla family and is quite interesting.

Drypetes lateriflora, Lyniani Plum, Guiana Plum: This and the next species are members of the Spurge family (Euphorbiaceae) and are not uncommon in the hammocks of extreme south Florida, also common in the West Indies. This species has red fruit. *D. keyensis* (*D. diversifolia*), Whitewood, grows also in hammocks in south Florida and has ivory-white fruits. Both species are small bushy trees, attaining a height of about 30 feet. Strictly tropical. Both are quite handsome, particularly when in fruit.

Eugenia [*E. axillaris*], White Stopper: There are four species of Eugenias in south Florida, and though belonging to the Myrtle family, they do not show much affinity to their relations in their foliage and growth. When flowering, however, their identity is immediately revealed. A native shrub, quite often confounded with the famous Old World Myrtle, and indeed closely allied to it, is our indigenous Large-leaved Florida Myrtle or White Stopper. I received my plants from Mr. Purdy, who collected them on shell mounds near his winter home at Ormond, together with *Ardisia pickeringia*

[= *A. escallonioides*] and *Psychotria undata* [= *P. nervosa*]. It is one of the most satisfactory and beautiful among all shrubs, being highly attractive at all times of the year, but particularly late in May or early in June when the whole plant appears as if covered with snow under its wealth of pure-white Myrtle-like blossoms. The foliage is fully as fragrant as that of the common Sweet Myrtle, but it is at least three times as large. The growth is more up-right and much more vigorous and the flowers appear always in masses and at least four weeks earlier. In good soil it attains a height of 15 feet. The habit is very dense, upright, and where enough room is allotted to it, it finally attains the size of very fine small bushy tree. The flowers appear in axillary clusters, being pure white and as large as Cherry blossoms. They are suc-ceeded by clusters of hard, dry black berries during the fall and winter months.

Easily propagated by hardwood cuttings placed in wet sand. There are a number of additional beautiful Eugenias indigenous to south Florida, but they are too tender for this region [Gotha]. Most all of them attain tree-size. The most beautiful appears to be Garber's Myrtle.

Eugenia [*confusa*]: Another fine hammock tree with pure white flowers. Fruit scarlet. It is usually known as the Ironwood. I pulled up a number of young plants in the hammock woods near Snapper Creek, and packed the roots in moist sphagnum moss. There are about six young plants now in my collection.

Eugenia [*foetida*], Spanish Stopper: This is also a beautiful evergreen tree, small, but of handsome shape. Found in the same localities with the former. Black fruit.

Eugenia [*rhombea*] Red Stopper: This also is a very handsome Eugenia with fine dense evergreen foliage. The berries are orange, tinged with red, and black at maturity. Fruits picked in their orange color supplied seeds that germinated without difficulty. These Eugenias ought to be largely propa-gated and used as ornamentals. All of them make fine, dense small trees when given sufficient room to develop. None of them do well in dry soil. Hammock soil, consisting mainly of rotted old leaves, is what they require.

Genipa [*americana*], Seven year Apple: A beautiful tree, long known as an inhabitant on sand dunes and coastal hammocks of the lower east coast. Mr. Walter M. Buswell found it recently quite common on Captiva Island, and I had an opportunity to come across it on Pine Island. The evergreen leaves are thick and obovate and the pretty white flowers are provided in abundance. The oval fruits are three inches long, and are said to need seven years to ripen. A very interesting tree and very ornamental at all times.

Guaiacum sanctum, Lignum Vitae: I have seen this characteristic tree only in dwarf specimens of no particular attractiveness, but it is said to grow sometimes 30 feet high. I have it in my collection, where it is an extremely slow grower. It naturally grows in hammocks.

Hamelia patens, Hamelia, Firebush: This singular native shrub is an old and well-established ornament of Palm Cottage Gardens,—one that I always liked and cherished. It is sometimes a lovely small tree, but more often it is a dense medium-sized shrub of a very characteristic and distinct appearance, belonging to the Rubiaceae or Coffee family—a group which contains such jewels as the *Gardenia, Bouvardia, Rondeletia, Guettarda,* Coffee, *Ixora, Mussaenda, Randia* and others of our most valuable and ornamental shrubs and trees. It is easily grown from seeds and cuttings and is easily transplanted from its native wilds. If properly used it is one of our most lovely garden shrubs.

I found it, together with its congeners, *Psychotria* [*nervosa*], [*Myrcianthes fragrans*], the Marlberry, and various other interesting plants on a shell mound near the ocean not far from Ormond, where at that time (1906) a most educated and well-informed lover of botany and plants, Mr. Purdy, resided. A few small specimens that I collected there are still growing in my garden at Gotha, one of them between a fine *Camellia sasanqua* (double white) and a *C. japonica* (also double white), in front of the east verandah of the house. It is quite tender and has several times been killed back to the ground by a severe freeze, but it always sprouted again vigorously from the roots. Several years later I found it in the woods of Pine Island, along the Caloosahatchee and still later in the hammocks south of Miami. It also grew abundantly on the shell mounds near Naples, usually in company of the Marlberry, the Satinleaf, and numerous other tropical plants.

Being always a conspicuous shrub when found wild, it is at its best in the garden when properly cared for. Its young branches and leaf-stalks are always bright red and the leaves themselves have a conspicuous red midrib and are often suffused with red. They are of a bright green color, with a satiny sheen, being wavy or plaited and are of elliptic or oblong form, In well cultivated specimens they are much larger than in their native hammocks. One leaf before me is 7 inches long and 3 inches wide, with a petiole almost

1 inch long. The very brilliant flowers appear in upright terminal cymes. Each flower is rather narrow and slender, with a vivid orange-scarlet tubular corolla. Humming-birds are very frequently seen soaring around these gleaming flower clusters. The shining black berries are as large as peas, growing in branched upright cymes. Each branchlet has a row of these berries. There is one bunch of berries before me while I write. It has six branchlets, and each branchlet again is subdivided into two smaller ones. Only these latter smaller ones carry the berries. The *Hamelia* is in flower and fruit all the year round. The berries are much relished by our winter birds. During the summer time they are scarcely touched, as birds always prefer insects when they can be had.

The *Hamelia* grows in rich, moist black soil, but always in well drained positions. It is a moisture loving plant, though it also will grow even on high pineland if well cared for. It is naturally quite a dense upright shrub or small bushy tree. It looks particularly well near water, where it can be associated with a number of fine native and exotic species. It has been in the trade for many years. The honor of its introduction belongs to Pliny W. Reasoner, who found it in the early eighties of the last century in the hammocks of south Florida. Indeed he was so struck with its beauty and distinct appearance that he collected it primarily for his own pleasure and for distribution later.

[*Picidia piscipula*], Jamaica Dogwood: This tree grows well from seed. It belongs to the bean family or Leguminosae, but is not particularly handsome, as so many of its congeners are. "A common and valuable timber tree for south Florida," says Dr. John Gifford. "Might be used to advantage as a shade and ornamental tree. Grows quickly, has an abundance of pea-like flowers in clusters which honey bees are fond of. As the name indicates, it is a fish poison. The bark and twigs are bruised and lowered in a basket into the water. A poison is dissolved which stupefies fish that come near it. They float to the surface and are easily captured. This tree grows well from seed and its propagation should be encouraged." There is a fine specimen near the river at Everglades.

[*Ardisia escallonioides*], Marlberry, Pickering's Ardisia, Shell-Mound Berry: The Marlberry, or Pickering's Ardisia, is one of our most valuable and best ornamental small evergreen trees or bushy shrubs. Though it is strictly tropical, I have grown it for years at Palm Cottage Gardens. It froze down repeatedly, but always sprouted again from the root-stalk as soon as warm weather set in. Mr. Purdy of Ormond and I found it quite common on a shell mound near the ocean, where it grew in company with the Florida-Myrtle, and another species of *Ardisia*, which according to the opinion of Dr. J. K. Small, is probably of Oriental origin. Mr. Purdy sent me later, in 1906, quite a number of small plants of all the three species which are still in my collection at Gotha and here at Naples. A few years ago I again visited the old shell mound near Ormond, but alas! It had disappeared with all its plant beauty. Road builders had hauled the shell away. None of the above named plants were found in the vicinity. Mr. Purdy had sent me the two Ardisias, similar at first sight, under the name *Ardisia pickeringia*. At close examination they are very different. The "ornamental" one is much less hardy, is smaller and denser in growth with larger and much more glossy leaves, and flowers that are not fragrant.

The Marlberry is a beautiful evergreen small tree or dense shrub, with ovate to lance-oblong leaves, not particularly glossy and with a peculiar rather dull tint of green. When well grown it is a handsomely shaped bushy tree, about 12 to 15 feet high, but we usually see it only in shrub form. Its main beauty lies hidden in the dainty, deliciously fragrant flowers, which are bell-shaped and appear in clusters during he autumn months. The spicy perfume is so strong and pronounced that the whole air for quite a distance is pervaded with it. These flowers appear in terminal panicles, with white or pink corollas and are often streaked purplish. When in full bloom these masses of flower trusses add a peculiar charm to the plant. The purplish-black berries, each as large as a pea, ripen in dense clusters early in spring. I have picked them as late as April 7 on a shell mound not far from my present home. Birds are very fond of these berries, which are not juicy, but quite mealy under their skin.

The rather dense and distinct growth of the Marlberry, its deliciously fragrant flowers and the masses of purplish berries combine to make it a first-class ornamental, well worthy of the attention of the plant lover and the landscape gardener. It is easily raised from seeds and young plants are easily transplanted. They flower when only a few feet high. I have raised hundreds of bushy seedlings and have offered them to many of my friends, but none was willing to plant them out in his or her garden. My enthusiasm about the plant was never contagious. I have invariably found that the beauty of this exceptionally fine plant is not appreciated at first sight. One has to care for it lovingly for several years and it will gradually reveal all its charms and attach itself upon your mind. And once in love with it, this love will be a lasting one.

It grows best in a fairly moist and rich soil. Undrained soils it seems to detest. In its wild state it is found along the east coast from Miami to Ormond. On the west coast I have found it abundantly on shell mounds near Naples and elsewhere. It is common on Pine Island, where I found it in 1916, and it also occurs on all the other nearby islands. Here, near Naples, I often enjoyed its beauty on a fine, large, but now well-nigh destroyed shell mound in company of the Satinleaf, Gumbo Limbo, *Hamelia,* the wild Papaya and many other plants. The soil of these shell mounds is naturally scant and rather dry, but it seems to contain special plant food for special plants. The spelling of its botanical name puzzles even the most expert horticultural writers. It is *Icacorea,* but half of my correspondents write "Icocarea," and I have seen it even spelled "Icaoroea" and "Icorea." The old name *Ardisia pickeringia* is distinct and beautiful, being still preferred by most horticultural writers.

Lysiloma [*latisiliquum*], Wild Tamarind: About six years ago I received from the Bureau of Plant Industry a small Acacia-like plant, which has developed into one of the most elegant and one of the largest and most conspicuous trees here on my place at Naples. Name and number were lost. Only lately Mr. R. A. Young, of the Bureau of Plant Industry, ascertained its correct name. It is about 12 feet high and almost as much through, and is of a very beautiful, though open form. The immediate impression is that it is a most elegant and graceful tree. It grows on high pineland in the neighborhood of a very fine and dense Nance (*Byrsonima crassifolia*) and a group of Kaffir Oranges. In its growth it reminds one somewhat of the Tamarind, hence its common name (Wild Tamarind), but it is not quite as dense and more elegant in form. Its bipinnate leaves are of a very lovely deep green, Along the stems where the leaves issue there is a shield-like green growth, closely adhering to the wood. This forms one of the characteristics of the species.

The flowers, which appear all the year round in more or less abundance, are brush-like, almost round, pure white in color and very sweetly, but not strongly perfumed. At their bottoms they show a deep purplish-red. Seed pods are thin, long and broad, dark brown when mature, and containing a number of thin flat seeds. It has proved a perfect success in my garden, being one of the handsomest trees in my collection, distinct from all others, evergreen and of great ornamental value. It would make an excellent avenue tree for towns and cities, and is also good for highway planting, reaching eventually a height of about 60 feet. Being an inhabitant of the hammocks of the Everglade keys and the Florida Keys, it seems to be exceptionally abundant in the Bahamas and the West Indies.

[*Licaria triandra*]: A most beautiful tree of the Laurel family. "One tree," says Dr. John Gifford, "eighteen inches in diameter, and a few small ones found by Miss Olivia Rodham in the Brickell hammock, near Miami. Identified by Prof. C. S. Sargent. Broad-topped, handsome tree, native of Cuba." This beautiful dark-leaved evergreen was pointed out to me as a special feature, and I was deeply struck with its beauty. It would be a gem in our ornamental plantations.

[*Myrcianthes fragrans*], Florida Myrtle: A most beautiful and interesting native shrub or small tree that I have grown at Palm Cottage Gardens for about twenty years, and which has been constantly confounded with the large-leaved form of the sweet European Myrtle. I received my first plants from Mr. Purdy, in 1906, who had collected them on a shell mound near his winter home at Ormond. It grew in company of a very fine *Ardisia* and our native *Psychotria* [*nervosa*]. The position where it grew in abundance was rather dry, but the soil was rich and well drained. Mr. Purdy, a man of culture and education, was an ardent lover of our native flora, of which he had an exceedingly good knowledge. He mistook it for the White Stopper *Eugenia* [*axillaris*], and sent it to me under that name. A celebrated botanist of the North determined it as *Myrtus communis* var. *latifolia*. This confusion came to an end when Dr. John K. Small, the greatest authority on southern plants, visited me last summer (1924) here at Naples. I have several small bushes here and he at once became deeply interested when he saw them, asking whether they came from this locality or from somewhere else. He was surprised when I told him that the original plant had been found on a shell mound near Ormond, informing me that this was a new species of [*Myrcianthes*], which he had named in honor of Prof. Chas. T. Simpson, who had found trees of it in April, 1917, in the Arch Creek Hammock on the lower East Coast.

Though I had seen the plants grow near Ormond, I was unable to tell him the exact position, as my notes, made at the time, had been lost. According to Dr. Small, it is a tree 15 meters (about 48 feet) tall or less, with a buttressed trunk, when well grown, and a smooth bark. Those I have seen in its native wilds near Ormond did not exceed 15 feet, and all were provided with branches from the ground up, forming very fine bushy trees. My plants at Gotha are fully as hardy as the Sweet Myrtle, and several have assumed a height of about 20 feet. One specimen forming a group with *Michelia* [*figo*] and a most floriferous pink Crape-Myrtle, with a big *Cycas revoluta* in front, is always a delight to the eye, being very dense and of graceful form.

It is one of the most satisfactory and beautiful among all the shrubs of my garden, and is a special favorite of mine. It is highly attractive at all times of the year, but particularly so late in May or early in June, when the whole plant appears as if covered with snow under the wealth of its pure white Myrtle-like blossoms, which are deliciously fragrant. The foliage is decidedly Myrtle-like, as are the blossoms, but it is fully three times as large. The very pleasant odor of the leaves also reminds one strongly of the Sweet Myrtle. The growth, however, is quite different, being much more upright and vigorous, and the flowers always appear in masses in the axils of the leaves. The habit of growth is very dense and upright, and where enough room is allowed for its development it finally attains the size of a small tree. The flowers appear in axillary clusters, being pure white, as large as cherry blossoms and are succeeded by small, hard, dry black berries during the fall and winter months.

7

Curious and Interesting Ornamental Plants

We south Floridians are really in a most wonderful region, because this region offers unlimited possibilities for the lover and cultivator of beautiful tropical plants, shrubs, trees and palms. When I look over my notes on these plants that should be tried I become bewildered, amazed. I have here at my Tropical Garden and Arboretum about 1,500 species and varieties, and this is only a beginning. There are many thousands more to add. Our soils are mostly very poor. They need lots of humus, organic fertilizers and often an addition of clay.

Tropical Looking Leaves

Trevesia palmata: I have two tall specimens of this most beautiful ornamental tree, fully 35 feet high and provided with large, palmate leaves from the ground up. They grow in rich, moist, mucky soil and are extremely effective, belonging to the most impressive of all the many trees and shrubs in my Naples garden. The Trevesias belong to the family Araliaceae and are natives of southern Asia and the islands in the region. There are about 8 or 9 species known to science, but with the exception of the species under consideration, none have been introduced into this country. *Trevesia* [*burckii*] and *T. sundaica* may, however, be found in some of our botanical gardens.

The subject of this note is not only conspicuous for its large ornamental leaves, but for their curious construction as well. These are divided into 7 to 9 large finger-like segments that are more or less contracted and narrowed toward their bases, and rested on the dilated, truncate base of the blade, that more or less resembles the foot of a web-footed bird. My most exquisite specimens have never flowered. The inflorescence is described as consisting of horizontal or pendulous panicled umbels of flowers, with fleshy, creamy-white petals, and a yellow disc. The smell is said to be rather disagreeable when fully exposed, but the flowers are extremely interesting, and are followed by globular berries about the size of Pears, and reminding one very much of Ivyberries. This *Trevesia* is a gem, perfectly hardy in south Florida, and of a unique and rare ornamental and distinct beauty.

The Traveler's Tree, or, as it is sometimes called Traveler's-Palm, is no palm at all. At the top of the trunk, of a mature plant, the leaves are in two rows,—distichous, as the technical expression runs—with long stalks, arranged like an enormous fan. As our wild air plants on the trees hold water, which is sometimes of service to hunters in the woods, so the sheaths of the leaf-stalks of the Traveler's Tree store up water for the plant's own needs, and each one pierced from below, will yield the thirsty traveler almost a quart of refreshing and pure water. The blades of the leaves are used for thatch. The flowers are supported by large bracts arranged in two rows along the stalk. The seeds in the hard, woody receptacles, or pods, are edible, as large as a small bean, and covered with a very deep indigo-blue, soft cottony substance. They yield an essential oil.

I have often admired the beautiful specimens of the Traveler's Tree at Fort Myers, Punta Gorda, Palm Beach, etc. Trees 30 feet high are not uncommon in tropical Florida. A deep, moist, rich, well-drained soil is necessary to cultivate this striking tree successfully. It usually suckers profusely. These suckers, if carefully removed, form excellent material for propagation. Large plants furnish a rich supply of seeds. Two years ago my friend, Mr. J. B. Donnelly of Palm Beach, sent me a few of the hard seed bunches and I have now quite a number of fine young plants set out in my Naples garden.

Its singular structure and masses of broad foliage impart so peculiar a character to the Madagascar landscape. It is a moisture loving plant, but it is also abundant on hillsides, covering vast tracts of country, intermingled here and there with the Raphia Palm.

I did not, at first, succeed well with the Traveler's Tree. As I have already stated, it requires a very rich, deep soil for its masses of fleshy roots. A starved specimen on dry poor soil does not reveal its beauty. And it should be planted in groups of 5 or 10, preferably on large lawns, or in the foreground of beautiful flowering trees and shrubs. The landscape gardener (I do not say the landscape "architect," who is in most cases an abomination) can use this tree with wonderful success in the formation of charming landscape effects. Young plants from pots grow well and rapidly if cared for in the proper way. [Nehrling apparently disliked the situation where there was too much "architecture" and too little natural landscape.]

If only for the sake of contrast this truly unique and elegant plant is well worth all our attention. The genus *Ravenala* consists only of [1] species; another closely related species from the Guianas and northern Brazil is known as *Phenakospermum guianensis,* a strictly tropical plant attaining a height of about 15 feet. It was introduced by Mr. E. N. Reasoner of Oneco, Fla., but I do not know if it has succeeded anywhere in the state.

Strelitzia nicolai: I had two large fine clumps of this beautiful plant, which is closely allied to the Traveler's Tree. It is the most robust of all the Strelitzias, having fine large foliage, and in good soil it will grow even more vigorously than the banana if given shelter from cold winds. It attains a height of about 25 feet. The flowers are quite large, of characteristic shape that reminds one of a huge butterfly in the act of alighting, and with large boat-shaped bracts of a purplish color, each about a foot in length and 3 inches broad. The sepals are white and the petals blue. [They are not all petals in the true sense.] If it is to be compared with any other species, that one must be *Strelitzia* [*alba*], which it so closely resembles that it was considered identical with that species until it spreads its flowers. These large-growing Strelitzias need rich, moist soil. Though coming from tropical Africa it is perfectly hardy in South Florida. I saw large fine clumps in the late Mr. Chas. Deering's place at Buena Vista, near Miami.

Panama Hat Plants: The Carludovicas form a most beautiful and interesting specialty in my collection of tropical plants. I have now about 9 or 10 species and it took a long time to find this number in the botanical gardens, as they are never offered in the trade. They form a handsome genus of foliage plants, which, from their general appearance show a great resemblance to palms, though in reality they are said to be related to the Pandanus or Screw Pine family. Carludovicas are of free and rapid growth when under congenial conditions, and deserve a more extended recognition as decorative plants than they have yet secured, for they are not only highly ornamental as greenhouse, lath-house and conservatory specimens, but may also be used in an out-of-door foliage bed together with Dracaenas, Pandanus, Palms and Crotons during the summer, provided they are not exposed to the full force of the sun.

All the Carludovicas are true children of the dark, moist, rich forests of tropical America, where they grow in very beautiful large tufts or clumps from 6 to 15 feet high. [Related genera] and species are even climbers, sending out aerial roots, which fasten upon the trunks of trees, or hang down like ropes.

Carludovicas are propagated by division as most all of the species sucker freely, or by means of seeds, when they are available. The genus *Carludovica* was named for Carol IV and his Queen Louisa of Spain, by Ruiz and Pavon, two Spanish botanists. They are also known as Panama Hat Plants, one species, *Carludovica palmata,* being the main source of these hats, and probably other species are also used for this purpose. These most exquisite and noble of plants are much admired in my collection by cultured visitors, while many of them simply look upon them as palms, on account of their remote similarity to these royal plants. A closer examination reveals, however, the fact that their flowers and fruits are vastly different and that their leaves are very soft and silky to the touch.

Carludovica palmata, a lovely palm-like plant, was introduced many years ago into Florida by the late E. N. Reasoner who disseminated it largely over the state. It is the most common of all species. I have seen beautiful dense, tall specimens in south Florida; the finest of them were grown at Four Way Lodge, Coconut Grove, where they flowered and fruited abundantly. They grew in shady position in a large lath house full of Aroids, Orchids, Bromeliads and many other dainty tropical plants. My friend, Mr. A. C. Splinter, the superintendent of this notable tropical paradise, has succeeded to ripen many seeds and has grown fine young plants from them. *C. palmata* is a native of Peru, Colombia, Ecuador, etc. where it is a common plant in shady, rather moist places. Its leaves are shaped and plaited like a fan and are borne upright on long slender stalks. They are tolerably large in size, and deeply cut into 4 to 5 divisions, each of which is again cut. The celebrated Panama hats are made of the young tender leaves of this Carludovica.

The Panama Hat Plant is undoubtedly one of the most elegant foliage plants we can grow. During the last 50 years it has assumed vast importance as a source of fibers used in the manufacture of the true Panama hat. This Carludovica was introduced into Europe in the year 1808. It is a stemless plant, the leaf-stalks and flowers shooting directly from the root. The leaves which are mounted on a solid triangular petiole, are palmate and folded like a fan. As they increase in size they split into three or more divisions. The leaf-disk or blade varies in diameter from 18 to 30 inches and even more, the leaf-stalk being often 6 to 9 and 10 feet in length. When carefully cultivated the leaf-blade is of a brilliant satiny green. The flowers, though they do not constitute the chief beauty of the plant, are nevertheless very interesting and singular in their way. They are, as in all Carludovicas, monoecious, on the same spadix, the female flowers being surrounded by four males. The spadix is most remarkable, both in form and color. The spadix on reaching maturity, bursts or heads up, exposing the inside of the fruit as well as the axis around which it is placed. These parts are of the most brilliant scarlet, which is rendered all the more intense by the strong contrast of the bright green surface of the spadix and of the leaves by which it is surrounded. Large healthy plants of this Carludovica flower regularly in extreme south Florida. The breaking up of the ripe spadix adds an additional beauty to that already possessed by this elegant plant.

In Weddell's *Travels in South Bolivia* I find an interesting account of the manufacture of Panama hats from the leaves of this plant. It may be here incidentally remarked that this is the same botanist after whom the beautiful palm, *Cocos* [*Syagrus weddelliana*], was named.

The Bolivians, according to Weddell, gave the *Carludovica palmata* the name of Jipagapa, a town in the Republic of Ecuador which is the principal seat of the hat manufacture, "Panama," like "Mocha," in the case of coffee, and "Brussels" in that of carpets, being a misnomer. Before the leaf begins to open—when, in fact, it resembles a closed fan—it is cut off close to the petiole, the base of which forms the center of the crown of the hat. It is then divided longitudinally into strips with the thumb nail, the thick part forming the midrib being rejected. The number of shreds into which it is divided of course depends on the fineness of the hat into which they are to be woven. The split leaf which is of greenish-white color, is next dipped into boiling water, then into tepid water acidulated with lemon juice, and lastly it is allowed to soak in cold water for some time, and afterwards dried in the sun. Each hat is, or ought to be made of one single leaf. They vary in price from a few to a hundred dollars. The damping and drying operations cause the shreds to assume a curled or cylindrical form, which much increases their strength without injuring their pliancy. Before plaiting the coarser qualities are damped with water, but the finest sorts are left out in the morning dew, and worked on before sunrise. A hat of the finest quality, made out of a single leaf, will take several months to make it complete, and the plaiting will be so fine as hardly to be perceptible at a short distance.

Dracaenas/[Cordylines]: These belong to the most beautiful and brilliant of tropical foliage plants. They are perfectly at home in moist shady spots of our south Florida gardens, but they will not be of much use in sunny, dry soil. I have had a wealth of wonderfully gorgeous foliage on plants being from 4 to 10 feet high in my lath house at Naples. Many flowered and bore branches of bright red berries late in fall. One of my most vigorous sorts—[*Cordyline terminalis*]—I crossed with the pollen of *Dracaena* 'Lord Wolseley.' The most brilliant branches of red berries attracted the attention of Mr. J. E. Hendry, Jr., a most enthusiastic plant lover, and he raised from the seeds quite a number of very choicest varieties. The three best beautifully variegated with pink, scarlet, white and green, have been names 'Mrs. J. E. Hendry,' 'Mrs. Arthur Kelley' and 'Mrs. B. P. Nehrling.' These and many other gorgeous Dracaenas can be seen and admired, in the Everglades Nursery at Fort Myers.

Years ago, when I first came to this part of the state, I found about a dozen most vigorous sorts of Dracaenas in Mr. Thomas A. Edison's garden. Being very luxuriant and of indescribable beauty I was at once convinced of the fact that the region south of the Caloosahatchee is particularly adapted for growing these plants out of doors in suitable soil and in shade. Last year I had over 55 species and varieties—mostly hybrids—in my collection here at Naples. My specimens of *Dracaena fragrans* and its variegated forms, *D.* [*fragrans*] 'Massangeana' and *D.* [*fragrans*] 'Lindenii,' were from 2 to 8 feet high and provided with reclining leaves from top to bottom. The first one flowered profusely, and during the night the air was scented with a delicious fragrance.

The following notes on the culture of these plants were made several years ago: The Dracaenas are very popular inmates of our glasshouses. Some of the species and hybrids require a very warm temperature; others do well in a cool house. They are all exceedingly attractive, some of them being most beautiful and conspicuous in foliage, while their habit is such as to render them most valuable for all kinds of decoration. They are easily grown and difficult to kill, although to bring them down to a ragged and unsightly condition is a very simple matter. Small plants are generally the most needed and serviceable for room and vase embellishment, and when used for this purpose, for which they are now and then in demand, they remain a long time in perfection. Larger plants are required frequently for stair-case, balcony, entrance hall and particularly for verandah decoration. The drooping foliage of some, the upright leaves of others, and the splendid tropical appearance of all render them ideal objects when used in such places. Some of the most tender and brilliant varieties can be used most successfully in tropical beds out of doors in south Florida. My plants—many of them of the most gorgeous varieties—scarcely suffered during the three cold nights—the thermometer went down to 26°F—early in January, 1927, and they suffered not at all, and again Jan. 1 and 2, 1928, when a thin crust of ice covered a bucket of water near where they are growing.

There cannot be any doubt, Dracaenas belong to the most beautiful of foliage plants we are able to grow in our south Florida gardens. They belong to the real plant nobility, like palms, Pandanus, Crotons and Cycads. They should be extensively cultivated on account of the extreme easiness with which they can be propagated. A single stem, 3 or more feet high, will produce 3 dozen young plants. When any plant becomes too tall or bare of foliage it should be cut into pieces about an inch long. These may be put in coarse sand, covered with sphagnum moss, and kept moist. Bottom heat assists materially to induce the cuttings to push forth healthy shoots from the dormant eyes, but I have found that they grow equally well during May and June in my Naples garden without artificial heat. These cuttings should never suffer from lack of water. As soon as the young shoots are about 2 inches high I take them out of their sand-bed, and pot each one in a mixture of muck, sand and powdered charcoal. Small pots are necessary for these rooted cuttings. The mixture must not be too fine, but sufficiently so to admit of a certain amount of all the ingredients being put in a 6-inch pot. This size pot will grow well nourished plants until they are 18 inches to 2 feet high. I have seen many fine specimens in 5- or 6-inch pots, which is the most convenient size for decorative work. Of course this treatment is not necessary in extreme south Florida. I transplant my young specimens—4 to 6 inches high—directly out in the moist soil under lath-covers. Here they grow most vigorously, and their fine and brilliant colors are always attractive and a delight.

Another means of propagation is found in the roots. At the base of large plants of each of these there is an eye. If an old stem be cut up, these eyes should be cut off, and together with the pieces of the stem, put in sand. In shifting well-grown plants into larger pots, these eyes may be taken off during the operation without injury or checking the progress of the specimen. In this way a fresh stock may be raised without even cutting down a large plant, and when only a few are required I prefer these root-cuttings to any other. Sometimes the tops are put in as cuttings, but they are rather slow in forming roots.

When propagated and in good growing condition, the daily requirements of Dracaenas are few, but a slight shading is necessary at all times. They are particularly sensitive to dryness at the roots, which usually causes the loss of the lower foliage and the tender young leaves are often injured and are withered from the same cause. The following species and hybrids—all extremely beautiful—I have, or have had, in my collection.

Nearly all the plants known in gardens as Dracaenas are, however, Cordylines, for instance, the red variegated plants, known as *D. terminalis, D. ferrea, D. shepherdii, D. terminalis* 'Baptisii,' etc., and the green, ensiform-leaved greenhouse plants, known as *D. indivisa, D. australis, D. stricta*, etc., are Cordylines. But even after these have been eliminated we have still left among true Dracaenas a heterogeneous collection of some 50 species, including such widely dissimilar plants as *D. draco* (the Dragon Tree of the Canary Islands), *D. goldiana, D. fragrans, D. cernua* [?], and the species here emphasized. It is difficult to believe that this plant, with its thin, wiry, branched, bamboo-like stems and ovate leaves, is a near ally of the Dragon Tree of Teneriffe, the stem of which was 60 feet high, and 15 feet thick, or even of the mottled-leaved *D. goldiana*. The differences in habit and leaves are, however, non-essential according to botanists, who found evidences of near relationship in the essential character of the flowers and fruits. The main difference between *Dracaena* and *Cordyline* is in the fruit, the former having one ovule in each of the three cells of the ovary, the latter having three ovules in each cell.

The Australian species, *Dracaena indivisa* [?], *D. stricta, D. australis* and their varieties all belong properly to the genus *Cordyline*, as do all those of brilliant foliage of the *D. termissolia* [?] group. These Australian species never succeeded with me in Florida, though I have seen tall specimens of the first named species in a garden of Avon park, and *D. australis* was admired in the open in the Royal Palm Nurseries many years ago. They are all very popular in northern glasshouses and are grown by the thousands annually.

The strictly tropical species, like [*Cordyline terminalis*] and its many hybrids, do splendidly in moist shady spots in south Florida. This species is a native of the South Sea Islands, and East India and Malaya. I have had it in splendid specimens 6 to 8 feet high. If cut down when young the stems push up quite a number of shoots, which finally make very bushy and brilliant plants. The color of the leaves is green, often streaked with red. They are from 1 to 2½ feet long and from 2 to 5 inches wide, elliptical or elliptic-lanceolate. In the autumn the large bunches of brilliant red berries, each as large as a holly-berry, ripen in profusion. If crossed with other more gorgeous sorts new and beautiful hybrids are obtained. The beautiful variety *C.* 'Lord Wolseley' is brilliant red, pink and crimson. It is similar in growth to [*Cordyline terminalis*]. The flowers of all these species and hybrids appear in large branched panicles. They are mostly pink, lilac and red and are very attractive.

[*Cordyline ferrea*], [*C.*] *guilfreylei*, [*C. terminalis*] 'Amabilis,' [*C. terminalis*] 'Baptisii,' [*C. terminalis*] 'Anerliensis,' [*C. terminalis*] 'Hybrida,' [*C.*] *metallica*, [*C. terminalis*] 'Imperialis' are all distinct and brilliant hybrids. *Dracaena* 'Youngii' [= *Cordyline terminalis* 'Youngii'] is perhaps the most distinct of all, having deep bronze-colored foliage. The young leaves are bright green striped with deep red and rose. This is one of the most easily grown and most robust in my collection. The latest hybrids, many of them raised by my friend Mr. Eugene Andre, of Trinidad, are outrivaling by far all the older sorts. I have [*Cordyline*] XMandaiana, a hybrid with dazzling red foliage. This is said to have originated with Mr. W. A. Manda of South Orange, N.J. My specimens came from the Missouri Botanical Garden. There are fine plants of it to be seen in the Everglades Nursery, Fort Myers. Mr. A. Kelly, the manager and one of the proprietors, intends to propagate this most brilliant [*Cordyline*].

It would lead too far to describe all the most beautiful hybrids of late years: I can only mention a few: *Cordyline* XMrs. Eugene Andre, *C.* XBertha Andre, *C.* XHarmony, *C.* XPink superba, *C.* XTricolor, *C.* XRuby, *C.* XTorch, *C.* XRedwing, *C.* XField of flame, *C.* XDawn and many others are all extremely beautiful, showing mostly a variety of dazzling red tints. All grow easily and are at home in moist shady spots of our south Florida gardens.

For the true Dracaenas—not including the Cordylines—I have the following: *Dracaena fragrans* with deep green pendulous, large and fine foliage. It grows with me up to 12 feet tall and flowers profusely. These flowers are very different from those of the true Cordylines, appearing in bunches on very short branches from the axils of the leaves. They are not showy but very fragrant in the evening. There are many varieties of it in cultivation, the best known being *D. fr.* 'Knerkii,' and *D. fr.* 'Rathiana,' both with showy, simple, green foliage. *D. fr.* 'Massangeana,' much like the type in growth, shows a yellow stripe in the center of each leaf. *D. fr.* 'Lindenii' has creamy-white stripes and *D. fr.* 'Victoria' is similar, but is not such a vigorous grower as the others. I have also had *D. hookerana,* a species from the Cape of Good Hope, with rather dull green leaves, similar to *D. fragrans,* and *D. umbraculifera* [?] from Mauritius. It attained a height in my Naples garden of 12 feet.

Dracaena deremensis, of tropical Africa, is a plant growing in a bushy form and from 6 to 10 feet high. The flowers have an unpleasant odor. I grew also *D. d.* 'Warneckii,' a variety of it. *D. goldieana,* also from Western Tropical Africa, a most distinct and beautiful species and very rare in collections. My plants came from Mr. August Koch of the Garfield Park Conservatories, Chicago. The finest one attained a height of three feet in the moist shady ground of my caladium-shed. The leaves are spreading, thick, oblong, 7 to 8 inches long and 4 to 5 inches broad, glossy green, conspicuously white spotted and horizontally branched. The young leaves are often tinged with red, particularly on the underside. There is a fine illustration of that species in Dr. L. H. Bailey's *Standard Cyclopedia of Horticulture* Vol. II, facing page 1069.

Dracaena sanderana from Kamerun, West Africa. I had many fine bushy plants from 3 to 5 feet high. The leaves are green, broadly margined with white. This is easily grown and very conspicuous in a collection. [*D. surculosa*], also from West Africa, does not look like *Dracaena* at all, the leaves being much like those of a certain Croton, glossy-green and densely freckled with white. My specimens grew in very moist mucky soil and were very bushy. The short flower-racemes were not conspicuous by any bright color, but the comparatively large berries, almost an inch in diameter and brilliant red when fully ripe, were very showy. I have another Dracaena with leaves much like the preceding, but they are spotted and clouded with light grayish-green on a deep green ground. [*Dianella ensifolia*] was admired many a time, the large bushy, exceedingly graceful and elegant specimen of this species in Horticultural Hall, Philadelphia. I have had just as effective bushy specimens in my Naples garden. They flowered profusely, but never set any seeds. The flowers appear in large, loose corymbs and are of a light lilac color. A beautiful and easily grown plant.

Dracaena kellerana [probably *D. surculosa* 'Kelleri'] also came from my friend, Mr. August Koch. It has fine spreading leaves, which are conspicuously banded with white. It is a most excellent ornament in my collection. My specimen of [*D. cincta*] has attained a height of 18 feet and carried on its top a bunch of narrow leaves, 12 inches long, deep green and margined with a narrow bright-red line. Several additional shoots were pushed up from the rootstalk. It is a very interesting plant, but not as showy as most other species and hybrids.

Plant lovers who are looking for something brilliant, beautiful, rare and easily grown should grow some or all of these plants in their collections. As I have remarked in the foregoing, they belong to the real nobility of the plant world and always attract attention. In south Florida south of Punta Gorda, they are hardy; farther north they can easily be grown in pots and tubs for verandah and other decorations.

Dracaena [*surculosa*]: Though I have given a short description of this fine distinct plant in one of my recent contributions to the columns of the *American Eagle,* I have received recently a number of letters requesting me to add a more detailed account. This is the first *Dracaena* that was distinguished by a fine color plate in the *Garden* (London). It is so totally unlike the plants popularly known as Dracaenas, that many will no doubt hesitate to accept it as one. The few fine dense specimens in the mucky soil of my Naples garden, with their mottled leaves—similar to a certain green leaved Croton, freckled with white—are always viewed with a good deal of doubt by most of my visitors when they see the label.

Of the about fifty species of Dracaenas, however, forty are native of Tropical Africa. These have been divided by Baker into eight sections, according to the form and arrangement of their leaves. *Dracaena* [*surculosa*] belongs to the fifth section, characterized by slender, much branched stems, with long internodes and leaves arranged in pairs or fours. In this section there are four species, and two of them are in cultivation—*D. surculosa* and *D. godseffeana.* It has been suggested that these two species are identical. Indeed in a recently published Flora of the Congo by Durand and Schintz, *D. godseffeana* is quoted as a synonym of the other. Botanists often do things that horticulturists fail to follow, and this is one of them. Anyone who knows *D. surculosa,* with its long straight stems, sometimes 10 feet high, its lanceolate leaves, 5 inches long, and about an inch wide, colored dull green, with gray mottling, and red fruits the size of a small pear, would never identify with it the plant growing close to it in my garden. I have seen fruits of *D. godseffeana* [= *D. surculosa*] an inch in diameter. It is possible that there may be intermediate forms between these two, which justify their being looked upon botanically as one species, but for garden purposes they are abundantly distinct, the one being a plant of botanical interest only, while the other promises to be to the tropical garden what *Aucuba japonica* is to the subtropical.

Dracaena [*surculosa*] is a native of Lagos, upper Guinea, where it was discovered in 1892 by Millen, curator of the Botanic station in that colony. The late Mr. Baker of Kew described it in the *Gardener's Chronicle* (1894, Vol. 16, p. 312). It forms a shrub a yard or more high, and with a little attention in the way of pruning or pinching it will develop into a compact bush crowded from top to bottom with leaves. The color of the leaves is deep glossy green, mottled with creamy white. The flowers are small, greenish-white, and they are succeeded by red, berry-like fruits from ½ to 1 inch in diameter. Cuttings of the branches root with me readily in sand.

Dracaena surculosa from the same country was introduced into cultivation in 1821. My specimens of both came from my friend, Mr. August Koch. Both require a moist, rich, mucky soil. They do not grow at all in dry spots. Shade they particularly demand. I have a specimen of *D. godseffeana*, 3 to 3½ feet high, and very bushy. They did not suffer from our very cold, icy spells in Jan., 1927, nor in Jan., 1928. This is a fine plant for shady, moist lath houses in south Florida. The *D. surculosa* I find very attractive and interesting. It should be grown as a companion with the former. An article of my late friend, W. Watson, of Kew Gardens, was used in the preparation of this account.

Dracaena thalioides: The many beautiful, often brilliantly colored, Dracaenas belong to the most valuable gems of our south Florida gardens. They are far too rare as yet, but where they have been planted—as for instance in Mr. Edison's garden at Fort Myers—they always form pictures of refined and gorgeous beauty. The Everglades Nursery has a fine collection of them for sale. The subject of this note is a most lovely and interesting plant, though it lacks dazzling beauty. A large example of this West African species was in full bloom in my garden at Naples during August and September. It has numerous stems, the tallest being 5 to 6 feet high, and the sub-erect, distichously arranged leaves are from 2 to 3 feet long, the upper half of which is a bright green lanceolate blade, 3 inches long, the lower half being a narrow-channeled gray-green petiole with a broad sheathing base. As a foliage plant it has its attractions, but it is much more ornamental when in flower, its racemes being 2 feet long, branched and crowded with long, slender, tubular flowers 1½ inches long, the segments linear, ¾-inch long and recurved, their color being white, tinged with purple; they are powerfully fragrant. It flowers freely every year. Like all Dracaenas it only will grow luxuriantly in a moist, rich, half shady spot. My plant came from the Missouri Botanical Garden.

Ornamental Sedges, Grasses and Bamboos

Cyperus alternifolius, Umbrella Grass (actually a sedge) from Madagascar, is a very elegant plant much grown in pots. It is perfectly hardy in Florida. My plants grow among Ferns and Fancy Caladiums where they look very beautiful, during the summer attaining a height of about 3 to 4 feet. There is a beautiful variegated form.

Cyperus papyrus, is the celebrated Egyptian Paper Reed or Paper Rush so common on the low lands of the Nile. The dark-green triangular stems without any joints support at their top an umbel of delicate drooping leaves 10 to 15 inches long which impart to the plant a very graceful and strikingly beautiful appearance. So unique is a large vigorous clump of Papyrus that it always excites exclamations of wonder. It grows well in rich, moist soil, but then it attains only a height of 4 to 6 feet, while in the mucky soil of shallow water it grows 8 to 10 feet high. It is perfectly hardy in Florida and should be planted in the rich black soil near the water's edge. The pith-like tissues of the larger flower-stems, cut into thin strips united together by narrowly-overlapping margins, and then crossed, under pressure, by a similar arrangement of strips at right angles, constituted the papyrus of antiquity.

Ornamental Grasses: Bamboos are nothing else but grasses. They are the giants of the family. The pygmies among them remind us of the true grasses as they cover the ground in dense masses, but they always have a very different aspect when closely examined. Many of the true Grasses are highly ornamental and extremely beautiful. In the temperate zone especially, grasses, next to forests, form the chief decorative material of Nature. They serve to cover the earth and color half of the landscape. But apart from their aesthetic value when growing together in a meadow or on the prairies, interspersed with Lilies, Phlox and a thousand other flowers, individual grasses have a beauty entirely their own—a beauty and elegance not half appreciated. We grow a number of exotic species,—not many,—and neglect our native grasses entirely. But one who keeps his eyes open may find about him in field and swamp and woodland very beautiful species well worth a place in gardens and on lawns. Planting them on lawns, however, to be kept closely mown is not enough, for it does not allow the often graceful and delicately colored flower spikes to be seen. Grasses are easily cultivated, requiring but a minimum of care. They will grow with great vigor provided the soil is moist and has been made rich by decayed manure.

Among the native species the Broom Sedges are undoubtedly the most showy. When living in Texas I always admired the beautiful light brown spikes of *Andropogon glomeratus* (*A. macrourus*), known as the common Broom Sedge. Then there is the Silvery Broom Grass, *Andropogon* [*tenarius*], with heads of silvery white bearded spikes. The Indian Grass or Wood Grass, *Sorghastrum nutans* (*Andropogon nutans*), is often met with in glades and along the woodland border. In autumn the tall straight stems bear handsome open panicles of silky brown spikelets. Then we have the various perennial Panicums, among them the Switch Grass (*Panicum virgatum*) which grows 3 to 6 feet high in good moist soil and the Reed Meadow Grass (*Panicularia americana*) and the nerved Manna Grass (*Panicularia nervata*). These last two are the *Glyceria grandis* and *G. nervata* of the trade.

It would lead too far to give a full list of all the fine ornamental grasses, native and exotic, that will grow well in our Florida gardens. I may be pardoned if I confine myself only to the very best and most striking exotic species. The following species are the most beautiful and impressive and should be largely planted: Arundo Cane, Bamboo Grass, Pampas Grass and its varieties, Palm Grass and the Japanese Eulalia. The next best three would run in about the following order, Lemon Grass, Ravenna Grass, Broad-leafed *Gymnothrix*. All are perennial.

Arundo donax, Arundo, Bamboo Reed, Great Reed Grass: An old inmate in all subtropical gardens from southern Europe and northern Africa. It is the most distinct of all our tall grasses, providing quickly a peculiar scenic effect in picturesque plantation, also for intercepting almost at once the view of unsightly objects, and for giving early shelter. "Cross sections of the canes are very convenient, placed closely and erect, for sowing into them seeds of Pines, Eucalyptus, and many other trees, seedlings of which are to be forwarded on a large scale to long distances, in the same manner as Bamboo joints are used in India" (Baron F. von Mueller). Here in my garden it attained a height of from 20 to 25 feet and the clumps spread in ten years over an area of 25 feet in diameter. It increases by very thick short rhizomes which gradually increase the size of the clump. The glaucous hue and the peculiar arrangement of the leaves which clothe the stem at regular intervals, combined with their robust character, render them strikingly effective objects, particularly if situated so as to give tall plumes, which appear in late July or early in August, and are very showy. Their color is a peculiar reddish-brown. They last a long time when cut just before flowering.

Arundo donax var. *variegata,* variegated Arundo with leaves striped glossy white, is everywhere preferred to the former in Florida. It grows about 12 to 15 feet high. There are large and imposing clumps in many gardens. In spring I cut the old stems down close to the ground, and the young leaves appear immediately in large masses, forming beds of indescribable beauty, being almost entirely glossy creamy-white. These new leaves are very large and very effective. Unfortunately the variegation is lost almost entirely when the plants grow taller. But I have numerous young sprouts appeared showing their predominatingly white stripes in a most striking manner.

In Florida the clumps of Arundos should be cut down close to the ground every spring, then a thick layer of well rotted stable manure should be spread over the entire clump. The result will be magical. Enormous masses of large leaves will appear immediately and the beauty will be striking.

Thysanolaena [*maxima*], Bamboo Grass of India, Flowering Bamboo, is a most strikingly beautiful large-leaved grass. Dr. David Fairchild of the Bureau of Plant Industry, the introducer of this valuable and highly important plant, wrote me under date of July 10, 1905: "I am sending you a small quantity of *Thysanolaena* [*maxima*] seed. We have made two attempts to introduce this beautiful flowering cane, which was found by Mr. Lathrop and myself in the gardens of Poona, India." The letter was accompanied by a very fine photograph showing several clumps taken by Mr. Fairchild in one of the gardens of Poona. The seed germinated rapidly and thousands of young plants made their appearance, but here in Florida almost everything sown in the rainy season is a failure. All the young plants damped off.

In the autumn of 1906 I received five fine young plants from the government gardens at Chico, Cal., which at once started into growth and soon formed fine dense and extremely ornamental specimens. The plants have attained a height of 7 feet and when in flower they are over 8 feet high; some stems even reached a height of 10 feet. The large dark-green glossy leaves are from 17 to 20 inches long and from 3½ to 4½ inches broad, standing 4 inches apart all along the stems from the ground up. In some places they are 8 inches apart and then a node on the stem is visible. Where the leaf clasps the stem there is a purplish black conspicuous spot. The stems are glaucous with a tinge of violet. The flower-spikes appear in October and last throughout the winter. They are very elegant, much branched and of a violet-brown color. The seeds are small, almost microscopical.

Grown in masses the Bamboo Grass forms pictures of elegance and tropical luxuriance. In such cases the plants should be set about 3 or 4 feet apart. Though always beautiful, they are most attractive when the numerous flowering plumes over-tower the green mass of foliage. On lawns single specimens are very effective. Groups with a background of palms arrest the attention of every plant lover. This grass grows on high pineland as well as on low land, provided the soil is rich. Being a strictly tropical plant, the Bamboo Grass is quite tender and freezes down easily, but in spring it sprouts up again vigorously. My plants were not injured when the thermometer registered a temperature of 26°F., and when *Carica papaya* and the Mango near it were cut down to the ground. It does not creep or send out rhizomes, but it forms elegant clumps. This beautiful grass will be one of the gems of our Florida gardens when it becomes more common and it will be a monument of everlasting beauty to its introducer, Dr. David Fairchild, the enthusiastic and painstaking agricultural explorer of the Bureau of Plant Industry,—a man of high ideals and a great lover of nature.

[*Setaria palmifolia*], Palm Grass, is a native of the West Indies and has been introduced to cultivation by Reasoner Bros. It is a strikingly beautiful grass resembling a cluster of young palms or a large clump of *Curculigo*, but it is much more imposing, forming large round masses of upright gracefully arching leaves, 28 inches long and 2¾ inches broad in the middle, gradually narrowing to a point on both ends. They are strongly fluted or plicate and have a white midrib. In good soil the clumps are 5 to 6 feet high, and the flower-stalks which appear in the middle of September, attain a height of 9½ feet. Last year I set out a small plant, and though it stands on dry ground and has not had special care, it is now,—a year and a half later,—4 feet in diameter near the ground and 8 feet at the top of the foliage.

A fine healthy clump of the Palm Grass is a very beautiful sight. Unfortunately it loses much of its beauty and elegance when the flower spikes appear. At first they stand erect, but gradually they bend to all sides and finally many of them lie prostrate on the ground, taking the fine foliage with them. By October 15 its fine dense and compact appearance is almost entirely lost. To prevent this the flower stalks should be cut away as soon as they appear. As there is no beauty in the green Sorghum-like flower panicles, we need not hesitate to remove them as soon as they appear. The Palm Grass, so successfully grown in Florida, should be largely used in parks and in the wild garden. I have seen large groups of it in the foreground of Bananas and evergreen shrubs in Mr. Harry L. Beeman's large and beautiful garden on Lake Sue, near Orlando. There it is planted everywhere in the woodland, along paths, underneath trees, and also in nooks in corners of the wild garden.

[*Lasiacis divaricata*] of West Indies, Central and South America, is a grass of scandent habit, ascending high up in trees; desirable for naturalization in forests, particularly in our Florida hammock woods. [It already occurred in Florida naturally.]

Cortaderia [*selloana*], Pampas Grass, is undoubtedly the most effective of all grasses in the gardens of Florida when in bloom, growing like a native on high as well as on low land, forming everywhere large and strikingly beautiful clumps. Its name seems to indicate, and this is also the general belief, that it is a native of the pampas, the vast grassy plains of Uruguay, Paraguay and Argentina, but really it is a native of the mountains.

The following varieties are found now and then in our gardens: *C.* [*selloana* var. *monstrosa*], a very large growing kind, and *C. sel.* var. *nana*, a dwarf form. *C. sel.* var. *elegans* has very narrow slender leaves. *C. sel.* var. *elegans niveo-lineata* has foliage striped with white, and in *C. sel.* var. *elegans niveo-vitta* the leaves show white spots. The plumes of all are silky white. The varieties, *C. sel.* vars. *rosea, violacea, purpurea, carminea* have plumes of various shades as the names indicate. Of these there are also varieties with variegated foliage. All have apparently originated in southern France (Riviera) and in Italy where the Pampas Grass is esteemed as one of the most beautiful ornaments of the subtropical garden.

Miscanthus sinensis (*Eulalia japonica*), Eulalia Grass frequently attains the height of 6 to 7 feet in good soil, and forms a fine tuft of erect stems, which are furnished with foliage from the ground to the extremities. The leaves are 3 to 4 feet long and not quite an inch in breadth, very rigid and channeled with a conspicuous white groove in the center. In color, they are dark green with a purplish tinge above and glaucous green underneath. The light and airy, much branched flower heads are dark-brown when they emerge from the sheaths, but as the numerous hairs around the spikelets expand, they become gray and feathery. *M. sinensis* 'Variegatus' has leaves which are striped with white.

Miscanthus sinensis 'Zebrinus,' the Zebra-striped Eulalia, is a most beautiful plant, a dense grower, forming elegant tufts of large size. All the leaves are beautifully banded cross-wise. If only one Eulalia can be grown, this variety should be selected. *M. sinensis* 'Gracillimus' has very narrow leaves. All come from Japan and China. *M. nepalensis,* Himalaya Fairy Grass, is sometimes grown.

[*Cymbopogon citratus*], Lemon Grass, common in many of our gardens, is a native of southern Asia and tropical Australia, extending to Japan. It is a very handsome grass, growing in clumps 5 to 6 feet high. The leaves are very broad and of a glaucous hue. It is not hardy, but sprouts again vigorously if the dead leaves are not removed before the young ones appear. Yields the strongly fragrant Lemon Grass oil and from the roots the Viri oil is obtained. The leaves are very fragrant when crushed with the fingers.

[*Cymbopogon nardus*], Citronella Grass, is another strongly fragrant grass, more tender than the former, but very successfully grown in Florida, where it soon forms large, beautiful clumps, 5 to 6 feet high. It yields the very strongly scented Citronella oil used in perfumery. In Ceylon [Sri Lanka] alone about 50,000 pounds of oil have annually been distilled from this grass. Dry leaves spread out among clothing keep out insects. A native of southern Asia.

[*Vetiveria zizanioides*], Vetiver Grass or Khus-khus, is also a native of India. It has delightfully fragrant roots, of which fans are made and also the fragrant Indian mats, etc. It is a vigorous species, soon forming large clumps. It used to be grown in many of the old gardens of Florida. I have not seen it lately.

Among the new and little known grasses, the following can be successfully grown in Florida:

Pennisetum [*setaceum*] 'Atrosanguineum,' Crimson Fountain Grass, is a new and very beautiful grass introduced by H. A. Dreer of Philadelphia from New Guinea. It is a strong grower, attaining a height of about 4 feet and forms beautiful tufts. The gracefully recurved foliage is of a crimson metallic red,—a color not to be found in any other grass. The plumes, arching to all sides, are also of a crimson-bronze color. It can be used in various ways in the garden, either in groups by itself, among other grasses or a border around Cannas, *Colocasia antiguorum* or *Alocasia odora*.

Phalaris arundinacea var. *variegata*, Ribbon Grass, so common in the north in old-fashioned gardens, is rarely seen here. It is very beautiful and does well here on rich, moist soil.

Aroids

The Strap-Leaved section of the large genus *Anthurium* has been hitherto little known beyond the limits of botanic gardens, or of other private establishments in which collections of them are grown. Their flowers, though singular in structure, and in many instances richly scented, are ineffective compared with those of some of the members of other sections, such as, for instance *A. lindigii* and *A. roseum*, belonging to the set with heart-shaped leaves, with waxy-white spathes and rose-colored spadices; and the well-known *A. scherzerianum*, belonging to the sagittate-leaves set.

The plants comprised in the present group are remarkable for the firm texture and permanent freshness of their foliage, and for the property possessed by them in luxuriating in shady situations in which plants of a like habit would fail to grow. The foliage in the section under notice, though belonging to the common type of form, is, according to its length and flexibility, so variously disposed in the different species as to present great variety in habit. A few weeks ago, my friend Mr. R. F. Deckert presented me with a fine specimen of *Anthurium hugelii*, which fairly illustrates the appearance of the acaulescent or stalkless forms, and it very closely resembles, both in foliage and habit, the *Anthurium acaule* and *A. glaucescens*. The foliage is of a deep green color, while in *A. glaucescens* it is of a glaucous hue, rising to the height of 2 to 3 feet from the broad root-stock, from which arise also the almost stalkless flowers.

The type of this stalkless set, and undoubtedly the grandest of the strap-leaved forms, is *A. acaule*, which may be compared with a large Bird's-nest Fern with an open center. Its vivid green leaves attain the height of 3 to 4 feet, with a breadth of nearly one foot. Not the least of its attractions are the long, rat-tail-like violet, or sometimes yellow flower-spikes, which rise above the foliage, and for a long period emit a fragrant odor.

A plant of nearly the same dimensions, but of a totally different character, is *Anthurium hookeri,* bearing dark green, deeply ribbed, almost spatulate leaves upon short footstalks. In this the root-stock becomes elongated so as to form an erect stem, some 2 to 3 feet high, the whole of which is clothed with stout waxy-white roots proceeding downwards to the soil. Such a plant would be a fine feature, as would also the majority of those enumerated here, for associating with planted out Ferns, Carludovicas (Panama Hat Plants), and shade loving Palms, in a tropical lath house of our south Florida gardens—all arranged in a natural style.

Anthurium tetragonum has narrow foliage and longer foot-stalks than the preceding; and the root-stock which never ascends, is quite hidden beneath a hillock of stout whitish roots, some of which measure almost half an inch in thickness.

In *Anthurium coriaceum* we have a robust plant, with bluish-green very thick leaves on round foot-stalks. It is seen to best advantage where its broad spear-like leaves stand out boldly from dwarfer foliage.

We next come to forms of a more slender habit, and therefore better adapted to small pot culture. *Anthurium lanceolatum,* around which are grouped a number of scarcely distinguishable species, produces an erect stem, furnished with roots all the way up, and long, slender, gracefully recurved leaves. The flower-spikes, which are of a dull red color, emit a pungent, but agreeable odor.

Anthurium consanguineum is a more majestic species, with red-stalked, fresh-green leaves upwards of 3 feet in length. *Anthurium galeottianum* is a gracefully habited plant, at first of tufted growth, but afterward forming a stem which requires to be supported. The leaves are stiff, deeply furrowed, and taper off into long points. Its flowers are inconspicuous, but the spreading arrangement of its singular leaves makes it a distinct and attractive plant.

Anthurium costatum, though possessing a slender stem, not unlike *A. lanceolatum,* differs materially from that plant in its glossy green, deeply veined leaves, having the texture of parchment. Its flower-spikes are ruby colored, and rather showy.

In *Anthurium bakeri* we have a very desirable small plant. Its foliage, which is of a delicate glaucous green, is disposed symmetrically all around from a short ascending stem. The main feature is the showy fruiting spadices, which when mature, are studded all over with small conical red berries. I saw many of these plants years ago in full beauty and in brilliant fruit in August Koch's good collection of Aroids in the Garfield Park Conservatories in Chicago.

Anthurium dombeyanum has foliage very broad in proportion to its length, and its arrangement in a rosette manner, surrounding the erect spadices, makes it a subject not to be overlooked.

Anthurium violaceum, when a number of its slender erect stems can be grown in a group, is a most interesting plant in a fruiting state. The berries, which are closely arranged in a spike about 2 inches in length, are at first white, but ultimately change to a mauve or blue. The true plant is very scarce.

All the above mentioned species, being natives of tropical America, require a moist, warm atmosphere to grow them satisfactorily. They prefer light peaty soil, mixed with potsherds and nodules of charcoal, and ample drainage. Every good garden in south Florida should have a small lath house. This can be very simple and cheap, or it can be very pretty and costly affair. A lath house 50 × 100 feet affords ample room for the most delicate, lovely and beautiful plants, such as many ferns, small *Chamaedorea* palms, Marantas, Selaginellas, Dracaenas and many of the beautiful Aroids such as I have mentioned in the above. Such houses can be kept constantly moist and shaded. And in winter some heat in cold weather should be provided. The most glorious assemblage of Aroids in this country is found in the Garfield Park Conservatories, Chicago, where Mr. August Koch, the specialist, has brought together a magnificent collection.

Calla Lilies, [Zantedeschias]: The Calla Lilies belong to our most popular and beautiful winter bloomers, and they are grown with much success in all northern glasshouses—not all of them, but those that have the showiest flowers. As a rule, two of them,—the yellow [*Zantedeschia elliottiana*] and the white *Z. aethiopica* (or *Richardia africana*),—do well in our Florida gardens, in rich, moist soil, but they drop off and rot in summer, when placed away in dry soil or in shady places. At Eustis, Mr. Bunek grew *Z. aethiopica* permanently in a mucky, shallow pond with much success. It was almost always in leaf and flower. Our tubers of both of the above species come usually from California, where they are cultivated in many thousands with great success. A large bed containing hundreds of thrifty plants and flowering profusely (of the two above mentioned species) is a glorious sight in our Florida winter gardens, but I prefer by far the yellow *Z. elliottiana* in full bloom.

The genus [*Zantedeschia*] has been brought in prominent notice within the last 35 years by the flowering under cultivation of several new and beautiful species, among them *Z. elliottiana* and *Z. pentlandii*. First, however, we much come to some decision with regard to their general title. They are certainly not Callas—though this name is in the headline. The only true *Calla* is the Bog Arum of some parts of Europe and North America, and which is *Calla palustris* L. The name *Calla aethiopica* is also a Linnaean name, but in 1818 Kunth, a German botanist, founded the genus *Richardia*, in compliment of Richard, a contemporary French botanist. He called the common and best known, and most popular form *R. africana*, while others retained the name *R. aethiopica*. This name *Richardia* for the genus has been accepted by botanists although it has not yet become generally accepted in horticulture. Another name, a frightful one, viz., *Zantedeschia*, has been proposed for the genus, but as *Richardia* was accepted by the Hookers, Bentham, Schott and others, we may reasonably claim to keep it. [The name accepted in modern taxonomy is *Zantedeschia*.]

The genus consists now of eight species, all African. They all have a perennial tuberous root-stalk, not unlike the Caladium, from which spring the annual leaves and flower-scapes, the former with folding stalks, which form a kind of stem, bearing sagittate leaves, the latter erect, stout, and bearing a large spathe. There is a noteworthy difference between *Zantedeschia aethiopica* and the others, the former having a rhizome and never naturally dying down.

[*Zantedeschia aethiopica*] was first introduced into Europe from South Africa in 1687. It is emphatically a Cape plant (Cape of Good Hope), and it is not found within 1,000 miles of the Nile. The name "Lily of the Nile" is therefore absurd. It was among the plants grown by Philip Miller in the old Botanical Garden at Chelsea in 1731. In some parts of England, for instance Cornwall, it has become naturalized, covering large areas of shallow water, spreading and flowering with the same freedom as in the ditches and swamps of the Cape. It varies considerably in the size of the spathes. I have seen them 10 inches long, and I am told that larger ones even have been grown by a cultivator who cut off most of the leaf-blades when the spathes are developing. The variety called 'Little Gem' is a pigmy form, the height, size of leaf and spathes being very small. I find, however, that liberal culture tends to destroy the chief characteristic of this variety. There are other varieties and named kinds.

I have experimented a good deal with this Calla Lily here in Central Florida. Those that I set out in spring invariably died, after having made a weak growth. On the other hand, the ones planted in October and November began to grow vigorously and flowered beautifully during the winter months. Late, usually in May, the leaves began to assume a sickly yellowish color and finally died, and the bulbs rotted. I have often tried to save them in various ways, but always without success. Those who have had better results should report their mode of culture. It may be possible to grow Callas permanently in rich, mucky shallow pools—a way that a few have successfully followed.

[*Zantedeschia albomaculata*] was introduced from Natal in 1899, but it never has become a popular garden plant. It has sagittate leaves, the basal lobes long and ear-like (much thinner in texture than in *Z. aethiopica*, green, and marked with irregular gray-white translucent spots and blotches. The spathe is about 5 inches long, 2 inches wide, dull creamy-yellow with a blotch of crimson at the base. It is folded for nearly its full length and hides the yellow spadix. Except in botanical collections it is not worth growing, though there may be a chance to use it in cross-breeding.

A variety of *Zantedeschia albomaculata* with pale greenish-yellow spathe called *Richardia hastata* was introduced from Natal in 1857 by James Veitch and Sons, who received it as a "yellow Calla, which from its smallness and beauty and being also hardy, will be much prized." It is not hardy, and the color of its spathe is dull pale yellow with a blotch of crimson at the base inside. In this species the leaves are broader than typical *Z. albomaculata*, thick, and dull green in color, not spotted, and the leaf-stalk bears a few short, soft hairs about the lower part. The spathe is broad at the base, more cup-like than trumpet-shaped, and the tail-like tip is short and erect. I have never seen the plant with spathes of so rich a yellow color as shown in the *Garden* (Vol. 18, p. 596, 1888). This species was re-introduced in 1892 and distributed afterward under the name of "Pride of the Congo." It was afterward informally named *Richardia lutwychei,* by Mr. N. E. Brown, who first thought it distinct from *R. hastata.* It would be interesting to know if the plant really came from the region of the Congo. The account given in the *Garden* (Vol. 42, p. 558, 1892) is after all, only an auction-room story. Who was the collector? I believe that the plant, distributed in 1892 by Mr. Delenil under the name *Richardia aurita* said to be of garden origin, is merely a form of this species.

Another variety of *Zandeschia albomaculata,* [*Zantedeschia melanoleuca*], was introduced from Natal in 1868. It is easily recognized by its broad, cordate, succulent leaves and the presence of scattered setiferous hairs on the lower part of the red-tinted petioles. The leaf-blade is from 6 inches to a foot in length, dark green, sometimes with a few oblong, semi-transparent white spots, following the direction of the nerves. The spathe is about 3 inches, not folded and trumpet-shaped, as in the others, but open to the base so that the whole of the spadix is exposed. The color of the spathe is straw yellow and there is a large vinous-purple blotch at the base.

[*Zantedschia rehmannii*] also has been introduced from Natal as the "Pink-flowered Calla," and although we have it on the most trustworthy authority that its spathes are wholly of a purple rose color in Natal, all the plants flowered in Europe have had white spathes faintly flashed with rose. It was first described by Dr. Engler, and first flowered in 1888 in the Cambridge Botanic Gardens. In December last year (1898) Mr. Medley Wood, curator of the Natal Botanic Gardens, sent to Kew tubers of plants which had flowered with him, and of which he had made the colored drawings which accompanied the tubers. The picture represented a flower of about the same size as that of the dwarf *Z. aethiopica,* viz., 4 inches long, erect, trumpet-shaped, with a tail-like tip an inch long, the whole colored dull rose outside, rose-purple inside, with a blotch of dark crimson at the base, seen only inside. One of the Kew plants flowered this year, and precisely as at Cambridge, the spathe was white, with a tinge of rose on the margin only. Apparently some condition essential to the development of the color is wanting in Europe, and probably this condition is bright sunshine. *Z. rehmannii* differs from all other species in having lanceolate, not sagittate, leaf blades. It is a pretty little plant with possibilities behind it in the propensity to produce rose-colored flowers under certain conditions.

[*Zantedeschia elliottiana*] is a glorious flowering winter plant at Orlando, where Mr. C. P. Dickinson, the well-known attorney, always grows large beds of them. They usually flower in March, and the brilliant yellow masses and the noble form of the flowers form pictures of indescribable beauty. They are planted usually closely together in rich soil, consisting of leaf mould and old cow manure. The show keeps on for weeks, and the foliage dies down in June. The tubers do not keep well in Florida, though Mr. Dickinson has often tried to save them till the next planting. As in the common Calla (*Z. aethiopica*) they rot invariably. He obtains his supply annually—several hundred tubers—from California, where they evidently grow and multiply without any trouble. The cause is undoubtedly found in our extremely humid summer climate, whereas that of California is very dry,—the air as well as the soil. Mr. Dickinson's garden is in summer replete with masses of exquisite fancy-leafed Caladiums, which do not grow in half-shade, but in the open in the center of his lawns, and in winter the brilliant Callas (*Z. elliottiana*) occupy their places.

[*Zantedeschia elliottiana*] is one of the two yellow spotted species which have lately here caused a lot of excitement in the horticultural world. They are almost as fine in stature, substance, size and form of spathe as the best varieties of *Zantedeschia aethiopica*, while the color of the spathe is a rich, clear, lustrous yellow, very different from the yellow of the older species. *Z. elliottiana* was introduced by Captain Elliott of Farnborough Park, Hampshire, who raised it from seed given to him in 1886 as those of a red Arum. Only one plant was raised, and it flowered in 1889, though it was not exhibited till the following spring, when it was sent to one of the meetings of the Royal Horticultural Society, where it caused a sensation. It ripened seeds from which plants were raised, which flowered and proved identical with the parent. This fact is noteworthy, as some have suggested that this species is of hybrid origin. Every year since its first appearance it has improved in the size of its spathe and depth of color. It differs from *Z. pentlandii* in having the leaves spotted as in *Z. albomaculata*. The tuber is like that of the ordinary Caladium; the growth is annual. The leaves are as large as those of *Z. aethiopica*, with mottled petioles and the blade is marked with a few gray-white translucent spots. The tuber is very proliferous, and every tubercle, if removed and potted, will grow into flowering size in two years. The spathe is yolk-of-egg color, clear and beautiful, becoming greenish with age.

[*Zantedeschia pentlandii*] is another new species which was first shown in flower by Mr. R. Whyte, Pentland House, Lee, in June 1892, when it was awarded a first class certificate by the Royal Horticultural Society. Mr. Watson was informed by Mr. Whyte that he did not import the plant, but a friend gave him in 1890, six tubers, among which he suspected there was a yellow-flowered Calla. The first two that flowered were *Z. aethiopica*, simply, but the third was the plant exhibited in 1892 and called *Calla pentlandii* by Mr. Whyte. This is as beautiful as *Z. elliottiana*. Some say it is more beautiful. It has the same sturdy habit, but differs from the latter in having thicker, larger, dark green leaves without spots, the petioles mottled with dull red, and the spathe, which is as large as that of *Z. aethiopica*, is bright golden yellow with a small blotch of crimson at the base. This plant also dies down every year, and its Caladium-like tuber is very prolific. Mr. Whyte did not know the origin of his plants, but in May, 1892, Mr. E. E. Galpin, F.L.S., then residing in Barberton, South Africa, paid a visit to Kew and brought with him six tubers of a yellow-flowered *Richardia* [*Zantedeschia*] which had been presented to him by a gentleman in the Transvaal, who obtained them from an artillery-man, who got them from a Basuto chief while in active service. One of these flowered at Kew in May last, and was identical with *Z. pentlandii*.

[*Zantedeschia albomaculata* subsp. *macrocarpa*] is the eighth one. We have not yet discovered the right treatment of the tubers during our summers. The plants themselves require more warmth than the common Calla Lily. As soon as the right treatment has been discovered these two latter, as well as *Z. aethiopica*, will be the most valuable of the genus in our Florida winter gardens. Both of these species,—*Z. elliottiana* as well as *Z. pentlandii*,—are so prolific that they are sure to become common in our gardens. They also ripen seeds freely.

Sir Joseph Hooker characterized *Z. pentlandii* in the following way in the *Botanical Magazine*: "*Z. Pentlandii* is much the largest-leaved species, and is the only one with deeply gamboge-yellow spathe within, which is much the largest and broadest of any." Its home is Basutoland, S. Africa. Most of the foregoing notes were adapted from an article by W. Watson, late Curator of Kew Gardens, in the *Garden* (1894, Vol. 46, p. 446–447). [The nomenclature has been revised to conform with C. Letty's "The Genus *Zantedeschia*," *Bothelia* 11 (1973):5–26.]

Monstera deliciosa: From Jamaica comes the following report of this fine plant: "Beware of this fruit whose praises have been sung by those who have little experience of it—*Monstera deliciosa*—delicious and Pineapple-like in scent, but those black threads in the fragrant flesh are flinty darts which will stick in tongue and throat and cause irritation. A tiny mouthful and you will say, 'I wish I had more'; as much as you want, and it will be, 'Never again!' The very look of the plant argues its unwholesomeness."

I have grown this beautiful plant, which was formerly known as *Philodendron pertusum,* in my greenhouse in Milwaukee, where it covered the entire east side of the glasshouse and flowered abundantly and ripened many fruits, which were a delicacy to all who tried to eat them. In my garden at Gotha I also had large plants with hundreds of fruits annually. The flowers are large, nearly white and each like large Calla Lilies. It is quite safe to eat the fruit, which looks like an ear of common Maize in its green state, and it is perfectly delicious to those who like it, if rightly prepared for the palate or the dessert table. It must be thoroughly ripe so that its coat of hexagons falls away with a touch, and then the pulpy segments are luscious and agreeable, despite the black threads which merely represent the defunct stamens of the flowers. It is the husk or outer coating only that is full of sharp and prickly raphides, not the ripe fruit itself. A fully ripe fruit of *Monstera deliciosa* is more delicious than any banana. The plant itself is of great ornamental value. The leaves are large and full of holes—natural holes—and it forms a most exquisite climber on walls and trees and even palms. Rich moist soil and half-shade in a warm spot are all it requires.

Water Lilies and Ferns

The hardy Nymphaeas are in their best condition here just now (June 10) and have been so since six weeks or more. All water lilies (hardy and tropical) grow so well in the open in Florida that all known species and hybrids have been introduced into cultivation, and the plant lovers have a wealth of material available. We have here the most congenial climate and have thousands of beautiful lakes; many of them with mucky and muddy edges. In most large places where an interest is taken in water gardens may usually be found not only hardy water lilies, but also the best tropical kinds, both day and night blooming. The Nelumbiums, as a rule, however, do not thrive, though there were fine flowering specimens to be seen of *N. speciosum* several years ago in the grounds of the Koreshan Unity at Estero, Florida. It will be seen that with this wealth of plants with such varying habits, we have an advantage over less favored localities. We have three native species of Nymphaeas,—*N. odorata, N. tuberosa* and [*N. mexicana*]—the first of which is very widely spread, and may be found in numerous forms and in various tones of pink, as well as pure white. Marliac's beautiful hybrids, however, have given a great impetus to the cultivation of hardy water lilies, they being without exception unique, as improvements of previously existing kinds. Of course they grow luxuriantly here and are well known. *Nymphaea alba* seems to be the largest white-flowered water lily—its blooms measuring 8 inches in diameter. It became naturalized in my little Lake Audubon where it is almost constantly in flower. It resembles *Nymphaea tuberosa,* a fine species, but to be avoided, as it will crowd out any other, owing to its strong growth and multiplication of tubers, buds and seeds. *N.* XMarliacea-Rosa has beautiful pink flowers, surpassing our native *N. odorata* var. *rosea* in size and fine coloring, and there are quite a number of yellow hybrids—beautiful and distinct. All the distinctly tropical species—blue, vivid red and yellow—grow luxuriantly in Florida. The beautiful *N.* [*capensis* var. *zanzibariensis*], blue in various hues, is my special favorite. Many of these flowers are deliciously fragrant. Water lilies do not thrive well in running water. They prosper in quiet pools of moderate depth, say 2½ feet, fully exposed to the sunlight. The original planting should be in good, heavy loam with a plentiful supply of well-decomposed old cow manure. The water should not be changed often—if grown in concrete tanks or tubs. Unfortunately the leaves of these water lilies are often eaten by cooters or water turtles.

A Forest of Tree Ferns: There is a forest of the most beautiful Tree Ferns, of the species [*Cyathea australis*], in the Everglades Nursery at Fort Myers. There are hundreds of perfect, dense palm-like specimens growing close together. Each one is planted in a tub. They are all as tall as, or taller than a man, 6 to 8 feet high, and almost as broad. All are perfect specimens and in the very best of health. The sight is one of the most beautiful, the most picturesque and impressive I ever have seen. There is nowhere in this country, and nowhere in Europe, I believe, such a picture of so many to be seen. Tree Ferns range with Palms and Cycads as the most decorative plants to be found. They are always inhabitants of tropical countries of the old and new world, but few of them grow in the hot lowlands. The majority of them are found in cool mountain regions from 1,000 to 5,000 feet of altitude. They are unable to stand frost—too much of it at least—but they also shun heat, and are always averse to drouth. Where they grow—and they are found all over the tropical world—they are always hailed with extreme pleasure and delight. In South Australia a number of the finest species grow in gullies—fern gullies—in shaded, moist, cool and well-drained soil.

Some of these Australians are doing well in many gardens of central and south Florida, particularly where the soil is mixed with lime-stone rock. They will not thrive well in sour soils, or land that is imperfectly drained. The true [*Cyathea australis*], the Australian Tree Fern, is the one most conspicuously seen in our gardens.

We—most of us—are deprived of the pleasure to admire them in their native haunts, though many as fine species grow close to our doors in Cuba and the Isle of Pines, but that forest of Tree Ferns I bring to reader's mind can be seen and admired by every one who is interested in the beauty of nature, in fine form, and palm-like grace and elegance. Every one who visits Fort Myers should not fail to enjoy this most exquisite sight.

I have grown many Tree Ferns at Palm Cottage Gardens, particularly the species in question, also the [New Zealand] [*Alsophila tricolor*], a fine tall, slender species; the extremely beautiful but very slow-growing *Cibotium schiedei* from Mexico; the fine rather small *Blechnum brasiliense*, and many others, in my large lath-roofed plant shed. The Alsophilas attained a height of from 8 to 15 feet. All were wiped out by the heavy freeze in February, 1917, except *Cibotium schiedei* which only lost its leaves.

Years ago there was a long gully or ravine in one of the large gardens in Orlando, running from Lake Lucerne to Lake Cherokee. It belonged to two most enthusiastic plant lovers I ever have met, the late Mr. and Mrs. Carpenter. It was beautifully planted with Seaforthia [Alexander] Palms, masses of Azaleas and many fine tall specimens of [*Cyathea*] *australis*. Some of these Tree Ferns were 20 feet high and of great beauty. All of these ferns and palms were killed outright by the heavy freeze. They never had suffered in the previous ten years, when only a white frost now and then occurred. Most of these specimens were from 10 to 12 years old when they were destroyed. In many of the gardens of Orlando, as well as of Winter Park, one often sees fine specimens of the Australian Tree Fern on shady lawns, and they are always a most attractive sight.

Tree Ferns are easily grown in shady, moist spots and in good well-drained soil. They do not thrive in excessively wet, sour, undrained ground. My specimens at Gotha grew with the greatest luxuriance, but they did not thrive in my Naples garden, where the soil conditions were not to their liking. The deep wet muck, where Dracaenas grow with utmost vigor, did not suit them. They gradually pined away, after having struggled eight years with unnatural conditions. Ferns are almost always planted in rich leaf-soil. In fact they are usually found in their wild haunts in well composted leaf mold. This soil also is used for Tree Ferns, but I found it very beneficial to apply also good manure. Commercial and chemical fertilizers should never be used. A liberal use of fresh cow manure of which a thick layer is placed over the soil in which each plant is growing, had a wonderful stimulating effect on the growth and vigor of my specimen Tree Ferns.

My correspondence of late has become so extremely large that I find it impossible to answer all letters promptly, During the past year 57 inquiries came on Ferns alone. There seem to be large Fern congregations in the State. Here I shall only take notice of a letter inquiring whether or not the Fern *Cibotium barometz,* the so called "Scythian Lamb," could be grown successfully in Florida and if it could be obtained from one of our nurseries. As I have had it in my collection at Palm Cottage Gardens for years, I quote from my Notebook: "*Cibotium barometz,* grown from spores received from Hong Kong, is a perfect success, a fine dense fern with large beautifully green leaves, which are covered on their stipes or leaf-stalks with soft brown wool. It is a native of southern China, Assam and Formosa, and the Malayan region. A magnificent woodland Fern."

This Fern, offered under the above name, is spurious, and is widely different from the true *Cibotium barometz.* The fronds or leaves of the true species are bipinnate, and rise to a height of 10 to 14 feet, produced from a procumbent and progressing caudex or stem, which is densely covered with long, light-brown, silky hairs (characteristic of the genus), when old looking like wool, and when lying on the ground having the appearance of a wool-clad animal. The story told to early travelers led them to describe it as a plant of flesh and blood. The traveler's tale upon the subject is that on an elevated plain of vast extent, in countries east of the Volga, grows a very wonderful plant, with the shape and appearance of a lamb, having feet, head, and tail distinctly formed, and its skin covered with soft down. The lamb grows upon a stalk about 3 feet high, the part by which it is sustained being a kind of navel, it turns about and bends to the herbage which serves for its food, and when the grass fails it dries up and pines away. The real facts are that the caudex or stem of this fern is decumbent, progressing in length a foot or more according to age, and is 3 or more inches in diameter. Its wooly appearance has led it to be likened to a lamb, the native name of it being *barometz,* and by travelers the "Tartarial Lamb," and by others, "*Agreus Scythicus,*" or "Scythian Lamb." Dr. L. H. Bailey in his great work *Standard Cyclopedia of Horticulture* gives on page 768 (Vol. II) a picture of this "Scythian Lamb," reproduced from an old book.

To make the story plausible the natives turn the woolly stipes upside down, cutting away the fronds, leaving a portion of the lower part of the stipes (leaf stems), four of which serve as legs, and thus the resemblance of a wooly animal is complete, and, being so manipulated, much resembles a weasel. The Chinese traveler and botanist, Lourier, was the first to describe it as a Fern.

About a hundred years ago the late John Reeves, who had long resided in Canton, succeeded in obtaining living plants of it, which he transmitted to England, and which first produced good spores.

[*Cibotium menziesii*], native of the Hawaiian Islands, differs from *C. barometz,* as being arborescent—real Tree Ferns—the stems attaining a height of 24 feet, the crown of fronds adding 12 feet more, making the total height of the tree 36 feet. The base of the stipes or leaf-stems of the fronds is densely furnished with fine silky hairs, which being permanent, clothe the stem, forming a thick wool-like coat, which is collected and used for stuffing cushions, mattresses and the like. Shiploads of this wool, known in the trade by the name of pulu, were sent to California, but lately it has fallen into disuse.

We need not only Palm specialists, and men of means, who can import the stems of the many Cycads from Africa, Australia and Mexico, and take up their cultivation in Florida. We need many other specialists, but the Ferns also should find numerous adherents. To be sure, Ferns are at present grown by the acre in central Florida, but it is only one genus that is grown,—*Nephrolepis* or Boston Ferns. In these large establishments we do not find a single species belonging to another genus, and their owners—who grow these plants only for the dollar,—have no knowledge, either scientifically or horticulturally, of ferns.

One is often misled by the sign "Fernery," our disappointment is complete. We see not a single Fern, but only *Asparagus* [*setaceus*], a plant not even remotely related to Ferns. It should never be called a Fern, but its really good, honest and correct name, Asparagus, should always be used.

Australian "Pine," Tonga Plant, and Upas Tree

An article in the *American Eagle*, "Palms and Pines," contains much timely advice. The planting of the so-called Australian Pine is overdone, in Lee (Collier) as well as in Dade County. It is a strictly tropical tree, and does not thrive even as far north as Orange County. These trees are called in Australia "beef-wood" and "she-oaks." The name Australian Pine is still more incorrect than the two others just mentioned, as it is no pine at all, not even distantly related to it. The botanical name is *Casuarina,* this species in particular being *Casuarina equisetifolia. Casuarina* is not only the correct name but also very pretty and easy to remember. Intellectual people and people of good taste and refinement should use it in preference to all others. It is supposed to be derived from the resemblance of the long, sweeping, leafless branches to the drooping feathers of the cassowary, which is a native of the same country as the majority of the Casuarinas.

The Casuarina has its place in nature and is invaluable as a windbreak along tropical shores. It is truly wonderful how it will grow under quite adverse conditions, standing the poor sandy soil and the salt spray better than most trees do. Originally a native of North Australia, it is at present found in eastern Africa, southern Asia, Polynesia, on our lower keys and the mainland of south Florida. And it is used and planted in larger numbers than any other tree I know of. Says young Mr. Reasoner (N.A.): "The good Lord never meant it for every use, which is about what you seem to expect of it. For seashore use, where salt and poor soil must be combated, it is without a peer, but that is about enough to expect of it."

It is the fastest grower I know. Four years ago, George Hendrie, of Naples, planted a wind-break of Casuarinas all around his fine garden, and all of them have attained a height of 50 feet, forming a dense wall of somber green. A seedling planted out grew 10 feet in less than a year. At Fort Myers it is largely planted, mostly in the form of hedges, for which purpose it is well adapted, as it stands clipping very well. Often I have noticed specimens trimmed in such a way that they suggested Italian cypresses.

The wood of this tree is hard and fine-grained. It is excellent for furniture, as it takes a fine polish. In India and elsewhere it supplies a valuable fire-wood, and for this purpose alone it should be planted largely on waste land in south Florida.

Another much more beautiful species, sometimes found in our gardens, is *Casuarina cunninghamiana.* I planted a small specimen received from the Bureau of Plant Industry, on my place at Naples, where it attained a height of about 25 feet in three years. It grows in the poorest white sand. In New South Wales, its native home, it reaches a height of from 60 to 70 feet. The hard, close-grained, pretty wood is used for many purposes.

In my collection I also grow *Casuarina glauca,* widely distributed through southeastern Australia, even in desert lands. It is of rapid growth and its wood is also very valuable. My specimens of [*C. stricta*] are small yet. In Australia it is called the coast she-oak.

Casuarinas are extremely rapid growers, forming an effective windbreak within a few years. They should never be used to border streets. For this purpose there is no nobler, no finer tree than our native Royal Palm. In comparison with it the Casuarina is plebeian.

Tonga Plant: A. L. F. writes: "Sometime ago I wrote to a northern botanical garden for information about a plant from the Fiji Islands, called the Tonga Plant. I received a friendly letter with the advice to write you about it, because you had made the study and the cultivation of tropical plants your specialty."

I do not know whether or not I can give the requested information, but I have made the cultivation of the above named plant, which I received under the name of Tonga Plant, a specialty. Years ago the public began to imagine what the meaning could be of the mystical word Tonga, which appeared in every railway station and as an inscription of every billboard on wooden fence in and about Chicago and other principal cities here and in Europe. I soon found, however, that it meant a specific for neuralgia and since that time (in the late 1870's) it has unlike most other novelties introduced in such conspicuous way, not only maintained its reputation, but as I believe, increased it.

When first introduced, Tonga was to be had only in the form in which it was sent here from Fiji, mainly in small bundles or balls, measuring only 4 to

5 inches by 3 in diameter. The wrapper in which the substance was contained consisted of portions of the fibrous sheath of the Coconut Palm, and the contents appeared like pieces of bark, leaf and woody fiber broken so small as to make it extremely difficult to identify it botanically. The instructions as to its use were as follows: "The bundle, without being unfastened, to be steeped in half a tumbler of cold water for ten minutes, then squeeze the liquid from the bundle back again into the tumbler, and take a claret glass of the infusion three times a day, about half an hour before each meal. Dry the bundle and hang it up in a dry place to prevent it getting mouldy. It will answer for 12 months." Since this, however, the medicine has been prepared in a more elegant form.

The only record of its use was that which accompanied it when first brought to this country, that it had been used for several years by the aborigines in the Fiji Islands, and a European who married a chief's daughter learned the secret from his father-in-law, in whose family the knowledge of the composition of this remedy had been an heirloom for upward of 200 years.

From a careful microscopical examination of the fragments contained in these bundles, Mr. E. M. Holmes, of the Pharmaceutical Society, arrived at the conclusion that they belonged to some Aroidous plant, and probably to [*Epipremnum pinnatum*]; some portions, however, belonged to a totally different order, but there was no doubt that the active principle of Tonga was found alone in the Aroid. Mr. Holmes' discovery, both to the botanical affinity of the plant forming the principal portion of the drug, and the absence of any active principle in the substance accompanying it, has since been borne out by other observers, some of whom have shown that this foreign matter, so to speak, is Verbenaceae.

The writer has *Premna taitensis,* a plant belonging to the Verbenaceae. He also has *Premna* [*pubescens*] in his collection. The true Tonga Plant is now referred to *Epipremnum mirabile* [?], and thus identification has been made by the famous botanist, N. E. Brown, of the Kew Herbarium, in whose hands a leaf of the plant was placed, and who immediately recognized it as being identical with a plant in Mr. Ball's possession, which had been received from the Fiji Islands by way of the Botanical Garden of Sydney. I have a fine specimen of it in my garden at Naples, which originally came from the Missouri Botanical Garden. It grows in rich mucky soil and climbs up the trunk of a Cabbage Palm, having grown up to about 9 feet at present. It reminds one somewhat of *Monstera deliciosa,* but the leaves are not perforated, but equally divided up into pinatifid segments. It is a very ornamental climber, and has not suffered from cold during the past few winters, though I believe that it will lose its fine large leaves during a real cold spell. The flowers are very much like those of the *Monstera,* only much smaller and not such a pure creamy-white color. Its fruits I never have seen. The plant seems to have a wide distribution, being also found in Java, Sumatra, other Malayan Islands and north Australia. It is usually found in damp, shady woods, climbing up into the tallest trees.

The Upas Tree: The following inquiry came several months ago: "I have read lately an account of the notorious Upas Tree, about its dangers and terrible poisonous qualities. I enclose a clipping from a paper, and would be glad to obtain some real trustworthy information."

In my opinion the Upas Tree (*Antiaris toxicaria*) is no more poisonous than our Poison Ivy,—perhaps less so. It is an interesting evergreen tree, belonging to the family Urticaceae, with quite large entire leaves, which look smooth, but have a rather rough feeling to the touch. The milky sap exudes plentifully from the broken-off leaf, or when a leaf is cracked. I found the small trees hardy in my lath house at Gotha from 1912 to 1917 when they were destroyed by a disastrous freeze early in February, 1917,—a month of calamity when I not only lost almost all my strictly tropical plants, but also about 75,000 Caladiums.

Previous to this freeze we had had mild winters and no frost. I had 4 crops of fine Mangoes and bushels of Rose Apples, and also a few West Indian Avocados. In 1912 I received seeds of the Upas Tree (*Antiaris toxicaria*), Cinchonas and *Hevea brasiliensis* from the celebrated Buitenzorg Botanical Gardens. All the seeds germinated, but I lost the Cinchonas after they had grown several inches. As the soil was rather moist and rich, the small Upas Trees and the Brazilian Rubber plants grew quite luxuriously, and had reached a height of about 3 feet when the freeze wiped them out. Both species are strictly tropical, but they never suffered from cold before.

Though I handled the leaves, as well as the cuttings, just as I handle Oleander cuttings, I never felt an ill effect. As I am perfectly immune against the poisonous properties of the Poison Ivy this experience may not be considered of much value, as many others may suffer. One of the plants stood close to a path, and visitors often came in contact with it, but I never have heard that anyone had been poisoned. Imagination, I think, has much to do with the bad reputation of the Upas Tree. The milky sap quite often stained my hands, but I never felt a burning irritation, as I experienced in the case of *Hura crepitans.*

The reports made by travelers in the tropics during the past two centuries were often of a very sensational character. Indeed, every account that was not greatly exaggerated was not considered of much importance. To attract the attention of the reader everything seen was described as of an abnormal character. The properties of the plant were vastly enlarged. The fruits were described as of a tremendous size, and produced in wonderful profusion. But the wildest statements in regard to the properties of plants were those made in regard to the poisonous character of the Upas Tree, which was fabled to diffuse a poisonous atmosphere around it, which was fatal to every living thing that came within its influence.

The most exaggerated statements about that tree were circulated by a surgeon about the close of the Eighteenth Century. The tree was described as growing in a desert tract of Java, with no other plants near it for a distance of 10 or 12 miles. Criminals condemned to die were offered the chance of life if they could go to the Upas Trees and collect some of the poison. They were supplied with proper directions and armed with due precautions, but not more than two out of every twenty ever returned. The Dutch surgeon, Foersch, states that he had derived his information from some of those who had been lucky enough to escape, although the ground around the trees was strewn with the bones of their predecessors; and such was the virulence of the poison that there are no fish in the waters, nor has any rat, mouse or any other vermin been seen there, and when any birds fly so near this tree that the effluvia reaches them, they fall a sacrifice to the effects of the poison.

It is now ascertained that the Upas Tree exerts a wholesome rather than a poisonous influence. That its fruit is poisonous does not admit of a doubt, and that the whole tree abounds in a white milky juice which is also an acid poison. "If a single drop of this juice," says a reliable authority,

> falls on the skin, it causes a sensation like the touch of a hot iron and raises a blister.
>
> Now let us look at its virtues. This tree is found in Java, growing in certain low valleys which are rendered unhealthy by an escape of carbonic acid gas from crevices in the ground, and which is given off in such

abundance as to be fatal to animals that approach too closely. These pestiferous valleys are connected with the numerous volcanos in the island. The craters of some of these emit, according to the best authorities, sulphuric vapors in such abundance as to cause the death of a great number of tigers, birds and insects, while the rivers and lakes are in some cases so charged with sulphuric acid that no fish can live in them. Now, while this tree had to bear the reproach really due to the volcanos and their products, they were undoubtedly created to take from the atmosphere those deadly gases and to transform them into healthy ones for the sustenance of animal life. This is abundantly shown by the fact that no other vegetable form can exist in those localities. This is the plant's work, and there cannot be found a spot where there is animal life, but there are plants whose mission it is to take from the atmosphere the gases that are injurious to animal life. (C. L. Allen)

This statement seems to me doubtful. At least it needs thorough investigation.

Nehrling's Favorite Places of Beauty

When I for the first time visited Fort Myers I was charmed with the beautiful gardens I found—the finest, the richest and the oldest being the one planted many years ago by the late Mrs. J. E. Hendry—the H. E. Heitman garden of the present day. Here I saw trees that I had never seen before in large and elegant specimens. It would lead me too far from my subject should I attempt to go into detail. I have somewhere else called Fort Myers "a precious tropical jewel put in a wonderful setting." The real glory of this enchanting city on the shore of the Caloosahatchee is found in the many tall, sublimely beautiful specimens of Royal Palms, but there are so many other tropical trees to admire that to mention them all, would require more space than is available for this sketch.

Tropical Fort Myers

When we enter Fort Myers, a most wonderful picture is placed before our eyes—color masses of the most exquisite hues. We have the feeling of entering fairyland. This impression is mainly caused by the masses of glowing purplish-scarlet Bougainvillea "Crimson Lake," beds of Crotons, Acalyphas, Screw-pines, and groups and avenues of Royal Palms, the most effective and beautiful of all Palms. The second time I entered the city, the Bougainvilleas only showed scattered color patches, but now (in June) the Royal Poinciana was a blaze of dazzling orange-scarlet.

This is the real home of tropical horticulture, as the climate is very perfect, the soil deep, rich and moist. Prof. Chas. T. Simpson, of Little River, Fla., has called Fort Myers "the gem" of tropical ornamental horticulture, and the writer fully agrees with this celebrated authority. With only little attention, the most beautiful plants in existence—such as Crotons, Dracaenas, the various species of *Pandanus, Hibiscus, Aralia* and particularly Palms—grow here to perfection. The picture is often marred, however, by the many old orange groves, even in the best residential parts, consisting of ugly, scraggy, almost leafless trees of no commercial value. Fort Myers is replete with the most beautiful seedling Mango Trees—tall, dense, massive and beautifully formed—from an ornamental standpoint the most charming shade tree imaginable.

Some of these giants must be at least 40 or 50 years old. The grounds of the Royal Palm Hotel contain the finest the writer has ever seen in south Florida. The gardener, Mr. F. W. Striebel, takes loving care of all his plants. He not only adds constantly to the list by exchange, but he attends to every plant with particular interest and studies its requirements. It is a pleasure to walk with this capable man over the extensive ground. Here we find a number of rare palms in full fruit such as *Livistona altissima,* and [*Aiphanes caryotifolia*], the latter with large bunches of vivid orange-colored fruits, each the size of a cherry. And there is a treasure of unspeakable value in these grounds, the Cannon-ball Tree (*Couroupita guianensis*) the only large fruiting specimen in this country. It flowers and fruits at the same time. The flowers are large, very difficult to describe. They appear in dense masses along the trunk and main limbs. Here we also see the clusters of round, hard-shelled fruits, having the shape and size of a cannon-ball. The tree is about 60 feet high, and near it stands a Mahogany Tree. The many Royal and Coconut Palms, the thickets of *Pandanus* and *Acalypha,* the dense masses of Areca Palms, the perfectly round specimens of Crotons combine to make this place an earthly paradise.

In front of the hotel grows an immense Rubber Tree (*Ficus elastica*) and several of the Date Palms are covered with intricate masses of Bougainvillea. The fine green lawn and the lovely landscape effects of the entire ground all around make this a first-class show-place. In walking around along First Street we find a large number of many rare and beautiful tropical Palms, trees and shrubs. There is a tall fine specimen of the Sugar Palm [*Arenga pinnata*] in Capt. Gwynne's garden, and Mr. Kingston's garden is extremely rich in rare palms, such as *Pritchardia thurstonii, Balaka* sp., [*Roystonea borinquena*], *Howea forsteriana,* and fine species of *Thrinax.* In walking around one sensation follows the other. What is that dense tree with immense banjo-shaped leathery leaves and deep red cherry-like fruits? It is one of the rare plants in northern conservatories, a Rubber Tree (*Ficus pandurata*), and on the opposite side of the street there is an immense native rubber or Florida Banyan tree (*Ficus aurea*). Approaching the business part of the town we come upon an old garden, consisting of dense broad Tamarinds, magnificent specimens of Sapodillas, one of the finest ornamentals, aside from its fruit-bearing importance; a *Ficus* [*racemosa*]—bearing its large clusters of fruit on the trunk and main branches; a tall spreading Pecan tree in perfect health, and underneath, thickets of *Ixora coccinea* and Aralias. There are tall specimens of *Bauhinia purpurea* and *B. variegata* var. *alba,* large Royal and Coconut Palms in this old garden. This is the old Hendry home, and the late Mrs. J. E. Hendry, a passionate plant-lover, set out most of these (now big trees) with her own hands. This love of plants and all that is beautiful was imparted to her son, J. E. Hendry, Jr., one of nature's noblemen, and one of the greatest benefactors of his native city. A fact most surprising is the great number of true plant lovers and horticulturists in Fort Myers—a class deplorably rare in most communities.

When the writer went around Fort Myers to enjoy the treasures of the various places he invariably inquired where and on whose advice these plants were obtained, and invariably the answer came—Mr. J. E. Hendry is responsible. I was informed that the beautiful arrangement of Crotons, palms and other plants around the Courthouse was due to him and that the street plantings, the avenues of *Caryota, Washingtonia,* [*Roystonea*], *Dictyosperma* Palms were his idea. The writer, of course, was very anxious to meet this exceptional man, and he had not long to wait. One fine morning he strolled down one of the side streets. About four or five squares from First Street he came suddenly upon a garden full of beauty and individuality. A magnificent specimen of *Cycas circinalis* struck his eye, then a number of rare palms, then masses of different Bougainvilleas in full bloom, large Traveler's Trees, a glorious display of *Beaumontia grandiflora,* and hundreds of other plants, many of them scarcely being found outside of botanical gardens. The beauty of this place was so impressive that I asked permission to enjoy the sight of the various plants more closely, and the gentleman, who noticed my interest, offered to conduct me around—a rather young man, browned by the sun and outside life, with energetic features and an exuberance of what people of today called "pep," and very courteous.

This proved to be Mr. J. E. Hendry, Jr., himself. I found a kindred spirit, and we became friends at once. The writer enjoyed a long visit with him. He found him exceedingly well posted on tropical plants and their culture. In the afternoon he was kind enough to show him all the fine places at Fort Myers, and pointed out to him all the rare and beautiful plants. Mr. Hendry is an ardent lover of plants, adding constantly to his private collection. He is the founder of the Everglades Nursery Co. Last spring he advertised that he would donate 300 Bougainvillea 'Crimson Lake,' the most gorgeous of all the tribe, to garden owners of Fort Myers. People came in flocks, and when closing time came, more than 300 plants (sold at $2.00 each in the trade) had been given away. Hundreds of Crotons, palms and tropical trees he has turned over to the city authorities. There are few men more liberal and more public spirited than Mr. Hendry and much of the floral beauty of the city is due to him. He loves the place of his birth, and he endeavors to get now, while it is possible, as much land for parks as can be obtained. There is no doubt that Fort Myers will be one of the leading and most beautiful winter resorts in the state. I know all the important places in Florida, but I do not know a more beautiful one, or a more tropical one.

So far the Everglades Nursery has only been a kind of side show, but Mr. Hendry is at present enlarging it considerably. It is under the management of Mr. Robert D. Mitchell, a graduate of the Missouri Botanical Garden.

A word must be said about Dr. Geo. S. Stone, one of the most passionate plant lovers and plant cultivators the writer has ever met. He is a real horticulturist, growing plants mostly from seeds which he received from many tropical countries, for his own pleasure and selling the surplus. His collection of rare Palms, Aroids, etc., is really wonderful.

Mr. Thomas A. Edison, the celebrated inventor, who has a most beautiful park-like winter home at Fort Myers on the south shore of the famous Caloosahatchee, replete with hundreds of rare tropical trees and shrubs, is particularly interested in all plants containing rubber. There cannot be any doubt that the tropical plantings of Mr. Thomas A. Edison on the shores of the Caloosahatchee, at Fort Myers, form one of the most distinct and enchanting garden paradises in Florida.

It is my particular intention to call your attention to Mr. Edison as a garden builder and a horticulturist. When he first came to Florida, about 50 years ago, he searched far and near all over the state, for the ideal spot to build his winter home. At last he found it at Fort Myers, a small and unimportant village at that time, and along the broad expanse of the famous Caloosahatchee. There were no railroads at that time in south Florida, no good country roads, no sawmills, no conveniences of life. The lumber for his house came by boat from New England. It was real pioneer life for quite a number of years. There were "Cuban" Pines on the place, and there were thickets of Mangroves along the water's edge. After the land had been cleared Mr. and Mrs. Edison made preparations to beautify it and to plant all the tropical trees, shrubs and palms, that were available. This was done with much consideration and after a thorough study of all the plant material that might answer the purpose. Mr. Ewald Stulpner a well educated professional gardener was employed, but Mr. Edison followed his own inclinations in planting the place. No landscape design was followed. Trees and shrubs were planted in positions where they promised to thrive best, and where whey would form most conspicuous pictures in the future.

Though the entire place impresses us as a large forest-like park of a tropical nature, there are many fine groups and open vistas, showing us the placid and glittering waters of the great river. There are many dense rare tropical trees everywhere in the grounds, and there is a wealth of fine dense shrubs everywhere. There is nowhere formality. Everything appears natural. There are three characteristics most evident—individuality, privacy and solitude. Even the tourist passing this wonderful tropical plantation is deeply impressed by its unique density and charm; by its outspoken individuality. The avenue of tall Royal Palms in front of the place is a sight that is never effaced from memory.

In order to keep out undesirable and curious visitors, who clamor by the hundreds and thousands to be admitted, a substantial fence lines the place along the highway. A gate-keeper is in charge of the main entrance. An avenue of fine old Mango trees lines the inside of the garden along the street. These large Mango trees are particularly adapted for air gardens. I have tied many fine tropical Bromeliads and Orchids to these old trees where they are growing with exceptional vigor. Last spring Dr. J. K. Small brought a few fine clumps of the noble *Oncidium* [*undulatum*] from the Cape Sable region, which were also fastened with copper wire to the trunks of these old Mangoes. There are also a few noble or dainty-growing ferns of an epiphytal nature tied to the trunks and stout branches. These air-gardens will, in the near future, form quite a feature in this unique garden. Cattleyas, Phalaenopsis, some Dendrobiums and many other gorgeous orchids, growing well in the open in south Florida, will be used largely on the trunks of the Mango and other trees. Mrs. Edison, an ardent plant lover and extremely attached to her garden, is particularly interested in orchids and bromeliads, in aroids and ferns.

There are no large open spaces and extensive lawns in this garden, but everywhere the soil is covered with a dense velvety carpet of grass, which is always kept in perfect condition. On the south side of the house and shaded by large overhanging Fig or Rubber Trees there are masses of ferns, Dracaenas, Screw Pines (*Pandanus*) and large and dense, and extremely impressive clusters or clumps of Areca Palms. There are large and noble specimens of the Traveler's Tree and of Cycads, Crinums and of Alpinias. On the north side of the house there is a row of fine old Royal Palms, some scattered Coconut Palms and a few very fine Seaforthia Palms (*Archontophoenix cunninghamiana*).

A few most interesting clumps of dwarf-growing bushy palms I have not yet been able to identify. There are also masses of bamboos in various species, giant tufts of Screw Pines, and a host of other smaller growing bulbous and perennial plants. Everywhere we find tree-like specimens of the Cattley-Guava, 20 to 25 feet high, and of fine ornamental shape. Orange trees, Pomelos and Kumquats are also doing well among the less dense tree-growth. There is a fine fruiting specimen of the Calabash Tree (*Crescentia cujete*) and most exquisite trees of the Golden Shower (*Cassia fistula*), the Pink Shower (*Cassia grandis*), and the Red and White Shower (*Cassia nodosa*), and large old specimens of the Variegated and Purple *Bauhinia,* and a very dense, tall and large *Dombeya* (*wallichii.*) These last three species are always in full bloom during Christmas time, which is also the case with several of the most glowing Bougainvilleas, of the blue *Thunbergia grandiflora* and of the glowing masses of [*Pyrostegia venusta*].

The verdure and density is more conspicuous just south, between the house and toward the highway. Here we find magnificent specimens of the familiar old Rubber Tree (*Ficus elastica*), of the Council Tree (*Ficus altissima*) tall, dense and broad; of the Cluster Fig (*Ficus* [*racemosa*]), covered with masses of fruit in dense clusters all along the trunk and the larger boughs; and a tall *Ficus infectoria,* with small cherry-like berries of a purplish-pink color. The finest of all these wonderful shade trees was a Moreton Bay Fig (*Ficus macrophylla*). During the hurricane of September, 1926, its top was destroyed, but it has almost recuperated and promises to attain its old beauty.

Here we also find an immense specimen of *Pithecellobium dulce* with a sturdy trunk bent over in a very picturesque way. There are so many rare and beautiful tropical trees in the grounds that I would need too much time to mention only the most interesting. Mrs. Edison has lately extended the ornamental plantings along the bank of the Caloosahatchee. The ground has been filled up, and she intends to have masses of moisture loving shrubs all along the borders, as well as some concrete water-lily pools. One of the latter has been completed, and there are a number of red, white, blue and yellow water-lilies already planted. Others will contain masses of real tropical night and day blooming species and hybrids as well as many other interesting water plants. [Written for the Fourth Annual meeting of the State Federation of Garden Clubs, assembled at Miami, Florida, March 20–21, 1929.]

Old Gardens

Old gardens planted by real plant lovers are always extremely interesting and very inspiring. Such gardens are rare, but they are found here and there in the state. Some of the gardens of north Florida are renowned on account of their very large specimens of Camellias and Indian Azaleas. The garden of the late Mr. Edward Hart at Federal Point was, up to the present day, an El Dorado for plant enthusiasts. Mr. Theodore L. Mead's grounds at Lake Charm are full of rarities. Bishopstead at Orlando is a jewel among gardens. Its large dense Silver-Leaf tree from India (*Pterospermun acerifolium*) being well known all over the county, as is the grand specimen of *Araucaria bidwillii* and the tree ferns in Mrs. Carpenter's garden on Lake Cherokee. Mr. Louis P. Bosanquet's garden at Fruitland park is replete with subtropical treasures, among them a large dense specimen of the Nepal Privet. Mrs. Marian A. McAdow's garden at Punta Gorda is a veritable fairyland of rare tropical plants.

The south Florida gardens, particularly those of Fort Myers, have a charm that is not found anywhere else in this country. They always remind me of a description from the pen of Lafcadio Hearn: "You observe curious orange-colored shrubs; plants speckled with four different colors; plants that look like wigs of green hair; plants with enormous broad leaves that seem made of colored crystal; plants that do not look like natural growths but like idealizations of plants, those beautiful fantasticalities of sculptors. All these we see in glimpses." (Horticultural notebook.)

The most interesting garden in Orlando was at that time the one we now know as "Bishopsted." Many of the rare and tender tropical plants I admired there in November, 1894, were later wiped out by the heavy freezes, but enough has been left to show the possibilities of what can be accomplished with a little love and care. There were immense clumps of three species of tender tropical Bamboos from India. The most beautiful in aspect and color was *Bambusa nutans* [?], the most massive and spreading, *B. vulgaris* and the most intricately impenetrable, *B. arundinacea*. I have all these in my garden, but they are always killed to the ground by a heavy freeze. Only *Bambusa nutans* should be grown in this region on account of its grace and singular bluish-green color.

In this garden I found a most exquisite rare palm, [*Polyandrococos caudescens*], about ten or twelve feet high with beautiful feathery leaves eight or ten feet long. The color of the upper side was deep glossy olive green, while the under side was silvery white. The trunk was not only short but very thick. The leaves curved gracefully to all sides. I scarcely ever saw a more elegant and massive palm. Its picture has never faded from memory. Many have been the attempts to add it to my collection, but I always failed. Near it stood a large clump of the Chinese Paper Plant or Aralia (*Tetrapanax papyriferus*), about fifteen feet high and as much in diameter, richly adorned by an abundance of large dense flower panicles. A gigantic *Dahlia imperialis* with single, pure white, bell-shaped flowers also attracted my attention. Fine, dense, well grown specimens of this plant are very ornamental and ought to find a place in every garden. Unfortunately many tropical plants in this garden and the immense clumps of giant Bamboos were killed to the ground by the unprecedented freeze of the early February days of 1895.

Dr. Petersen's place at Redlands (or Homestead) is mainly an assemblage of valuable economic tropical plants, but my first glimpse of it told me that here a man of good taste, of artistic attainments and scientific knowledge has taken up his abode—a man of culture, energy, systematic training and high ideals of life. I did not expect much along the lines of ornamental horticulture. The doctor never had mentioned it. But the first sight of the place along the highway tells another story. The grounds between the street and the home consist of a beautiful green velvety lawn. Near the highway we see two magnificent Canary Island Date Palms. Only four years old, but of a symmetry and beauty I have rarely seen before. On one side there is a bed of *Plumbago capensis* and a little farther inside there is another bed of *Cryptostegia madagascariensis*. The beds are quite large, the plants massed and full of blossoms. The foundation planting consists of masses of gorgeous Crotons and some fine specimens of *Pandanus veitchii*. Clumps of *Alocasia macrorrhiza* grow on both sides of the steps. Underneath the Crotons there are numbers of beautiful fancy-leaved Caladiums. In the rear of the home we find a small lath-shed. Here are hundreds of pots, containing Crotons, Caladiums and hundreds of small seedling plants. The roof of this shed is covered with a most beautiful specimen of Lady Briggs' *Ipomoea*, a sheet of glowing purplish-rose. On the north side of the home grows a dense and very large specimen of *Monstera deliciosa*.

Dr. Petersen's place does not show many large palms. He has just begun to set out many new and rare palms, but they are still quite small. Along the drive there are hundreds of Rose bushes, many of them in full bloom. I understood that there are about 150 varieties of Roses. The entire arrangement of the dwelling and its surroundings is so exquisitely beautiful,—so tastefully planted, so symmetrical and accurate, that it would require a long article to point out only the outstanding characteristics to do it justice. In the main garden everything is planted in a symmetrical way. The plants are 10 feet apart each way. All are seen in long lines. Each plant is properly labeled. In his book of design the doctor has given two pages or more to each row. Every plant is found in its proper page of the book. There is not a weed to be seen anywhere. Everything is clean, accurate, perfect, and my surprise was complete when I walked along the rows of these plants. There are thousands of ornamental shrubs and trees—hundreds that I never found anywhere else. The soil is rocky mixed with red clay. Around many of the shrubs there in a tasteful way, vegetable beds are arranged—beets, carrots, turnips, etc., and there are even carpets of parsley and celeriac. Many beautiful annual flowers are grown amid the shrubs and trees. I particularly admired masses of a glowing red *Pentstemon* in full bloom. The Pentstemon is a most gorgeous flower, being found in many species in the drier West. I never succeeded to grow these exquisite plants, with their thimble shaped, many-colored tubular flowers.

I found here many rare and important shrubs that I never saw before. The collection of Pittosporums consists of most all of the fine Australian species,—plants that grow so well in California. The fine *Pittosporum floribundum* from Himalayas was also there. The Myrtaceous plants, mostly all Australian, were represented in many species, particularly the members of the genus *Callistemon, Melaleuca* and *Metrosideros*. I never was able to grow the fine *Meterosideros [excelsus]* from New Zealand, but here I saw a fine healthy specimen. The Melaleucas,—in fact all the above named plants,—are most popular in the gardens of California. In Dr. Petersen's place I found a lonely plant of *Melaleuca styphelioides*, a tall tree from Australia, the trunk being covered with thick spongy bark. The flowers, produced in bottle brush-like racemes are very white. This and other fine dense species grow extremely well here.

Among the fruit trees the Governor's Plum (*Flacourtia ramontchii*), a beautiful ornamental also, was found in dozens of symmetrical dense specimens. The plum-like fruits, delicious to eat out of hand, just began to ripen. And there were fine species of *Spondias,* several Lucumas and Annonas, fine Garcinias, etc.,—all important as first-class ornamentals. It is impossible, at this time, to give a more complete description of the treasures in this wonderful garden.

The gardens of Mr. Deering are extremely rich in tropical plants, though they are scarcely more than fifteen years old. New material is constantly added. During certain days of the week the public enjoys free admittance. That Mr. Deering is an enthusiastic plant lover is vividly brought before everybody who has the good luck to visit his grounds. But this is not what I like to emphasize here. Mr. Deering is just as much a lover and protector of our native birds. He has his special favorites among his plants, because they supply the birds with food and shelter. [Horticultural notebook.]

In 1913 Dr. C. F. Baker of the College of Agriculture at Los Banos in the Philippines, introduced into this country through the Bureau of Plant Industry in Washington a very beautiful berry-bearing shrub, which he thought might be easily acclimatized in south Florida. It was a success in Mr. Deering's grounds from the beginning, growing very luxuriantly and soon formed large, conspicuous specimens. This particular exotic belongs to the family Verbenaceae, and is known under the name of *Premna odorata* (*Premna pubescens*). Its leaves are large, pubescent and of an oval-oblong form, 6 to 8 in. long and 4 to 5 in. broad. It grows to a height of 12 to 15 feet and is quite dense and very ornamental. The berries are borne in large umbels, reminding a little of those of our Elderberry, though the latter cannot compare with it in size or number of berry-clusters.

To Miss Eleanor Bisbee belongs the credit to have made this fine shrub known to the public. A good account from her pen first appeared in the column of the *Miami Metropolis*. The following lines are adapted from her article: "To attract birds, especially mocking-birds, *Premna odorata* is indispensable. It thrives well in Dade County. Elderberry is the nearest like it of common bushes. Berries from it are somewhat of a licorice flavor, and mocking-birds, as well as many other birds, are extremely fond of them. The leaves of the shrub are fully as valuable as the berries." When sending the seeds to the Bureau of Plant Industry Mr. Baker advised

> that the leaves are rich in an unknown essential oil which possesses marked insecticidal power. The leaves, dried and powdered, are used by the natives for lice on poultry and animals.
>
> Mr. Deering has made use of the bushes for a heavy border hedge, reaching high above one's head, and bordering one of the drives, and thus the birds are brought constantly into the heart of the estate. Along a cement walk there might be a possibility that the dropping berries would leave unsightly stains, but set back a little way or on a lawn or planted around an arbor they would prove a great attraction to birds and be a thing of great beauty.

Mr. Chas. Schmidt, whose name was mentioned in Mrs. Bisbee's article as Mr. Deering's gardener, was approached by me with the request to send me some cuttings. They soon came, and also a lot of seeds, and I have now quite a number of fine young plants. Though my soil here in my "Tropical Garden and Arboretum" is of the poorest kind, they appear to do well and promise to prove a distinguished and beautiful addition to my collection. (Horticultural notebook.)

Our Proposed National Park

When I for the first time had the pleasure to ramble around in the primeval forests of Paradise Key I was overwhelmed by the dense, truly tropical vegetation, the lofty Royal Palms raising their noble heads high above the other trees. The huge Live Oaks were real air-gardens, covered with orchids, bromeliads and ferns. Mr. Mosier, the care-taker, had hewn out miles of winding paths along which we rambled for long distances. It is easy to specify the individual objects of admiration, but it is not possible to give an adequate idea of the higher feelings of wonder, astonishment and devotion which fill and elevate the mind, while walking along the paths of Royal Palm State Park, as it is now called.

The day seems to dawn. A bright light will soon be cast over south Florida, and I hope over the entire state. The question of making the Cape Sable region and parts of Collier County a National Park is now agitating the eminent scientific and cultured men and women of the nation,—not only of Florida. Dr. David Fairchild and Mr. Ernest F. Coe, seem to be the main promoters of this plan, and there are many helpers such as Prof. W. M. Buswell, Dr. John K. Small, Mr. C. A. Mosier, Dr. John B. Seeds, Mr. R. F. Deckert and many others, who are deeply interested in this National Park plan. As Mr. S. C. Singleton points out: "And now . . . we have become the center interest for a new group of admirers who would not pay the slightest attention to commercialized sport, who are not interested in land speculation and who have never clamored for industrial development." True and well said! And we need a whole legion of such spirits. All the intellectual people of the state should help, should assist. Such a national park in our most tropical part of the state is an urgent necessity. If not carried out at once there is danger that much of the wild beauty will be destroyed.

I do not know the Cape Sable region intimately, having made only two short trips to several of the finest hammocks and to the Gulf Coast region. My time was limited. I could only obtain the lasting impressions from closer study that I desired. The nature lover, the naturalist, the plantsman should spend days and even weeks in that incomparably beautiful and unique region. Such men as Dr. John K. Small, the eminent botanist, Prof. Chas. T. Simpson, John Soar, Richard F. Deckert, and last but surely not least, Mr. C. A. Mosier, have explored the Cape Sable region very thoroughly. Both Dr. Small and Prof. Simpson have given us very interesting accounts of the entire Cape Sable region.

I admired particularly the forests of Coconut Palms, the masses of Butterfly Orchids (*Oncidium* [*undulatum*]) and the clusters of Everglade Palms [*Acoelorrhaphe wrightii*], as well as the many Palms of the genus *Thrinax* and the many huge Rubber Trees, *Ficus aurea* and *F.* [*citrifolia*].

The orchids, as well as many bromeliads, ferns and strange tropical trees and shrubs, were found along the shady borders of the hammocks, which I had no time to penetrate. In order to enjoy fully such an excursion it is absolutely essential to have an understanding companion with you—a kindred spirit. The one who accompanied me had no eye for the beautiful, and he simply could not understand my raving and enthusiasm. He only said, "This is fine land for tomatoes. It will be cleared as soon as we can get a passable road." Such remarks have always pained me, and in this case I really felt sad. I am rejoicing now. All will be saved, and I hope much more. The great lights of our country and time will join hands to help us to preserve the beauty of Florida, and add to it. I hope that Dr. David Fairchild's favorite idea to create a Tropical Botanical Garden in south Florida, may also find staunch supporters. We ought not to stay behind California in this respect, and there is splendid work done in Los Angeles along these lines, as they have millions of dollars at hand for building up such a scientific institution.

While musing about all this I feel that I should not omit to call the attention of all nature lovers, of all admirers of Florida scenery to the Big Cypress, situated in the eastern part of Collier County. Dr. Small has partly explored it and has given an interesting account of it. It is indeed a wonderland of interest. Usually all the Cypress growth is covered with water. Only the many higher situated islands, usually small in size, but extremely fascinating and overgrown mostly with masses of Cabbage Palms and some tall and dense trees, are more or less dry even in the rainy season. At present (January) on account of lack of rain since three months, the water has receded and we are able to walk for miles without getting wet. On the larger of these islands the remnants of the Seminoles have built their house-like tents, thatched with palm leaves. There are some sweet potatoes, corn, pumpkins and other vegetables growing on small areas of ground usually fenced in. Some of the large Cypresses show in their tops immense clusters of the Bee-swarm Orchid (*Cyrtopodium punctatum*) large enough to fill a good sized trunk.

It is a thrilling and exhilarating experience to spend a night with a good friend on one of the Palmetto covered islands. The weird hooting of numerous owls alone is worth all the troubles to walk miles to listen to it. You may hear the gobbling of several turkeys and the voices of many strange birds. If you are lucky you may be able to listen to the call notes and loud hammering of the ivory-billed woodpecker, a noble bird, almost extinct. The puma, the wildcat and even the bear may cross your tracks, not to speak of many a deer. You will see numerous white and blue herons, egrets, wood ibises and anhingas leaving their roosts early in the morning and returning to them when the evening falls. Coots and gallinules, bitterns and night herons and numerous ducks are also present where there are small ponds and water-holes.

Alligators are still in evidence everywhere. Otters, not as common as they were a few years ago, may now and then be seen, while raccoons are quite abundant, feasting on the berries of the Palmetto and the fruits of the Pond Apple (*Annona glabra*).

The plant lover and botanist is here in a rich field of plant life, new to him in many respects, but always full of new charms. The masses of Florida Bird's-Nest Ferns (*Asplenium serratum*) and the clumps of Strap Ferns (*Campyloneurum phylliditis*) always attract attention, while the luxurious and the incredibly long leaves of the wild Boston Ferns (*Nephrolepis exaltata*) fascinate even the hunter and the common woodsman. The Pond Apple trees, usually loaded with a lovely growth of bromeliads and various orchids, mostly overhang the water. In its southern part the Big Cypress is showing a different plant life, as here we find the Royal Palms [*Roystonea elata*] in large communities. Hunters and their guides have assured me that there are at least 2,000 of these, the most beautiful of all palms, growing closely together. Collier's Royal Palm Hammock, on both sides of the Tamiami Trail, is said to be due west of them.

This large Royal Palm Hammock is situated about forty miles from my home here (Naples), and as it is quite difficult to reach, for a man of my age, I have not yet been able to enjoy perhaps the most unique, the most enchanting sight that can be experienced in Florida. All the hunters and their guides agree that this Royal Palm Hammock surpasses in grandeur and magnificence anything that can be seen in Florida. They assert that many of them are over a hundred feet in height. I have studied the group of the Collier Royal Palms more closely. There are two groups, one on each side of the trail, and though not very evident from the highway, they soon will be taken care of, so that their beauty can be enjoyed by thousands of tourists. In June I found on the smooth trunk of one of these Royal Palms a cluster of four pure white conspicuous blossoms of [*Polyrrhiza* or *Polyradicion lindenii*], a rare orchid without leaves, but with a dense matting of somewhat green roots which stretch to all sides like an octopus. It seems to have a predilection for the smooth marble-gray trunk of these most glorious palms. I found plants of the *Dendrophylax* on the stems of many other specimens.

I most earnestly urge that the Big Cypress, and particularly these Royal Palm Hammocks, may be included in this new National Park System. I maintain that the Big Cypress and the Royal Palms are quite as important and valuable as anything that can be recommended for this purpose.

The state Federation of Garden Clubs is doing wonderful work and as the members belong to the most cultured, distinguished and sincere, we can already see the good work they are doing everywhere. There are hundreds—thousands—of wealthy men all over the country searching for a congenial climate and to enjoy nature's beauty in their old age. These men have nothing to do but to eat and sleep and read the papers and to crave for sensational sports and rough games. They have no ideals and are fast dying out. If they would occupy themselves with one or the other branch of ornamental horticulture, they soon would become interested and assume a new lease of life. There is no greater pleasure, none more elevating, none more satisfying, none more healthy than the work in nature's garden—in the ornamental field. Everyone who comes to Florida with the idea of regaining his health or prolonging his life should make ornamental horticulture his special field, because nothing is more satisfactory and health and pleasure giving than the work along these lines.

9

Landscaping and Visions of the Future

Owners of low rich hammock woods made grave mistakes in destroying the indigenous forest flora when selecting a place for their dwellings. The majestic Live Oaks, Magnolias, Sweet Gums, Cabbage Palmettos and other beautiful native forest trees cannot be replaced, and it takes a lifetime to grow exotic and native ornamental trees planted for adornment into large and attractive specimens. These low, rich hammocks form ideal places for parks and ornamental grounds. Only a slight thinning out of unattractive spots, laying out of the paths and walks curving and leading in all directions to particularly attractive points, to dense thickets and to meandering water courses, is all that is necessary. In some favorable spots the thick underwood can be removed for the planting of shade loving plants which will not grow successfully anywhere else. Many ferns, among them several species of Tree Ferns, Aroids, Gloxinias, the beautiful and deliciously perfumed *Dapheodora,* and hundreds of other dainty plants thrive splendidly in such cool and shady places. The dwelling can be erected in an open space in front of such a tract of woodland with exotic ornamental shrubs and trees in the forest and along the sides.

Landscaping the Home Grounds

Prof. Charles T. Simpson of Lemon City is the happy owner of such a hammock on the shores of Biscayne Bay. It is the most charming and the most attractive spot I ever have seen. This hammock consists of a large number of native tropical trees and shrubs. Though the soil is quite rocky the growth is dense and many of the trees are quite large. The undergrowth consists mostly of evergreen shrubs and ferns. Paths leading to all directions have been laid out with an eye for harmony and beauty. They lead us to spots where large clumps of ferns grow or where beautiful specimens of epiphytal orchids, such as Cattleyas, Laelias, Oncidiums, Epidendrums, Dendrobiums and even Phalaenopsis are fastened artificially to the trunks of large and curving forest trees.

Aroids, such as Anthuriums, Alocasias, Spathiphyllums, Philodendrons, and large tufts of Bird's-Nest Ferns (*Asplenium nidus*) are found on trees as well as in beautiful nooks and corners in the shaded soil. Now and then we come to the rustic seat from which our eyes can feast on the beauty of a group or single specimen of rare palms or other beautiful shade-loving tropical plants, exceedingly effective bromeliads, Tillandsias, Nidulariums, Aechmeas, Billbergias and masses of small palms, like Chamaedoreas, Geonomas and members of the genus *Synecanthus, Calyptrogyne* and others. Indeed Mr. Simpson has changed this primeval forest into a fairyland of beauty and enchantment.

While the climate along Biscayne Bay has every advantage for growing of strictly tropical plants, Mr. Theodore L. Mead of Lake Charm, Seminole Co., had to combat heavy freezes and other disadvantages, but he succeeded in acclimating many hundreds of shade-loving tropical species in his hammock,—a piece of low and rich moist forest land. He had wonderful masses of *Azalea indica,* magnificent Tree Ferns, large clumps of terrestrial and epiphytal orchids, aroids and bromeliads, and hundreds of small delicate shade-loving plants in many places of his hammock. A beautiful large growing fern [*Thelypteris torresiana*] escaped from this forest land and is now found in many rich moist woodlands all over Seminole County. Recently it has been found even near Sanford. Unfortunately the roving herds of semi-wild hogs (razor-backs) uprooted almost all the charming plants Mr. Mead had introduced with so much care and expenditure. What Prof. Simpson and Mr. Mead have done thousands of others could do. The necessary requirements are love for the beautiful, enthusiasm and perseverance.

Landscaping Larger Areas

In planting out large and extensive grounds one mistake is very commonly made,—that of dotting the trees around at regular distances apart, giving the appearance of a checker board in a great degree. We noticed this defect in the arrangement of the grounds of the Punta Gorda Hotel recently. Although the Bermuda Grass lawn is the finest we have ever seen, the effect was partly spoiled by the methodical arrangement of the palms, which had been planted on the lawn. A clump here and there with now and then a single specimen apparently planted indiscriminately, but really, an eye to the future and general effect, would have made a great difference in the beauty of the picture. No rules can be laid down, however, upon this subject, but good taste, common sense and the general fitness of things should go hand in hand with careful thought as to how it will look in the future, in laying out such grounds.

These lines were written in 1888 by the genial enthusiast, the late Mr. W. P. Reasoner.

Beautifying the Cemetery

One of the weakest—I should say, one of the most horrid—points of our Florida civilization, are the cemeteries, particularly in rural districts. There are no beautiful trees or shrubs, no artistic planting, no flowers or lawns anywhere to be seen. They are usually found on the highest, driest and poorest soils. Show me the cemetery in one of our communities and I shall tell you what class of people populate the surrounding country.

A few little hints of my own experience, perhaps, may not come amiss. If they should be the inducement to beautify only one or two deserted cemeteries I would feel well repaid for my trouble.

By all means have the entrance to the graveyard well paved, so that you will not have to wade through six inches of dust, or mud puddles. It should be marked by a neat looking gate. The whole cemetery should be surrounded by a substantial fence or neat hedge, which should be kept in good trim. We have here in Florida many beautiful subtropical evergreen trees and shrubs for this purpose. The dense and beautiful Florida Cedar *Juniperus* [*silicicola*] I especially recommend. It grows on dry land, is exquisitely beautiful while young, and can be kept in any form and size by the use of the pruning shears. Oleanders also make dense and beautiful hedges, and so does the very dense evergreen Laurel Cherry (*Prunus caroliniana*), which can be kept low by the use of pruning shears. Some of the smaller clump bamboos, *Bambusa* [*glaucescens*], and *B.* 'Alphonse-Karr' make splendid and dense hedges in the course of time. Some of the fine large-leaved privets, *Ligustrum* [*indicum*], *L. japonicum*, *L. lucidum,* etc., form wonderful hedges in the course of a few years, and there are many others.

In the cemetery, near the entrance, I would lay out a lawn, which should be planted with evergreen shrubs and flowers of various kinds. From these, well-made driveways of easy grade and giving the shortest access to the different parts of the cemetery ought to be made. These should always be kept in the best possible shape. Where such driveways cannot be kept tidy I would prefer to have none at all, but would have everything sodded down, for nothing looks uglier than a roadway overgrown with weeds. None of the northern grasses will do here, but we have the Bermuda Grass and particularly the new and very dense and fine growing Centipede Grass (*Eremochloa ophiuroides*) which latter makes a dense sod with some good care bestowed on it. Have the sides of the driveways and also the cemetery proper planted with some of the beautiful broad-leaved evergreen trees, such as the glorious *Magnolia grandiflora,* the Loblolly Bay (*Gordonia lasianthus*), the Laurel Cherry (*Prunus caroliniana*) and the Live Oak.

There are sometimes old picturesque Live Oaks found on such cemetery grounds. They should be carefully preserved, and young ones should be planted in addition. Groups and single specimens of Cabbage Palms (*Sabal palmetto*) should never be missed in any of the Florida cemeteries. The various varieties of the Crape-Myrtle, though deciduous, light up their surroundings in a most lively way all summer long. I have had the beautiful pink forms in flower from June to October. They need little attention. The various Hollies, particularly the native *Ilex opaca* or Christmas Holly, though a slow grower, makes a first-class cemetery tree, and so does the dense Japanese Othera (*Ilex integra*).

In Houston, Texas, I was struck, many years ago, with the beauty of the dense Gardenias or Cape Jasmines and the bush and tree-like specimens of the *Pittosporum tobira* in one of the well-kept woodland cemeteries along Buffalo Bayou. Here and there under the trees seats ought to be made so that visitors may sit down and rest. Wells and pumps ought to be provided so that the lot owners can water their plants. By all means have some groups of such shrubs as *Plumbago capensis* (blue and white form), of the Golden Dewdrop (*Duranta* [*repens* or *erecta*]), of Sweet Myrtles (the ancient classic *Myrtus communis*), of Banana Shrubs ([*Michelia figo*]), of the fragrant *Illicium* [*anisatum*] and the lovely *Abelia* [*chinensis*]. Of climbing plants on the trees and trellises none is better than our native dainty Yellow Jessamine

(*Gelsemium sempervirens*), with its intensely fragrant yellow flower-trumpets, and the Malayan Jasmine (*Trachelospermum jasminoides*). This is a sheet of pure white fragrant flowers in March and April. There are many other beautiful climbers available, such as [*Pyrostegia venusta*] and the blue *Thunbergia grandiflora,* but they are usually of such gigantic growth, that they cannot be recommended for cemetery planting.

The so-called Sago Palm (*Cycas revoluta*) is a splendid plant for single lots or individual graves. One of the most celebrated graves in Florida is the one of the great botanist and medical man, Dr. A. W. Chapman (author of the *Flora of the Southern States*), at Apalachicola. It is planted with dense masses of the native Coontie (*Zamia*), one of our most beautiful evergreen cycads. It never grows taller than about 2½ feet. I have used in the same way another dense Coontie, *Zamia* [*integrifolia*], on my graves at Gotha. These plants are the most appropriate and beautiful dense plants I know for the planting on and around graves. They grow in sunshine and shade.

Some of the lilies form beautiful masses in the cemeteries of the North. None of them will thrive in our Florida climate. We have a number of Crinums (*Crinum scabrum, C. amabile, C. asiaticum*) that can be used in the place of lilies. Our "Red Lily,"—not a lily at all, but an Amaryllis,—will do very well on graves, and flowers in orange-red sheets in March and April. It is one of the best plants for cemetery planting.

The best dense small evergreen shrub I know for low hedges around the graves is the comparatively new *Severinia buxifolia,* a native of southern China, Hong Kong and Formosa. Belonging to the orange family, it bears small black berries and is quite spiney and very dense. The leaves resemble the Box,—*Buxus sempervirens.* As it is a slow grower it can be used with much success as a cemetery plant. It can easily be kept small and dense by the use of the pruning shears. Wherever the Box is used up North this little *Severinia* can be used in Florida. It seems to be hardy all over the state. The finest specimens I saw about fifteen years ago in the Laughlin place at Zellwood—fine dense specimens 6 to 7 feet high and full of black berries as large as small cherries.

One of the most exquisite of all small evergreen Japanese trees is the upright Temple Tree *Ternstroemia japonica* [= *T. gymnanthera*]; sold sometimes as *Cleyera japonica.* Of upright, dense growth, beautiful shiny foliage, fragrant perfect white flowers and showy red fruit, I regard it as one of the most distinct and lovely of all our trees, and it is well adapted for cemetery planting. These specimens should be planted together, 15 feet apart. It is a narrow tree, and never spreads its branches. They are always upright,—one of my special favorites, and should be used abundantly by the landscape gardener.

In winter many of the brilliant annuals should be used, such as Petunias, *Phlox drummondii,* etc. Among perennials, a few of the Blanket flowers (*Gaillardia*), and the new and finer *Gerbera jamesonii* (Barberton Daisy) can be used. The German Iris, Paeonies, Perennial Phlox, Golden Glow, Delphiniums, etc., cannot be used in Florida, and even Roses are usually a failure in cemeteries. Do not overcrowd your lot with rank growing plants like Zinnias, Marigolds, Balsams, etc. They are all very beautiful in a garden, but the cemetery is not the place for them. Even the Crinums should never be planted on the graves. They might find a place in a corner of the rear lot, or if there is room enough, along the sides. The only species that could be used is *Crinum* [*jagus*], resembling so much the Amazon Lily *Eucharis* [*grandiflora*], but it needs shade and very rich moist soil.

I do not advise to plant grass on a small cemetery lot; there it needs too much attention because the grass cannot very well be cut with a machine, and the sickle is not a very good instrument in the hands of an inexperienced man. Rather I would propose to lay out the ground in some matforming perennials. There is for instance the blanket-flower (*Gaillardia*); perhaps also one or the other Verbena, or still better, the fine Japanese *Ophiopogon jaburan* and its near ally *Ophiopogon japonicus.* These make fine dense grass-like tufts.

Monotony in Gardens

Perhaps the most grievous source of wasted effort in gardens is monotony arising from everybody growing what his neighbor grows, so that we lose any chance of variety. Thus it comes that the nurseryman who grows new or rare trees or shrubs often finds them left on his hands, so that many state nurseries only grow a very limited number of a few stereotyped things, which means monotony in gardens. For instance, we see public gardens and squares given over to common Privets, Oleanders, Hibiscus and a few other like plants. The temptation is strong on the part of trade growers to keep and grow only things that people want to grow freely, and to recommend things, like common privets, which are without beauty and offensive in odor when in flower. The presence of such things is one of the causes of the miserable aspects of shrubbery and trees in many gardens, which might be extremely beautiful with varied life.

There are thousands of the finest tropical and subtropical plants available for Florida gardens, and there are other thousands awaiting introduction, but the common nurseryman with little or no education is simply at sea. He knows nothing except a few common easily grown plants, and these he tries to unload on the uncultured collector. There are exceptions. Prof. Harold Hume of the Glen St. Mary Nursery,—not to forget his immensely practical head man, August Schubel,—knows Florida conditions, knows plants and what to plant. There is also J. E. Hendry, Jr., a lover of tropical plants and who knows them botanically and horticulturally, and there is his assistant and co-worker, Mr. Arthur Kelly of the Everglades Nursery. Last, but not least, there are the Reasoner Bros. of Royal Palm Nurseries, the introducers since half a century of thousands of rare tropical plants. These are the men who can break the monotony of our average garden by these fine new introductions and by their variety of plants they have on hand.

The presence of many shrubs and trees of little beauty often destroys by their vigor the rare and beautiful garden vegetation. There are too many Water and Laurel Oaks; too many Eucalyptus; too many old scraggy Arbor Vitaes, coarse growing and otherwise unsatisfactory trees in our city parks and streets, and far too few Live Oaks, *Magnolia grandiflora*, *Magnolia glauca*, Pittosporums, and kinds of Palms and Cycads and hundreds of other distinct and beautiful tropical and subtropical trees and shrubs. Another fact remains to be mentioned here,—the fact that the coarse and vigorous growing things have overrun and killed many precious and rare plants, and hence we see many shrubberies worn out.

Lovers of gardens and wide-awake horticulturists could do a lot to check this fatal tendency to monotony by taking up some family of plants for themselves, which perhaps they are unable to find in the established nurseries. It is not only beautiful species of plants which are excluded from ordinary nurseries, but those making a specialty of certain groups often leave out the very best and most satisfactory species. There ought to be specialists in every line of ornamental horticultural pursuit. There ought to be special collections of Palms, Cycads, Crotons, Dracaenas, Ficus, members of the Myrtle family, Amaryllis, Crinums, the broad-leaved evergreen Japanese, Chinese, Australian and South African shrubs and trees, and particularly experimental gardens for strictly tropical trees and shrubs. Besides special Rose gardens, there should be such for Azaleas and other members of the Heath family.

The writer of these lines has experimented with tropical and subtropical plants since 1886 in Florida. Such experiments are extremely costly and often quite unsatisfactory until a plant is found that finds our soil and climate conducive to its health and well-being. Before a paternal government and a mischievous bureaucracy interfered, he had imported from foreign countries in large consignments, and often by parcel post, about 2,000 different plants. There were 300 among these that proved particularly fine and most exquisite for our Florida gardens. Other experimenters, like the late Mr. E. H. Hart of Federal Point, Mr. Theodore L. Mead of Lake Charm, and Prof. Chas. T. Simpson have worked in the same direction. The late Mr. E. N. Reasoner was one of the foremost, if not the foremost of experimenters in Florida. His introductions are so numerous and important that a large volume could be written about them. He was not only a practical horticulturist and an excellent financier, but also a plant student who was exceedingly well informed on the literature of the subject. No new plant escaped his attention. There are hundreds of new and rare plants scattered about Florida that come from him and that form conspicuous features in our gardens.

It would be too much to expect that the enormous number of Roses now available should be grown by any one man, or even by any half dozen growers; but the fact remains that even nurseries devoted to special subjects may be too exclusive. We say so much to show that even in the branches of gardening that seem best known, there are neglected sources of interest, while among little known plants there are many. But it is not only the introduction of new plants or species we have to think of here, but other things equally important—the raising of new forms of hybrids, the fine collection of new groups, as the beautiful Gerberas (Transvaal Daisies), Crinums, Amaryllis, Gaillardias and hundreds of others; the making more artistic use of old and well-known plants; the skilful adaptation of plants and trees to the soil so as to get the highest beauty of which they are capable without excessive care or cost, and without the mourning and death that are visible in many places after hard winters.

It is necessary to form true ideas of trade limitations, as many people seem to think that the nearest nurseryman possesses all the known art of gardening, and has all the plants worth having, whereas he probably is in a very narrow groove as regards either of these subjects. Therefore those who seek to vary monotony of gardens must be prepared to face some little trouble, and not take the least notice of what is considered right in the neighborhood, or what can be obtained from the nearest nursery garden, or even from some of the largest nursery gardens. The farther afield they look, probably the better in the end it will be for them if they would escape from the trammels of monotony. At the same time if local men have good things they ought to be encouraged. It is a misfortune for gardens that there are not more local nurseries of an interesting character.

The foregoing notes have been based on a similar article in the *London Field*. It has been the endeavor of the writer to point out during the past seven years in the columns of the *American Eagle* the most beautiful and interesting plants available for our Florida gardens. These articles appear to have created a good deal of interest among the lovers of beautiful plants, as the hundreds of letters we have received will testify.

Visions of the Future Are Before Me

I see residences, built more or less in the colonial style—elaborate modern winter homes and architecturally fine villas—homes where cultured and refined people have taken up their abode. Wonderful tropical gardens surround these homes,—gardens replete with tropical trees and shrubs. Royal Palms are the glory of all of them and all are arranged in the most effective and tasteful way. One in particular strikes my fancy. The house,—not an expensive structure,—is covered with vines, mostly Bougainvilleas, Allamandas and *Pyrostegia venusta*. In the foreground, near the road, on both sides of this Palm avenue, are groups of [*Syagrus romanzoffianum*], of *Livistona chinensis* and of *Acrocomia aculeata* and *A. totai*.

In front of the house there are six fine large Coconut Palms and among them groups of *Cycas circinalis, Dioon edule* and *D. spinulosum* flanked by groups of Royal Palms, each group on each side of the walk, but a little distant from the formal avenues, consisting of about a dozen specimens. Dense bushes of various Crotons are planted among the groups of Cycads on each side. The smooth white trunks of the Royal Palms are nowhere obliterated by tall trees or shrubs, being set off by a fine green, grassy lawn. The edges of this palm avenue toward the walk consist of dense specimens of the low-growing, but beautiful Coonti *Zamia* [*integrifolia*]. A little distant from the lines of Palms there is a background consisting of the Norfolk Island Pine *Araucaria* [*heterophylla*], the Bunya-Bunya (*Araucaria bidwillii*) and tall feathery Bamboos, and these again are mixed with numerous Rubber or Banyan Trees, Terminalias, Sterculias, Royal Poincianas and Jacarandas. In the spaces of the groups of [*Syagrus romanzoffianum*] in front of the avenue masses of Crotons add color to the picture. Though rather formal, this combination is very effective and beautiful. In other parts of the grounds, which cover several acres, a more natural arrangement prevails.

No other palm forms such beautiful avenues within comparatively so short a time. The Royal Palm is one of the fastest growers of all palms. E. Otta has left us a graphic description of the famous avenue of this species attached to the Angerona Coffee Estate of Cuba. It is 1,900 feet long, and consists of four rows, each row numbering a hundred trees, the whole forming a splendid natural colonnade, protected by a roof of magnificent foliage.

I know that in my own case the *index expurgatorius* would of necessity include the names of plants which my friends at Orlando, Punta Gorda, Miami and elsewhere—even my friends a few miles away,—grow with perfect ease, while they are unable to succeed with subjects that are satisfactory with me. Then again the minds of men, not being, fortunately, cast in identical molds, show even greater dissimilarity than do the soils and the climates of their gardens. That which to one is an object of reprobation, to another is a matter of beauty and enthusiasm.

The long protracted drouth is broken, at last. The first delightful showers of the rainy season have fallen. It has rained day and night. The hot and dry air has become fresh once more. Rain-drops are hidden in verge; they glisten like diamonds on the brilliant leaves of the Caladiums. The pent-up fragrance is set free again, and the incense of the flowers ascends with the breath of morn and floats in the evening air. Nature is indeed rejoicing, and so are they who feel her every mood.—June, 1, 1923.

The foregoing notes represent a part of my latest conclusions on horticulture in Florida, after thirty years of practice and experiments on my own ground, at my own expense, and with no other object in view than to promote by precept and example the cultivation and enjoyment of tropical and subtropical plants as the noblest, the most delightful and the most satisfactory of all earthly pursuits and pleasures. (From a Horticultural notebook.)

10

Some of Nehrling's Favorite People

[Throughout the works of Henry Nehrling occur digressions regarding people he knew and admired. Often the digressions were unrelated to his subject and seemed to call for a chapter devoted to Nehrling's friends. Hence, the following passages may seem disjointed but are intended to bring together sketches about people who enlivened Henry Nehrling's life.]

Thomas Alva Edison, Garden Builder: Mr. Edison, the celebrated inventor, who has a most beautiful park-like winter home at Fort Myers on the south shore of the famous Caloosahatchee, replete with hundreds of rare tropical trees and shrubs, is particularly interested in all plants containing rubber. Recently (April 27, 1927) he and Mrs. Edison spent almost an entire day with me in my garden here at Naples, where I have accumulated a collection of about 100 species of *Ficus*. Though having celebrated on Feb. 11, his eightieth birthday, he showed himself as alert and enthusiastic, as interested and desirous of knowledge as any young student. In fact, I have never met with anyone who was so elated and delighted about all the species of *Ficus* and all other plants that attracted his attention. He made notes of all the species I cultivate, the correct botanical name, their age, where they came from and about the quantity and quality of their milky sap. With the exception of *Ficus elastica*, he found only one other species that met with his approval as a rubber yielding plant—[*F. nikbudu*] of southeast Africa. I have a third one that is described as a first-class rubber yielding plant,—*F. vogelii* of tropical West Africa,—but my specimen was too small to be used in Mr. Edison's tests. My three most beautiful small-leaved species [*F. microcarpa*], *F. benjamina* and [*F. obliqua*] only showed a small quantity of milky sap and this was full of resin.

After we had looked over all the plants in the grounds we retired to my little house, where both Mr. and Mrs. Edison looked over with profound interest my books, my manuscripts and my photographs of *Ficus* species. In every respect this famous inventor, one of the greatest men of all times, showed himself as a model of modesty, as a thorough scientist and as a most systematic worker—a most wonderful man. It is only necessary to come in contact with him to feel the power of his eminence and greatness and charm of his personality.

We all know Mr. Edison as the great inventor. But he is much more than that. He is one of the greatest men of our time and of all times. Intensely interested in science and its practical application, he is extremely systematic and accurate in everything he does, and he is a constant hard worker. Being the acknowledged master in his own chosen field, he is much more than most men of our day are—interested in literature and all branches of natural history. Nothing ideal and elevating in the life of humanity fails to gain his appreciative attention. Only those who have the rare opportunity to come in close contact with him feel the wonderful power of his personality. (Mr. Ewald Stulpner was the former gardener to Thomas A. Edison.)

Dr. David Fairchild, for whom the Fairchild Tropical Gardens, in Coral Gables, is named was head of the Plant Exploration and Introduction branch of the Bureau of Plant Industry, U.S. Department of Agriculture. Dr. Fairchild visited both Palm Cottage Gardens in Gotha, after the big freeze of 1917, and Nehrling's Tropical Gardens and Arboretum at Naples-on-the-Gulf. He was instrumental in making Nehrling an associate in order to receive and test new plant introductions.

Paul C. Standley, Young and Noted Botanist: A few days ago the writer had a very pleasant and most interesting call from Dr. Paul C. Standley, a young and very celebrated botanist, whom he had always admired, with whom he had corresponded, but never had met. Mr. Standley is the assistant curator of the United States National Herbarium of the United States National Museum, Washington, D.C., and the author of that great work in five volumes, *Trees and Shrubs of Mexico*. I can scarcely recall to my mind a more interesting, a more scholarly and thorough work than this.

Dr. Standley follows somewhat in the footsteps of that great scholar and ideal American, the late Dr. E. W. Safford. This work does not merely consist of dry descriptive matter, but is interspersed with numerous and highly interesting notes and of quotations from many of the old Spanish authors, such as Hernandez, Mocino, Urbina, Clavigero and others. Last winter Dr. Standley explored the wonderful mountain forests of Costa Rica. The writer had the pleasure of receiving a most interesting and valuable letter from him, in which he described the exquisite and beautiful orchids and bromeliads with which the trees are loaded in the cool rain forests near Cartago, C.R. This winter he spends with his parents on the Tamiami Trail, between Fort Myers and Estero.

Many of my friends know my weakness, not only for bromeliads, but also for the members of the Ficus or Rubber tribe. There are at present about 100 species of Ficus in my collection, though the freeze may have killed about 25 of them outright. Some of the most tender are really dead, but many of the finest survived, among them the Sayula Rubber Tree, one of the grandest and densest shade trees in existence. I did not know that I had it until Dr. Standley pointed it out to me. This is the true *Ficus padifolia* of Humboldt. I had craved it since I read the late Mr. Pringle's description of it in *Garden and Forest* about 35 years ago. This description I cannot refrain from quoting. Pringle says: "A prominent feature in the landscape about Sayula is a wild Fig, *Ficus fasciculata.* Its horizontal, far-reaching branches make it a remarkable flat-topped tree, and as it grows to immense size and lines the roadsides in the neighborhood of the city, the Fig avenues of Sayula are among the grandest of Mexican avenues." This species is identical with *F. padifolia.*

Last fall (1925) I received the fruits of seven species of Ficus from a friend in Vera Cruz, of which five germinated and are now in my collection, and this one,—the treasure I had so long craved,—is among them. I hope to be successful in its cultivation, and to distribute it later among my tree-loving friends.

Dr. Standley will also have the kindness to identify the four remaining Mexican species for me, as all of them are extremely beautiful and most important. This young botanist has another important work (on the trees and shrubs of Panama) in preparation, which will soon be published by the United States National Museum.

The late Mr. Pliny W. Reasoner [Royal Palm Nursery], whom we must call the real pioneer of ornamental horticulture in Florida, not only brought together large collections of beautiful tropical and subtropical plants for commercial purposes, but was an excellent plantsman, a good cultivator and an enthusiast. He did more for the promotion of ornamental gardening in Florida than anyone else. He loved plants intensely and he told about favorites in glowing language. His writings would fill a good sized volume. Mr. Walter N. Pike, and later Mr. W. C. Steele, worked along the same line and contributed their share in the columns of the *Florida Agriculturist* to make known the possibilities of tropical gardening to the plant loving world.

It is always a great pleasure to me to study the gardens and collections of other plant lovers, and many are the discoveries of beautiful things I never had seen before. Even in the early pioneer days beautiful gardens were planted in this part of the state. In the garden at Federal Point the late Mr. E. H. Hart has erected for himself an everlasting monument. Here we find the largest specimens of the Canary Island Date Palm and the Sugar Date Palm (*Phoenix sylvestris*), of the Chinese Fan Palm (*Livistona chinensis*) and the Washingtonias, in the State. The large and very dense specimen of *Podocarpus nagi*, showing the most singular green with a slight violet cast, is the most exquisite coniferous tree I ever have seen. Small groups of rare tropical Zamias and extremely interesting clumps of the Australian *Macrozamia spiralis* proclaim, more than anything else, the intense love and enthusiasm of the one who planted and cared for them. I owe much of my knowledge of plants adapted to our soil and climate to his correspondence.

At Lake Charm, near Oveido, Seminole County, another scholarly enthusiast, Mr. Theodore L. Mead, never sought publicity; a man of high culture, a scientist, an accurate observer, a scholar; a man controlling several languages—in short, a man of a classical education and a hybridizer of the first rank. The first most beautiful hybrids of the fancy-leaved Caladiums in this country came from him. A number of the most lovely crimson Amaryllis, Gladiolus, etc., were added by him to our garden flora. But his name has been placed with indelible letters in the list of orchid hybridizers.

Mr. Mead, started in 1885 a most beautiful tropical garden, well laid out and richly stocked with rare plants. His particular hobby was the cross-breeding of Orchids, and in order to get a good start for his seeds he had erected high up in the Magnolias and Live Oaks little lath houses which he only could use by the aid of very long ladders. He grew many plants under glass as well. In his rich shady hammock he naturalized tropical ferns, gesneriads, terrestrial orchids and a host of other beautiful and dainty plants. Most all the plants did well, but the constant fight against the ravages of the Florida "razor-back" forced him to discontinue his experiments along these lines. His collection of Palms and Bamboos was the most complete and beautiful in the early nineties of the last century.

Dr. Petersen was a chemist with a hobby and expertise in Tropical Plants with economic value for south Florida. He gave a lecture at Estero on Oct. 27, 1929 in the Art Hall. His home was at Bonita Grove on Hainlin Rd., Redlands, south of Miami. [Andrews notes that Dr. Petersen later moved to 5420 N. Miami Ave., Miami, where he had a tropical garden and operated a large fruit preserving factory.]

Some time ago my wife and I enjoyed the royal hospitality of Dr. and Mrs. J. Petersen at Bonita Grove, near Homestead, Fla. In 1918 he was known only as a chemist, not having entered the field of horticulture as yet. But the love for plants and their cultivation slumbered in him, and when this love was awakened, no power in the world could have kept him from entering the field, and he entered it with all the enthusiasm that is necessary to make a success. His training as a chemist was a most powerful help to him.

Though he speaks lightly of his botanical knowledge, it is nevertheless true that he had an excellent training in the rudiments of botany. Before he entered the universities of Kiev and Heidelberg he had made his preparatory studies in one of the German gymnasiums (the classical high school). The study of botany in these schools is compulsory. Every student has to collect and study the native flora. Herbarium specimens are collected, properly identified and placed in herbarium sheets for further study. While our high school boys spend their time on the baseball grounds, etc., the students in this gymnasium are required to accompany their teachers in excursions through woods, meadows and fields to collect and study natural history objects—particularly plants. Dr. Petersen admitted all this, and I further learned that he had on hand the works of Leunis and had collected hundreds of plants. "Leunis" is the natural history college book and the botany of this author is crammed with interesting and important notes of plants. Here Dr. Petersen had laid his foundation. Here his love and enthusiasm for plants was born, though it also may have been partly an inheritance.

The owner of the greater part of the county that bears his name, Mr. Barron Collier, is a man of vision and high ideals. He will not only preserve the glorious groups of Royal Palms along the Tamiami Trail, but he intended to beautify all the land around them and along the Trail. Mr. Collier of Everglades will not only preserve the beautiful Royal Palm Hammock along the Tamiami Trail as a state park for coming generations, but he will pay special attention to creating many beauty spots in the new county, which was named in his honor. Mr. Collier is a man in his best years; a man of broad ideas; a man of vision, and very liberal. His generosity will support men of knowledge and genius who are willing to make a mark in the beautification of his domain. Experimental horticulture will be encouraged and aided. As he is not a man with closed pockets (the word parsimonious is not in his dictionary) only looking out for himself and what he can get out of his fellow men. He is bound to succeed, and his success as a community builder will be phenomenal.

Mr. Charles Deering, of Buena Vista, in this state, is one of America's real noblemen. His ideals are of the highest and the purest kind. He has enabled Prof. Chas. T. Simpson to give to the world the best that was in him. Dr. J. K. Small, the famous botanist, has received the most substantial aid in exploring south Florida botanically. These are only two examples. Mr. Deering's gardens and grounds have a world-wide fame. They are extremely rich in tropical plants, though they are scarcely more than fifteen years old. New material is constantly added. During certain days of the week the public enjoys free admittance. That Mr. Deering is an enthusiastic plant lover is vividly brought before everybody who has the good luck to visit his grounds. But this is not what I like to emphasize here. Mr. Deering is just as much a lover and protector of our native birds. He has his special favorites among his plants, because they supply the birds with food and shelter.

Mr. Deering's example as a lover of nature and horticulture is apparently followed by other men of wealth and refinement. Mr. Glenn Curtis is collecting material for a real botanical garden. These are the men we need to make south Florida an earthly paradise.

Dr. Charles Torrey Simpson of Lemon City and Biscayne Bay, a man "possessed of a keen wit that is continually effervescing." Dr. Simpson was a naturalist, scientist, author, for many years connected with the Smithsonian Institution in D.C., having written several authoritative works on botany, tree snails and Florida wildlife. His bayshore home was in the northern section of Miami, where he grew masses of Cattleyas, Dendrobiums and Phalaenopsis in his garden and hammock on Biscayne Bay.

Charles Mosier: Warden of the former "Paradise Key" (the Royal Palm State Park) of the present Everglades National Park, south of Miami.

John Kunkel Small was an authority on the higher plants of the southeastern United States, an indefatigable field collector throughout that region, and author of the most comprehensive work on its flora, *Manual of the Southeastern Flora*, New York, 1933.

Judge E. G. Wilkinson: "Here at Naples is also the home of Judge E. G. Wilkinson, the first elected Mayor of Naples-on-the-Gulf." He is one of the most ardent plant hunters I have ever met, . . . an enthusiastic plant lover and an exceedingly good woodsman, having as a young man often accompanied the late botanical collector, A. H. Curtiss, in his expeditions through unknown primeval forests.

Mr. E. W. Safford: "One of the great and noble scientific Americans, and years ago vice-governor of the Island of Guam." He wrote the *Useful Plants of Guam*.

Mr. James E. Hendry, Jr.: A kindred spirit, an ardent lover of plants, adding constantly to his private collection, and exceedingly well posted on tropical plants and their culture. Mr. Hendry was founder of the Everglades Nursery Co. in Fort Myers. There are few men more liberal and more public spirited than Mr. Hendry and much of the floral beauty of the city is due to him. He loves the place of his birth. His mother was responsible for planting a lovely large garden and instilled in her son the love of gardens.

Dr. P. J. Berckmans, of Berckman's Fruitland Nurseries at Augusta, Ga. was the leading spirit of ornamental horticulture in the South Atlantic states for almost half a century. A scholar, a botanist, a horticulturist and nurseryman.

Prof. C. S. Sargent, of Harvard University and Director of the Arnold Arboretum is an authority on Japanese trees and shrubs. He is the author of the *Sylva of North America* and numerous papers on oriental plants.

Mr. E. W. Crayton, Manager of the Hotel Naples, at Naples-on-the-Gulf, Fla.

Mr. Henry Pfister was a good friend and for many years was in charge of the White House Conservatory.

Mrs. Marian McAdow, a close friend of Dr. Nehrling, with a fine collection of mature plants at her home in Punta Gorda. Nehrling frequently comments on the large, beautiful, most gorgeous specimens grown by Mrs. McAdow. She apparently also maintained a garden in Fort Myers.

General W. B. Haldeman's home directly on the Gulf is mentioned occasionally, but more importantly the younger Haldemans' loan of a couple thousand dollars enabled the Nehrlings to purchase the Naples property.

Dr. Harold L. Lyon, Forester and Botanist of the Hawaiian Sugar Planters' Experiment Station. Dr. Lyon sent many seedlings of *Ficus* to Dr. Nehrling. He was attempting to introduce the pollinators of figs into Hawaii. The Harold L. Lyon Arboretum at Honolulu is named in his honor.

Dr. C. A. Purpus of Zacuapan, Huatusco, Vera Cruz, Mexico was a celebrated botanist and botanical collector. He also sent many seeds of *Ficus* to Dr. Nehrling.

Mr. & Mrs. C. Wittgustain Codwise: A dear friend of Henry Nehrling and a passionate flower lover and expert horticulturist. He build their home south of Imperial River near Bonita Springs.

[To these figures of importance, we might now add the name of A. H. Andrews, his editor. Our record of Nehrling's pioneering horticultural work in Florida and of his continuing excitement at the beauty of the plants he could grow there would be much the poorer had Andrews not published such a wealth of the material during and after Nehrling's lifetime.]

Selected References

Andrews, Allen H. *A Yank Pioneer in Florida; Recounting the Adventures of a City Chap Who Came to the Wilds of South Florida in the 1890's and Remained to Grow Up with the Country.* Jacksonville, Fla.: Douglas Printing, 1950.

Baensch, Ulrich, and Ursula Baensch. *Blooming Bromeliads.* Bramsche, Germany: Rasch Druck und Verlag, 1994.

Benson, Lyman David. *The Cacti of the United States and Canada.* Stanford, Calif.: Stanford University Press, 1977.

Broschat, Timothy K., and Alan W. Meerow. *Betrock's Reference Guide to Florida Landscape Plants.* 4th printing. Cooper City: Institute of Food and Agricultural Sciences, University of Florida and Betrock Information Systems, 1996.

Burch, Derek, Daniel B. Ward, and David W. Hall. *Checklist of the Woody Cultivated Plants of Florida.* SP-33. Gainesville: Florida Cooperative Extension Service, Institute of Food and Agricultural Sciences, University of Florida, 1988.

Dransfield, John, and Henk Beentje. *The Palms of Madagascar.* Kew [Surrey: UK]: Royal Botanic Garden and the International Palm Society, 1995.

Godfrey, Robert K. *Trees, Shrubs, and Woody Vines of Northern Florida and Adjacent Georgia and Alabama.* Athens: University of Georgia Press, 1988.

Graf, Alfred Bryd. *Exotica.* 7th ed. E. Rutherford, N.J.: Roehrs Company, 1974.

Harper, F. *Proceedings of the Biological Society of Washington.* D.C. 59:29. 1946.

Hawkes, Alex D. *Encyclopedia of Cultivated Orchids.* London: Faber and Faber, 1975.

Hitchcock, Albert Spear. *Manual of the Grasses of the United States.* 2nd ed. Washington, D.C.: United States Government Printing Office, 1950.

Hortus Third: A Concise Dictionary of Plants Cultivated in the United States and Canada. 2nd printing. Ed. L. H. Bailey and E. Z. Bailey. Revised and expanded by Liberty Hyde Bailey Hortorium staff. New York: Macmillan, 1977.

Jones, David L. *Cycads of the World.* Washington, D.C.: Smithsonian Institution Press, 1993.

———. *Palms throughout the World.* Washington, D.C.: Smithsonian Institution Press, 1995.

Lellinger, David B. *A Field Manual of the Ferns and Fern-Alies of the United States and Canada.* Washington, D.C.: Smithsonian Institution Press, 1985.

Long, Robert W., and Olga Lakela. *A Flora of Tropical Florida: A Manual of the Seed Plants and Ferns of Southern Peninsular Florida.* Coral Gables, Fla.: University of Miami Press, 1971.

Luer, Carlyle A. *The Native Orchids of Florida.* New York: New York Botanical Garden, 1972.

McClintock, Elizabeth May, and Andrew T. Leiser, *An Annotated Checklist of Woody Ornamental Plants of California, Oregon and Washington.* No. 4091. Berkeley: Division of Agricultural Sciences, University of California, 1979.

Meerow, Alan W. *Betrock's Guide to Landscape Palms.* Cooper City, Fla.: Betrock Information Systems, 1992.

Moore, Harold E., Jr. "An Annotated Checklist of Cultivated Palms." *Principes* (Journal of the Palm Society) 7, no. 4 (October 1963): 119–84.

Morton, Julia Frances. *Some Useful and Ornamental Plants of the Caribbean Gardens.* Naples, Fla.: Caribbean Gardens, 1955.

Neal, Marie C. *In Gardens of Hawaii.* Honolulu: Bishop Museum Press, 1965.

Nehrling, H. *The Plant World in Florida.* Ed. A. and E. Kay. New York: Macmillan, 1933.

————. *My Garden in Florida and Miscellaneous Horticultural Notes / From the Manuscripts of Dr. Henry Nehrling.* Ed. A. H. Andrews. 2 vols. Estero, Fla.: Koreshan Unity Press, 1944–46.

Nicolson, Dan H., with Robert A. DeFilipps, Alice C. Nicolson, and others. *Flora of Dominica. Part 2, Dicotyledoneae.* Smithsonian Contributions to Botany, no. 77. Washington, D.C.: Smithsonian Institution Press, 1991.

Small, John Kunkel. *Manual of the Southeastern Flora: Being Descriptions of the Seed Plants Growing Naturally in Florida, Alabama, Mississippi, Eastern Louisiana, Tennessee, North Carolina, South Carolina, and Georgia.* Chapel Hill: University of North Carolina Press, 1933.

Smith, L. B., and R. J. Downs. *Flora Neotropica.* Monograph no. 14, pt. 2 (Tillandsioideae). New York: Hafner Press, 1977.

Wunderlin, Richard P. *Guide to the Vascular Plants of Central Florida.* 3rd printing. Tampa: University Presses of Florida, 1992.

Index

Names preceding (=) are used by Nehrling; modern equivalents follow.